the writings and documents of **richard cruz** and católicos por la raza

Chicano Liberation Theology

Edited by
MARIO T. GARCÍA

Kendall Hunt
publishing company

Kendall Hunt
publishing company

www.kendallhunt.com
Send all inquiries to:
4050 Westmark Drive
Dubuque, IA 52004-1840

ISBN 978-0-7575-6236-5

Printed in the United States of America
10 9 8 7 6 5 4 3 2 1

To Richard Cruz, his family,
and to the veteranos of Católicos Por La Raza

Contents

Acknowledgments ix
Introduction xiii

Part 1: The Chicano Movement and the Catholic Church 1

César Chávez
"The Chicano y la Iglesia [Church] 3

Rodolfo Salinas
"Of the Church" 7

Antonio J. Sclabassi, O.F.M.
"The Catholic Church and La Raza" 10

Agustín Garza
"The New Chicano Priests" 12

Part 2: The Origins of Católicos Por La Raza 17

Richard Cruz
"Católicos Por La Raza and Mexican Americans: Part One" 19
"Católicos Por La Raza and Mexican Americans: Part Two" 21
"The Church and La Raza" 24
"The Church: the MODEL of HYPOCRISY 27
"Demands of Católicos Por La Raza" 29

Part 3: Católicos in Action 33

"The Camp Oliver Take Over" 35
"Demands of Católicos Por La Raza in San Diego County" 38
"Confrontation with the Church" 40

Richard Cruz
"Católicos Por La Raza" 42
"Católicos Por La Raza Press Release" 44
"Congress of Mexican-American Unity" 47
"Católicos Por La Raza Revisited-Three Years Later (1972) 50
"Join us for a Christmas Eve Candlelight March" 52
"No Room at St. Basil's for Chicanos" 53
"Letter to Rev. James Francis McIntyre" 54

Pedro Arias
"Testimony of Pedro Arias" 57
"Church Response to Demands" 59
"Open Letter to the Church" 62
"Pedro Arias to Cardinal Francis McIntyre" 66

Wellin Reidder
"District Attorney Wellin Reidder on Trial of the St. Basil's 21" 69

Oscar Zeta Acosta
"Oscar Zeta Acosta's Opening Statement in Trial of St. Basil's 21" 72

Oscar Zeta Acosta and Richard Cruz
"Trial of St. Basil's 21: Testimony of Richard Cruz" 76
"Church vs. Católicos" 96
"Católicos Por La Raza: A Moral Struggle" 99
"Católicos Por La Raza: Bautismo de Fuego [Baptism of Fire] 102

Part 4: Testimonios [Oral Histories] 105

Ray Cruz and Paloma Martínez-Cruz on Richard Cruz and CPLR 107
Rosa Martínez on Richard Cruz and CPLR 135
Camilo Cruz on Richard Cruz and CPLR 152
Miguel García on CPLR 170

Part 5: Richard Cruz: People's Attorney 191

Richard Cruz, el.al.
"Letter to Rev. Charles C. Casassa, S. J." 193

Richard Cruz
"People's Declaration of April 29th, 1972" 195
"The Fight for Miguel García and Richard Cruz" 197

Manuel Barrera
"Chicano Lawyer-Activist Subjected to California State Bar Hearing" 199

Richard Cruz and Miguel García
"Administration of Justice?" 203

Richard Cruz
"Ricardo Cruz: People's Lawyer" 209
"Abogados de Aztlán" [Attorneys of Aztlán] 212
"Some Novel Concept: Lawyers & Social Change" 220

Part 6: Richard Cruz: Pensamientos and Other Reflections 225

Richard Cruz
"Chicanos in Mexico: Some Emerging Themes" 227
"Untitled" 233
"Untitled" 236
"Untitled" 238
"Untitled" 239
"Untitled" 240
"Chicano Interview: Chicanos, Catholicism, and Political Ideology (1976)" 241
"An Ode to Chicanos & Chicanas" 263
"Untitled Poem" 264
"Untitled Poem" 265
"Letter to His Parents" 270

Part 7: Eulogy of Richard Cruz by Camilo Cruz 273

Acknowledgments

I have been fascinated by the history of Católicos Por La Raza for many years. As part of the Chicano Movement in Los Angeles, Católicos or CPLR was an openly Chicano Catholic group espousing reforms within the Church that would support the Mexican American community. As I developed an interest in Chicano Catholic history, I first focused on researching the role of Católicos. The first paper I presented at a conference on Chicano religions back in the mid-1990s was, in fact, on Católicos. Hence, I have spent almost fifteen years researching the history of CPLR and of its dynamic leader, Richard Cruz. This volume is part of this research and intended to provide the most comprehensive presentation of the history and ideology of both Católicos and Richard Cruz.

In my research, I have been indebted to a number of people who have provided incentive, support, and materials for my research on CPLR. These include Gastón Espinosa, Camilo Cruz, Ray Cruz, Paloma Martínez-Cruz, Raul Ruiz, Pedro Arias, Miguel García, Bob Gandara, Richard Martínez, Father Patrick McNamara, Lydia López, Rick Sánchez, and Alberto Pulido. Special thanks to Salvador Guerena and Ed Fields for their assistance in accessing the Ricardo Cruz/Católicos Por La Raza Papers in the California Ethnic and Multicultural Archives in Special Collections in the Davidson Library at the University of California, Santa Barbara. Needless to say, I am thankful to Kendall Hunt Publishing Company and in particular Joe Wells and Ryan L. Schrodt for their support in the publication of this volume.

Finally, I am very grateful to Edith Cruz, my research assistant whose help in transforming the original documents into a publishable manuscript was invaluable. I also want to acknowledge my other research assistant, Colleen Ho who also aided me in this work by ably transcribing the oral histories included in this volume.

About the Editor

Mario T. García is Professor of Chicana and Chicano Studies and affiliated with History and Religious Studies at the University of California, Santa Barbara. He was born in El Paso, Texas and attended local Catholic schools there. He received his B.A. and M.A. in History from the University of Texas at El Paso and his Ph.D. in History from the University of California, San Diego.

He is the author of several books on Chicano and U.S. Catholic history including *Desert Immigrants: The Mexicans of El Paso, 1880-1922* (1981); *Mexican Americans: Leadership, Ideology & Identity, 1930-1960* (1989); *Memories of Chicano History: The Life and Narrative of Bert Corona* (1994); *The Making of a Mexican American Mayor: Raymond L. Telles of El Paso* (1998); *Migrant Daughter: Coming of Age as a Mexican American Woman* with Frances Esquibel Tywoniak (2000); *Padre: The Spiritual Journey of Father Virgil Cordano* (2005); *Católicos: Resistance and Affirmation in Chicano Catholic History* (2008). He is also the editor of Ruben Salazar, *Border Correspondent: Selected Writings, 1954-1970* (1995); *The Gospel of César Chávez: My Faith In Action* (2007); *Mexican American Religions: Spirituality, Activism, and Culture* with Gastón Espinosa (2008); *A Dolores Huerta Reader* (2008); and *Bridging Cultures: An Introduction to Chicano/Latino Studies* (2000). He is a Guggenheim Fellow and a Fulbright Scholar.

Introduction

CATÓLICOS POR LA RAZA

The Chicano Movement of the late 1960s and early 1970s represented the most significant and widespread protest by Mexican Americans in the history of the United States. Reacting to a legacy of conquest in the Southwest in the nineteenth century, to a history of labor exploitation, and to experiences as second-class citizens characterized by various forms of discrimination and segregation including lack of access to quality education, Mexican Americans by the 1960s challenged the system as never before. The Movement was a Chicano "intifada" or uprising.

Courtesy of Special Collections, Davidson Library, Univ. of Calif. Santa Barbara

CPLR Christmas Eve Vigil at St. Basil's, Dec. 24, 1969.

As part of its agenda, the movement gave birth to Chicano Studies defining it in very strong ethnic nationalist terms. In turn, Chicano nationalism was largely portrayed as an expression of secular values and goals. The role of religion, especially Catholicism, was not perceived by early students of Chicano Studies to have played a major role in the movement. And yet while secularization characterized a good deal of movement politics, religion was not absent. Religion, primarily but not exclusively Catholicism, played a role in the formation of a movement value system focused on social justice including the direct and indirect expression of liberation theology or the stress on a preferential option for the poor and oppressed. Religion in some cases also proved to be the basis for community organization. Andrew Greeley refers to "cultural Catholics;" however, there is also what I would call "political Catholics."[1]

This volume is a case study of the role of Catholicism in the Chicano Movement in Los Angeles as exemplified by Católicos Por La Raza.[2]

Origins Of Católicos

Católicos Por La Raza began as an extension of some of the early movement activities in Los Angeles that had sprung up first in reaction to the inspirational struggle of César Chávez and the farm workers when they struck for union recognition in 1965. The 1968 school "blowouts" in East Los Angeles during the spring of that year when several thousand Mexican-American students walked out of their schools inspired by teacher Sal Castro to protest inferior education likewise helped to ignite the movement in Los Angeles.[3]

Católicos was organized as the result of the coming together of three groups: the Chicano Law Students Association at Loyola University School of Law (a Jesuit institution), part of a statewide association; La Raza newspaper/magazine (a community-based Chicano publication); and UMAS (United Mexican American Students) a Chicano student group at Los Angeles City College. Richard Martínez, who at the time was the head of UMAS (later to be re-named Movimiento Estudiantil Chicano de Aztlan), recalls that he and other Chicano students began to question the role of the Catholic Church in Los Angeles with respect to Chicanos. "If you have the Church standing with you in making a demand," Martínez remembers thinking, "it's a hell of a lot more powerful than you standing by yourself. If the Bishop is next to me, I'm in good shape."[4]

Martínez convinced other UMAS students at his school that they should make the relevance of the Church to the Chicano community one of their top priorities. At Loyola, the Chicano Law Students Association appears to have started when Richard (Ricardo) Cruz and Miguel García, the only two Chicano law students, along with other progressive students protested what they claimed was the failure of the school to recruit and support, financial and otherwise, Chicano law students.[5]

Cruz and García were also incensed that there were more Jewish students enrolled at this Catholic institution than Chicanos.[6] This local grievance soon expanded to include the Church's general neglect of the Mexican-American community.[7] Of particular concern was the closing of a Catholic parochial school, Our Lady Queen of Angeles High School, with an 87% Mexican American enrollment at the same time that the Archdiocese had finished construction of a new $3 million St. Basil's Church in the trendy Wilshire district.[8]

At La Raza newspaper, Joe Razo, one of the organizers of the paper, appears to have already been involved with various dissident Chicano priests in Los Angeles who less than a year later formed a branch of PADRES, an association of Chicano priests in the Southwest, who likewise wanted to make the Church more sensitive to the conditions of Mexican Americans. Razo, himself, was not a priest.[9]

At some point, in late October or early November of 1969, Martínez recalls meeting with Richard Cruz, the chair of the Loyola group, to discuss their common concerns. Cruz, whom Martínez characterized as thoughtful, intelligent, quick-minded, determined, and possessing clear organizational thinking along with a high intensity level, was part of what Martínez referred to as the "Cathedral Mafia"—a group of graduates from Cathedral High School in Los Angeles, a Catholic school run by the Christian Brothers just north of China Town and bordering the eastside of the city. Besides Richard and his brother, Ray, members of this "mafia" included Tómas Varela, Percy Duran, Miguel Duran, and Peter Navarro.[10] Raul Ruiz of La Raza considers Cruz to have been "a courageous, articulate, and charismatic young man."[11] Members of the "mafia" went on to college and became activists in the Chicano Movement including in Católicos.[12] According to Martínez, the Cathedral Mafia, including Cruz, because they were graduates of parochial schools during the period of the liberal reforms of Vatican Council II championed by Pope John XXIII, knew much more about the politics of the Church than those like Martínez who had been raised Catholic, but who had not gone to Catholic schools.[13]

Richard Cruz, who emerged as the key leader of Católicos, a former altar boy and product along with his brothers of the Catholic schools, recalled in a 1976 interview that he considered the Christian Brothers to have been great teachers and who were philosophical and spiritual and yet taught their students about applying their religious beliefs to the world. "They related to reality more than they [did] to any trimmings and trappings," he observed, "and what I call the dark ages and dark mentality of religion." Cruz further noted that what he and other students took from their Catholic education involved a sense of morality, about good and evil that they could apply to their social world.[14]

Some years later, Cruz noted that he had been influenced by the life of Jesus—a life that he had studied. "More than any of you have," he wrote his parents in 1974, "I at one time loved, sacrificed, understood and, a rare thing indeed, also studied the person, life and times of J.C."[15]

Ray Cruz, Richard's older brother, remembers Richard as a natural-born leader, a great debater in high school, and someone who took his Catholicism seriously, and even, at one point, considered a religious vocation. Rosa Martínez, his later companion, notes that Richard belonged to a "model Catholic family."[16] In his undergraduate years at Cal State, Los Angeles, where both Richard and Ray participated in the radical Students for Democratic Action (SDS), Richard majored in philosophy and told Ray: "I am a Hegelian." Although not a Marxist, he appears to have read widely in philosophy including Marx and Marxist thinkers.[17] "Richard acquired a philosophical and more revolutionary orientation during his undergraduate studies at Cal State Los Angeles," Ray Cruz observes.[18]

Shortly after the meeting between Martínez and Cruz, Católicos Por La Raza was formed to launch a Chicano Movement assault on the Church in Los Angeles. The actual time line of the organization of Católicos is not certain although it clearly was in 1969. Miguel García recalls that the group might have been formed earlier than the fall of that year.[19] According to Raul Ruiz, who became the editor of La Raza, Católicos was the brainchild of Richard Cruz. García concurs. "Richard was the key, the sparkplug," he stresses, "He kept things moving. Without Richard, Católicos wouldn't have happened."[20] Católico member, Bob Gandara, agrees. "That son-of-a-bitch was good," Gandara fondly notes of Cruz; "he was articulate, worked hard, was open-minded, and believed in what he was doing." As a result, Gandara adds, "we made sure that Richard was the man."[21]

Although Cruz was referred to as the co-chair of the group, in fact, he represented the agreed upon leader and main spokesperson for Católicos.[22] The name of the group, especially the term Católicos, was deliberately chosen in order to stress that the members were not anti-Catholic.[23] The term "La Raza" instead of Chicano was chosen because Cruz believed that it represented a more open and inclusive term and one that integrated the concept of the people and community into the title. The full title expressed the view that the Catholic Church belonged to the people. "Richard was well beyond just being a devout practicing Catholic," his brother Ray stresses, "at the time of Católicos, my brother was focusing on the very meaning of the Church."[24]

Richard Cruz later observed that meeting César Chávez inspired him to think about forming a group such as Católicos. He first met Chávez when Cruz spent time as a law intern with the California Rural Legal Assistance helping farm workers in Salinas in 1969. What particularly impressed Cruz was when the farm labor leader lamented that while he had received support from a variety of Protestant and Jewish denominations, he had not gotten the public support of the Catholic Church. Upon being introduced to Chávez, Cruz promised that he would do what he could do bring the Church to "la causa." Chávez would later express support for Católicos.[25]

As it prepared to protest against the Church, Católicos moved from being strictly a student effort to an off-campus one as a way of expanding its base. Raul Ruiz stresses that Católicos was a good example of how the movement was always a mixture of students and community and not just students as some contend.[26] Still, the three key pillars of Católicos were the Loyola law students, La Raza newspaper and later magazine, and UMAS at L.A. City College, but which in a short time also included UMAS or MEChA students from other schools such as Long Beach State. Functioning primarily in Los Angeles, Católicos, as Alberto Pulido has noted, inspired the formation of at least one other Católicos' group in San Diego.[27]

To announce its formation, Católicos arranged a press conference and invited the media. Cruz recalled that the only mainstream reporter who showed up was Ruben Salazar of the Los Angeles Times.[28] At that press conference held at the Los Angeles Press Club, Cruz announced the key objective of Católicos: "We have committed ourselves to one goal—the return of the Catholic Church to the oppressed Chicano community." He added that Católicos wanted the Church "to become as radical as Christ."[29]

A Católicos Theology

Influenced directly and indirectly by various political and theological developments, Católicos put forward after its organization its own ideological views and critique of the Church. First and foremost, members of Católicos made it very clear that they identified as Chicano Catholics. In its founding proclamation, Católicos stressed that it was precisely the Catholic background of its members that made them conscious of the contradictions of the Church. Although Católicos was not a mass organization, it reminded the Church that Mexican Americans as well as other Latinos were predominantly Catholics and made up a large percentage of U.S. Catholics especially in the Southwest.[30] "Mexican-Americans have been most faithful to Catholicism and its traditions," a Católicos press release addressed to Cardinal Frances McIntyre and to the Catholic clergy of the Los Angeles Archdiocese stressed, "We have produced saints and martyrs; have given and continue to give truly sacrificial donations to our Catholic Church and for the most part have attempted to live up to Christ's mandate that we love our brother. We believe that you, our spiritual leaders, know these things to be true."[31]

As Catholics, members of Católicos stressed that one of the Catholic traditions that they embraced was an identity with the poor. This was an identity that Christ himself had established. This stress on the poor resonated with the emergence of liberation theology in Latin America as a response to the reforms of Vatican Council II (1962-65) and the Council's emphasis on making the Church relevant to the modern world. In Latin American, many of its clergy interpreted this as re-focusing the Church's priority on the poor and oppressed.

As Catholics and as Christians, members of Católicos believed that they had no option but to identify with the poor as Christ had done. [W]e have the duty," Católicos insisted, "to not only love the poor but to be as Christ-like as possible."[32]

It was because poverty existed in the barrios—in the parishes—that Católicos, like liberationists in Latin America, called attention to the contradictions within the Church concerning the poverty of the people and the wealth of the Church. Católicos believed that this contradiction represented hypocrisy on the part of the Church. It preached, on the one hand, that the poor through their devotion to Christ would acquire ever-lasting rewards ("Blessed are the poor"), while, at the same time, the Church as an institution accumulated wealth beyond the imaginations of the poor.[33]

The contradictions between the poverty of the poor and the wealth of the Church could especially be seen in housing conditions in the barrio and the Church's ownership of property in Los Angeles. While most Chicanos lived in inadequate and deteriorating homes, the Church, despite its own vast property holding, did nothing to reform barrio housing conditions.[34]

To further document what Católicos claimed was the Church's hypocrisy with respect to the poor, La Raza published a partial listing of Church-owned property acquired from the County Assessor's office. According to Católicos, these holdings amounted to a billion dollars. Moreover, this amount only covered Los Angeles County and not the rest of the Archdiocese that included Orange, Ventura, and Santa Barbara counties. La Raza further noted that this value might only cover part of the Church's property since it did not include corporations owned by the Church. These properties listed, Católicos believed, did not just include churches, schools, and rectories, but also private homes, apartments, and businesses. According to Raul Ruiz, these holdings involved many slum dwellings.[35]

Católicos contrasted certain displays of Church wealth with the conditions of most Chicanos. "We know that the stained glass in Los Angeles' newest Catholic church is worth approximately two hundred and fifty thousand dollars ($250,000)," it pointed out, "We know of this wealth; yet Chicanitos [little children] are praying to La Virgen de Guadalupe as they go to bed hungry and will not be able to afford decent education."[36] Católicos further added: "Compare such wealth to the plight of our people and you begin to wonder, as CPLR [Católicos Por La Raza] has wondered, just who has taken the vow of poverty—the Chicanos or the Catholic Church."[37]

Part of the Church's neglect of the poor, contended Catolicós, included a lack of Chicano representation within the Church's structure. Católicos noted that of the twelve million Spanish-speaking people in the United States over 90% were Catholics. This made the Spanish-speaking the largest single ethnic group within the Church constituting almost a quarter of all Catholics and 67% in the southwestern states. Latin American countries with smaller populations including Puerto Rico possessed their own native church hierarchy and institutions. By contrast, despite their numbers, Spanish-speaking Catholics in the United States had little representation. There was not a single Spanish-speaking bishop. Of over 720 priests in the Los Angeles archdiocese only 5% were Spanish-speaking.[38]

Católicos believed that the Spanish-speaking had to be represented at all levels of the Church and that both Chicano clergy as well as laity needed to be part of the decision-making process of the Church in order to give priority to the needs of the poor.[39]

What needed to be done given the contradictions, hypocrisy, and insensitivity of the Church was, according to Católicos, to transform the Church from an elite institution to an agency of the people. Católicos stressed that this transformation was justified based on Church doctrines and traditions themselves. "Saint Thomas says that concrete attribution of an authority is made by the people," Católicos noted. "When there is an authority opposed to the people, this authority is illegitimate and tyrannical. As Christians and Catholics, we can and must fight against the mismanagement of OUR Church."[40] Quoting St, Matthew (Matt: 20:28), Católicos reminded the Church of Christ's mission: "I came not to be served, but to serve."[41]

In their own way, Católicos were asserting the profound, new emphasis out of Vatican Council II that all Catholics, not just the clergy, represented the Church. According to Fr. Patrick McNamara, a Jesuit scholar at Loyola University during this period, this new conception of the Church, in his words, "the Church as the people of God," was the most significant pronouncement out of the Council. It meant, McNamara notes, that the laity, including Católicos, would be agents of change within the Church.[42]

In their struggle to re-convert the Church, members of Católicos believed that they had no better role model than Christ himself. Católicos as well as other Catholic activists in the movement in their version of a Chicano Christology reinterpreted Christ as a revolutionary. "Jesus Christ is being seen as the radical he really is," one New Mexican movement activist proposed. "He is seen as a revolutionist through the eyes of the revolutionaries, for it is from him that we draw strength."[43] As a revolutionary, Jesus, as the Chicano poet Abelardo Delgado wrote, represented the "New Christ" bearing the "New Cross" that would establish the "New Church."[44]

In its call for a "New Church," Católicos made it very clear that they were not attacking Catholic beliefs and doctrines, but the current leadership of the Church that had deviated from these beliefs and doctrines. "I think that we went to great lengths," recalls Raul Ruiz, "to explain every time we spoke or wrote that we were not writing about the ideology or the religion itself, but rather the human aspect of the Church which we felt was very defective."[45]

Richard Cruz later observed that Católicos was simply telling the Catholic clergy "to live like your so-called leader, the one who says . . . 'Be like me'. . . . So live with the poor, feed them, get going in other words." Jesus, in Cruz's opinion, lived a "socialistic-communistic life."[46]

Católicos did not see itself as leading a schism from the Church, but of leading it back to its own principles. "It is not the Church or more specifically the religious views that are inadequate to meet the needs of today's poor," Católicos pointed out," but some of the men who help run the Church." One of these men was Cardinal McIntyre who, according to Católicos, ran the Los Angeles Archdiocese with a tyrannical hand suppressing both clergy and laity especially those who identified with the poor. Jesuit Fr.McNamara referred to McIntyre's administration as an "authoritarian regime."[47] "Social action, to the Cardinal," Católicos stressed, "is regarded in the same vein as hell."[48]

Defining their beliefs and their objectives, members of Católicos shortly after organizing likewise drafted a list of demands that it hoped to present to Cardinal McIntyre. These demands reflected Católicos' philosophy, but in a more concrete manner outlined the specific changes it hoped to pressure the Church into accepting. Key to the demands was acquiring a substantive input by the Chicano community into Church decision-making. This would be achieved by the creation of a Commission on Mexican American Affairs within the hierarchy of the Church in Los Angeles. The Commission would be composed of representatives of Mexican American community organizations as well as of Mexican American priests and nuns. This Commission would concentrate its efforts into re-orienting Church policy in the following areas: (1) Education; (2) Housing; (3) Health; (4) Shared Governance; (5) Leadership and Orientation; (6) Assignment of Clergy to the Chicano Movement; (7) Freedom of speech for all priests and nuns; (8) Use of Church Facilities; and (9) Public Commitment to the Chicano Movement.[49] [see specifics of demands in volume]

Católicos stressed that they would persist in their struggle until their demands were met irrespective of the consequences. "Further understand that we shall enforce our demands with whatever spiritual and physical powers we possess even if it means we must be jailed," they told the press.[50]

Confronting The Church

With demands in hand, Católicos into the fall of 1969 proceeded to devise a strategy to force the Church in Los Angeles, specifically Cardinal McIntyre, to agree to them. Meeting at the headquarters of La Raza magazine and later at the Euclid Community Center on Whittier Boulevard in East L.A., members of Católicos (around twenty hard core-members) concentrated in devising the steps they would take. According to Miguel García, the members of the Chicano Law Students Association of Los Angeles involving students from various L.A. schools represented the most active members of Católicos.[51] Rosa Martínez, who volunteered to represent Cal State, Northridge at Católicos meetings, remembers between thirty to forty people at these meetings.[52] It does not appear that these were the occasion for any philosophical discussions. Richard Martínez notes that the issues-oriented and pragmatic aspects of these meetings coincided with what he considered to be Católicos' more populist base as opposed to a philosophical one.[53]

Católicos' initial strategy further involved publishing an open letter in La Raza to Cardinal McIntyre concerning its demands and attempting to present a copy personally to the Cardinal. When Richard Cruz and a few others visited the Chancery office to do this on October 15, McIntyre refused to see them - instead leaving his office through a back door and calling the police. No arrests were made. After Católicos persisted in seeing the Cardinal, he agreed to meet with them two days later only to tell them "say what you have to say or get out!" Cruz later recalled: "I kiss[ed] [the] Cardinal's ring but he treats us like trash and we split."[54] The Católicos left without presenting their demands since McIntyre refused to treat them with respect. "Do we have to stay out of our own Church?" Cruz remarked, "A Church that is not only hypocritically wealthy, but which does not respect our culture. It is our duty, as Chicanos and Catholics, to return the Catholic Church to us."[55]

Following the Cardinal's rebuff, Católicos devised a new two-fold but interrelated strategy. It would call for another meeting with the Cardinal and, at the same time, commence picketing of the Cardinal's residence at St. Basil's Church in order to force such a meeting. The strategy of confrontation had been part of the debate within Católicos. It appears that some, including Ray Cruz and Bob Gandara, had concerns about a strategy of direct confrontation either because of their lingering loyalty to traditional Church authority or whether it was a sound tactical decision. Such reservations, whether expressed or not, did not win the day. Richard Cruz, Richard Martínez, and Raul Ruiz, as the key inner circle, forcibly and successfully argued for confrontation. They insisted that the only way to get awareness in the community about the failures of the Church was to get publicity and the only way to get publicity was through confrontation. Not only would publicity be gotten, they observed, but confrontation, almost as a form of guerilla warfare, would expose the contradictions of the Church. Cruz and the others were convinced that the Church would overreact and even use violence against Católicos. This would proof their point that the Church was a rigid, conservative institution that had no sympathy or support for Chicanos.

Picketing included a prayer vigil on Thanksgiving Day in front of St. Basil's.[56] This vigil continued the following week on December 7 at the end of the Sunday Masses. The protestors attempted to see the Cardinal whose residence was at the rear of the church, but neither he nor any of his staff would meet with Católicos. After receiving no response from the Cardinal, Católicos decided to raise the ante. On December 18, 1969, members of Católicos—between fifteen and thirty—visited the Cardinal's offices at the Chancery to demand a meeting. They had decided not to take no for an answer.

A decision was made to force their way into the Cardinal's office. Rosa Martínez, who was part of the contingent notes that Richard Cruz was not a very patient person and that he finally told the others "let's just go in."[57] They forced open the door into the inner corridor in search of the Cardinal's office. As startled priests emerged from their offices, they ran down the corridor. Joe Razo led the charge and when one of the priests tried to stop him, Razo, perhaps an ex-football player, threw him a perfect body block, taking the priest completely off his feet, and freeing the other Católicos to move down the hall in search of the Cardinal's office. "That's it!" Richard Martínez and the others yelled out. Miguel García tried to open the door only to have it shut on him from the inside pinning his arm between the doors. García recalls acting as if his arm was in serious pain in order to try to get the door open. His ploy worked enough to allow him to force it ajar. As García pushed his way into the office, there standing no more than three feet away was a red-faced and very nervous Cardinal McIntyre. "Call the police. Call the police," he in a faint voice ordered his staff of two or three other priests.[58]

"No, no, we don't need to call the police," Martínez remembers one of the staff responding, "calm down, calm down."[59] Rosa Martínez observes that the Cardinal was visibly shaken and that some of his staff seemed to think that she and the other Católicos had come to rob the Chancery office.[60] In fact, Rosa Martínez, herself was somewhat shaken at what was transpiring. "I remember thinking," she says, "that the Holy Ghost was going to come down, as all of my

Catholic upbringing came back to me, and I was in terror of being struck down by God."[61]

A livid Cardinal agreed to meet with the few Católicos who had managed to enter the office. Other priests who had blocked the entryway to the corridor prevented the other Católicos from doing so.[62] McIntyre listened to their demands, but only promised to look into the issues presented to him. Richard Cruz did all of the talking for Católicos. After several minutes, having forced their meeting with the Cardinal, members of Católicos retreated believing that they had at least won a moral victory. "We weren't very sophisticated," Martínez notes, "but that was our strength because with our energy and our enthusiasm we just charged ahead."[63] Miguel García recalls that it was a very short encounter with the Cardinal because he and the other Católicos believed that the police had been called and would arrive shortly.[64]

A few days passed and Católicos did not hear back from the Cardinal. As a result, the decision was made to organize a large demonstration outside of St. Basil's on Christmas Eve and to disrupt the Cardinal's midnight Mass. Since the service was also going to be televised, Católicos hoped to take advantage of this to publicize its demands.[65] This more dramatic strategy may have been inspired by the actions of the Católicos group in San Diego who on November 30 had taken over Camp Oliver, a Catholic youth camp in Descanso just east of San Diego. The San Diego Católicos used the seizure to bring attention to their own demands. The take-over ended on December 1.[66]

The strategy for the intervention at the Cardinal's Mass involved several steps. The assembled crowd would first have an alternative "people's Mass" outside of the church at the same time as the Mass inside of St. Basil's. Both Masses would commence at 11:00 p.m. and conclude at around midnight. The alternative Mass would be officiated by some of the priest supporters of Católicos including Father Blase Bonpane. It would be timed to end a few minutes before the conclusion of the Cardinal's Mass. The group would then line up in a candlelight procession and enter the church. Going through the vestibule, they would enter the sanctuary and proceed down the main aisle. At the foot of the altar railing, they would spread out and face the congregation. Three of them including Cruz and Martínez would then take turns reading their demands. This strategy, according to Martínez, "sounded good."[67]

The actual events, however, did not quite turn out that way. It appears that somewhere between two hundred and three hundred fifty people gathered to participate in the demonstration. Not only were activists encouraged to attend, but also families.[68] They grouped to the side of the main entrance and next to the large nativity scene. The front entrance to the church is small in space so that the hundreds of Católicos supporters spilled out into the street.[69]

As people arrived for the midnight Mass, some verbal altercations took place between those entering and members of Católicos. Blas Bonpane said the Católicos Mass in Spanish using a table for the altar. Instead of the regular wafers for communion, he used bits of flour tortilla. Ray Cruz remembers the alternative Mass as "radical but fun."[70] When their Mass ended, the Católicos group formed into a procession with lighted candles and prepared to enter the vestibule around 12:15 AM.[71]

At this point, the sequence of events is not perfectly clear. Oscar Zeta Acosta, the attorney for CPLR, later claimed that Católicos had made prior arrangements, presumably with St. Basil's, to enter the church as long as they left their banners and candles outside the church.[72] Richard Cruz in a letter to Cardinal McIntyre on December 26 also noted that prior to the commencement of the Cardinal's Mass that a Sergeant Domínguez of the Los Angeles police had talked to him and other Católicos about their intent with respect to the Mass. "We told him that we had no intention whatsoever of disrupting the service," Cruz wrote. "He advised us that you [McIntyre] had instructed him to inform us that so long as we did not carry our banners and candles within the sanctuary, that we would be welcome to participate in the celebration of the Mass, and that the doors would remain open."[73] On the other hand, Bob Gandara recalls that some priests came out of the church and informed the group that no further room was available.[74]

It appears, however, that discovering the huge and heavy front doors of the church electronically shut, a small contingent of Católicos proceeded to enter the church through a side door. Miguel García who earlier that evening had walked to the church parking lot on the west side of the church and had seen a side door leading into the church led them. Curious, he entered and discovered that he was in a large basement sanctuary where a second midnight Mass was in progress. He walked down the side aisle and at the back discovered stairs that led him up to the main vestibule or lobby of the church outside of the main sanctuary where the Cardinal was saying Mass. When Católicos had failed to open the outside door later, García informed some key people of the side entrance. García notes that about twelve to fifteen people followed him into the basement sanctuary that included Joe Razo and Zeta Acosta. Richard Cruz also joined the group. At least three others, including Rick Sánchez, found still another side entrance that led to the vestibule. Upon ascending the stairs to the main vestibule, García moved to open one of the main doors to allow the others outside to enter the church. "I went directly for the door," he remembers, "and I put my hand on the bar, when this big old undercover cop lifted me up away from the door."[75] In the vestibule, that is quite small, the Católicos had encountered a number of "ushers" who later turned out to be undercover county sheriffs. Monsignor Benjamin Hawkes, the pastor at St. Basil's, later testified that he had requested "extra ushers" from the Anchor

Club, an organization of lay Catholics holding public jobs such as the county sheriffs. He requested them not only because of an anticipated large attendance at the midnight Mass, but because an informant within Católicos had reported the group's strategy for confrontation that evening.[76] Cruz later referred to this encounter as an "ambush." "When one of us merely reached for the door handle to the outside door," Cruz explained the effort by García to open the door, "the usher struck the man in the back of the neck. Immediately, the usher in charge ordered the others ushers to throw us out, and in the twinkle of an eye, they viciously beat upon us and attempted to eject us."[77] However, when García had put his hand on the bar of the door, the automatic doors swung open allowing some on the outside to come in.[78]

Richard Martínez recalls that as he and other Católicos entered the vestibule, they realized that it was not going to be easy to go into the sanctuary or main part of the church. Blocking the doors to the sanctuary were the "ushers." Martínez notes that they were "not small." As Martínez and the others approached the "ushers," they started to chant, "Let the poor people in! Let the poor people in!" As they attempted to open the sanctuary doors, as Martínez remembers, "all hell broke lose."[79]

As the melee erupted, additional "ushers" entered through the side of the vestibule. Fisticuffs, wrestling, and shouting filled the area and apparently also in the choir loft and basement. Raul Ruiz remembers that the congregation inside the church raised their voices in singing "O Come, All Ye Faithful" in an effort to drown out the calls of "Let the poor people in!" Although the Mass was being televised by KTLA, Channel 5, viewers never saw the fighting although the audio did pick up some of the shouting.[80]

Within a few minutes uniformed Los Angeles police in full riot gear that, according to Católicos, had been waiting behind the church in busses reinforced the "ushers".[81] Declaring the demonstration to be an "unlawful assembly," the police or "juras," as Bob Gandara refers to them, moved into the crowd wielding their riot sticks and spraying mace both outside and inside the vestibule. "I felt a strong stream of something cold on my forehead," Pedro Arias, the "old man" of Católicos, later described being maced, "and almost immediately I felt my eyes sting. Because of this, I could hardly see."[82] Ray Cruz still remembers the "angry, ugly faces of the police. You could see the hate in their eyes."[83] Acosta referred to the conflict as a "religious war, a holy riot in full gear."[84]

Inside the church, as the Mass came to an end, an irate Cardinal McIntyre, aware of the disturbance in the vestibule, condemned the action of Católicos. "We are ashamed of the participants," he told the congregation, "and we recognize that their conduct was symbolic of the conduct of the rabble as they stood at the foot of the cross, shouting, 'Crucify Him!'" However, the Cardinal asked the congregation to forgive the demonstrators "for they know not what they do." The Tidings, the archdiocesan paper, later referred to the action of Católicos as the "new barbarism."[85] And one church official called them "militant revolutionaries."[86] In addition, a newscaster, former Los Angeles Chief Tom Reddin, accused Católicos of practicing extortion against the Church.[87]

Outnumbered, the demonstrators retreated outside of the church and onto Wilshire Boulevard. In retreating some from the group smashed one of the main doors of the church by picking up, according to Bob Gandara, a heavy cigarette receptor or pot and throwing it at the door.[88] As the people inside the church began exiting, Martínez recalls, seeing one of the churchgoers literally flatten a young student demonstrator who had to be taken to the hospital. In addition, the police arrested five of the protestors whom the Los Angeles Times the next day referred to as the "club-swinging mob." One of those arrested, Alicia Escalante, was held by two police officers from behind holding her arms back. Gandara recalls seeing another "jura" approach her as if to possibly hit her with his nightstick. He never got the chance. "I don't know where she got her strength," Gandara says of Escalante, "but she picked up her right foot and kicked the cop right in the huevos [testicles]." The officer went down on his knees while television cameras caught Escalante's action. Those arrested were charged with conspiring to start a riot and assaulting an officer. Two of those arrested were Razo and Ruiz who had to spend the rest of Christmas Eve in jail until bailed out the next day. Charges were later dropped at least for those arrested that night. Oscar Zeta Acosta would later call the events of that evening a "police riot."[89] A Católicos news release further protested the actions of the police and of Cardinal McIntyre: "Women, children and innocent bystanders were clubbed without mercy from the police, the Church officials and the Cardinal who allegedly speaks for the Pope and Jesus Christ."[90] Those maced included senior citizens who had attended the Católicos mass.[91]

The next day, Christmas Day, between fifty and one hundred protestors returned to St.Basil's and held a vigil across the street from the church in an empty lot on Wilshire. They also picketed in front of the church, some carrying pictures of those who had been injured and arrested that evening. They exchanged angry comments with the mostly Anglo parishioners as they entered for Mass. "Go back to Mexico!" some of the churchgoers shouted at the demonstrators. Police in civilian clothes in the meantime snapped photos of the protestors.[92] Outside the church, Richard Cruz told a reporter: "We're not going to stop demonstrating. The Cardinal will have to kill us to get us to stop."[93]

The vigil was marred, however, by the actions of Gloria Chávez, a member of Católicos and a community activist, who entered St. Basil's during one of the Christmas Masses with a golf club in hand and proceeded to march down the main aisle before the ushers were aware of what was occurring. Acosta noted that it was a number seven wood.[94] When she reached the altar, she waved the club, scaring the priest away, and then pulled the altar cloth off spilling the items on it including the chalice onto the floor. Police arrested Chávez "on suspicion of disrupting a religious meeting."[95] Lydia López recalls that Chávez's actions were "beyond the pail," and was a polarizing issue. Martínez observes that Chávez's action was disavowed by most Católicos who expressed disbelief that Chávez would go so far as to desecrate the altar.[96] Miguel García was not particularly surprised that Chávez would do such a thing because, according to him, she was "a gutsy woman."[97]

Although Católicos had only been in existence a couple of months, their demonstration at St. Basil's represented the climax of its short history. St. Basil's symbolized the differences and tensions between Católicos and the Church in Los Angeles. The Christmas Eve protest led to a variety of repercussions. As far as the Church was concerned, it denied the charges that it had been unresponsive to the Mexican American community. At the same time, Monsignor William Johnson told a reporter that social action was not the main task of the Church. "The Church," he said, "tries to inspire people to live Christian lives, not to dictate particular solutions to social problems."[98] Although rhetorically holding its ground, the Church nevertheless moved to meet Católicos' challenge by instituting certain reforms or at least the appearance of reform.

These moves on the part of the Church were aided by the announced retirement of Cardinal McIntyre in early 1970. Whether the protests initiated against him by Católicos played a role in his retirement is hard to determine. One reporter believed that the Cardinal's retirement was welcomed by the Vatican due to the Cardinal's seeming inability to deal with what the reporter called a "theology of resistance" carried out not only by Católicos but by other discontented Church sources.[99]

Political And Legal Ramifications

With Cardinal McIntyre's departure, the Church was in a better position to address the demands made on it by Católicos. McIntyre's successor, Archbishop Timothy Manning, was more disposed to pursue a conciliatory policy within certain limits. Miguel García found him more "approachable."[100] Shortly after assuming office, Archbishop Manning met with representative of Católicos and while Manning never conceded the issue of shared governance, he did proceed to address some of the other concerns of Católicos. For one, he emerged as one of the leading Catholic bishops who helped end the grape boycott with the growers agreeing to recognize the farm workers' union. Manning authorized additional funds for the

Church's social and educational services in East Los Angeles. To deal with the issue of representation, Manning established an inter-parochial council of clergy and laypeople for the East Los Angeles parishes to serve as an advisory group to the Archbishop. Cultural reforms included permission for Spanish-speaking parishes to include Latino music such as mariachis at Mass. Although it is not clear if Manning met again during the next several months with Católicos, he, on his own initiative, visited the home of Richard Cruz later that September and met with some members of Católicos. Ray Cruz recalls that while he, Richard, and the other Católicos present were diplomatic with Manning that his parents, by contrast, were in awe of the Archbishop's visit to their home on Avenue 37.[101] Outside of Los Angeles, similar changes also took place in other California and southwestern dioceses.[102]

At a larger level, the protests by Católicos as well as a growing restlessness on the part of Chicano clergy made an impression not only on the U.S. hierarchy but in Rome as well. In 1970, for example, the Vatican approved the appointment of the Reverend Patricio Flores of San Antonio as the first bishop of Mexican American decent in the United States. One year later, the Reverend Juan Arzupe, a Latino of Ecuadorian origin, was appointed Auxiliary Bishop in Los Angeles, a clear concession to Católicos and other Chicano demands for more Latino representation in the Los Angeles Church. By 1974 three additional Latino priests were appointed bishops in the United States. Moreover, within the U.S. Church, working committees and conferences on the Spanish-speaking were organized into the 1970s. This included the Primer Encuentro Hispano de Pastoral (First Hispanic Pastoral Encounter) that met in Washington, D.C. in 1972 under the U.S. Catholic Conference for the Spanish-Speaking and recommended a number of changes to make the Church more relevant to the Latino communities.[103]

Although Católicos continued its criticism of the Church, it was significantly hampered by having to defend itself against new legal actions against it. One month after the St. Basil's demonstration, twenty-one members or supporters of Católicos were arrested for their participation in the Christmas Eve protest. Oscar Zeta Acosta referred to them as the St. Basil Twenty-One.[104] Officers arrested Richard and Ray Cruz at their parent's home where they both lived on and off.

Oscar Zeta Acosta was retained as the attorney for the defendants who were split into two separate trials that together lasted until June of 1970. Acosta accused the Catholic Church in Los Angeles of prosecuting not only Católicos, but also all Mexican Americans.[105] The trials were characterized by Zeta Acosta's theatrical antics, as Ian Haney López so well documents concerning other Acosta cases as does Acosta, himself, in his semi-fictional account of the trial in The Revolt of the Cockroach People, questioning the legitimacy of the legal process especially with respect to the exclusion of Chicanos from the jury selection process.[106] He also requested that all Catholics be excluded from the jury since the Church had publicly censured the defendants. According to Acosta, the state was unconstitutionally interfering in a purely religious matter. The court rejected his request.[107] During the trials, the presiding judge found Acosta in contempt of court and sentenced him to three days in jail.[108] Miguel García notes that at one point in the trials, Acosta had to be suspended because he had not paid his bar dues.[109]

In the end, twelve were found guilty. Some, like Martínez, Joe Razo, and Richard Cruz, served from two to four months in jail for disrupting a religious service. Others, such as Ruiz and Arias, received minor fines.[110]

The distraction of the trials clearly affected the ability of Católicos to maintain its momentum. In addition, Chicano activists, including members of Católicos, because they wore many hats in the movement, were further distracted by the organization of the Chicano anti-Vietnam war movement during 1970. This built-up would itself climax on August 29 when over twenty thousand, mostly Chicanos, demonstrated against the war in East Los Angeles. Richard Cruz and other Católicos helped organize for the demonstration. Like the St. Basil protest, but on a much larger scale, this example of growing Chicano discontent and militancy over the war was forcibly attacked and destroyed by the Los Angeles County Sheriffs that led to a full-scale riot in East Los Angeles. Three people were killed including Los Angeles Times reporter Ruben Salazar. Richard Cruz saw this as another example of police overreaction as had occurred at St. Basil's.[111] By that tragic day, and certainly into the fall, Católicos for all practical purposes had ceased to exist as still other venues of social protest arose.

The Legacy of Católicos and Richard Cruz

Because of his leadership in Católicos including his arrest due to the St. Basil's demonstration, Richard Cruz later after his graduation in 1971 from law school continued to pay a price for his convictions. He met resistance, along with Miguel García, in being certified as a practicing attorney despite passing the bar. The State Bar of California claimed that Cruz had committed "moral turpitude" due to his arrest for disturbing a religious service. Cruz fought this unjust opposition and with the support of the American Civil Liberties Union along with Chicano community support gained his right to practice law in 1973. Archbishop Manning, to his credit, testified in support of Cruz. Like other members of Católicos, Cruz would remain a committed activist and champion of social justice until his early death in 1993 at age fifty, the victim of lung cancer.[112] Camilo Cruz observes that his father was considered a "Chicanos' Chicano" due to his leadership.[113] His fellow attorney, Miguel García besides admiring Cruz's passion for the underdog, at the same time notes that he had a quick wit and great sense of humor. Cruz also loved to party and could out-party all others of his friends and colleagues. "In his fifty years," García observes with much fondness, "Richard lived a good seventy-five."[114]

Hermán Sillas, a founding member of the Mexican American Legal Defense and Education Fund (MALDEF), in an obituary on Cruz recalled as a young attorney meeting Richard and some of the other Chicano law students in the late 1960s. "It was quickly apparent that there were those who would never go back to the barrio and help its residents," he observed. "Richard was different. You knew instantly that he would go back and have an impact." Sillas referred to Cruz as a lawyer always on the right side.[115]

For Richard Cruz, the legacy of Católicos, besides the political issues involved, also had to do with more philosophical and even theological ones. "Personally," he wrote in 1976, "to myself and quite a few others, what it [Católicos] did was allow many of us to really once and for all get down to [the] . . . realities of who are we? Do we need religion?"[116] Cruz, himself, would later leave the Church, became an atheist, although still believing in a spiritual force in the world. Richard, Rosa Martínez notes, "was a spiritual person but not religious."[117] Católicos Por La Raza in an existential way proved to be not only a confrontation with the institutional Church, but also a confrontation with the Catholic soul of its participants. Although Cruz moved away from his faith, indeed he no longer was a practicing Catholic by the time of Católicos; he continued to believe that the Catholic Church had to be always made accountable to the people and had to serve the people. "He never abandoned his principles," Ray Cruz says of his brother.[118]

After Richard Cruz died on July 27, 1993, his son Camilo paid tribute to his father's commitment and, indirectly, to that of Católicos as a whole. He noted that the struggle had not been in vain and that their story would not be forgotten. "Dead Dad," Camilo eulogized, "Although I can't embrace you physically, I can embrace what you've done for me and our people. I want to especially thank you, my mother, and all the other brave warriors who challenged and fought the many hateful and oppressive institutions of this country. Because of the rebellion of the 1960s young Chicanos of today and the future have a few more chances at making it in this society. We don't have to worry as much as you did about having a voice, an existence, and about calling ourselves 'Chicanos.' In thinking of you Dad, I think of the tremendous 1960's and the people you were involved with in creating the beautiful Chicano Revolution. Many things are still wrong, of course, but [we] are better now because of what you and others have left for us."[119]

Nature of Volume

This edited volume Chicano Liberation Theology: The Writings and Documents of Richard Cruz and Católicos Por La Raza is a compilation of primary sources on CPLR and its key leader, Richard Cruz. It represents the most extensive collection of records pertaining to this important movement associated with the Chicano Movement. Many of these documents are housed in the Ricardo Cruz/Católicos Por La Raza Papers in the California Ethnic and Multicultural Archives in Special Collections in the Davidson Library at the University of California, Santa Barbara.

This volume is divided into five sections. Part 1 is on The Chicano Movement and the Catholic Church. Part 2 is on the Origins of Católicos Por La Raza. Part 3 is on Católicos in Action. Part 4 is Testimonios or oral histories of Richard Cruz and CPLR. Part 5 is on Richard Cruz: People's Attorney. Part 6 is Richard Cruz: Pensamientos and Other Reflections. Part 7 is a special Eulogy on Richard Cruz by Camilo Cruz.

[1] See Andrew Greeley, The Catholic Imagination (Berkeley and Los Angeles: University of California Press, 2000).

[2] For a study of the Chicano Movement and the Church in Houston, see Roberto Trevino, The Church in the Barrio: Mexican American Ethno-Catholicism in Houston (Chapel Hill: The University of North Carolina Press, 2006), pp. 176-205.

[3] On the movement in Los Angeles, see Ernesto Chávez, Mi Raza Primero! Nationalism, Identity, and Insurgency in the Chicano Movement in Los Angeles, 1966-1978 (Berkeley and Los Angeles: Univ. of California Press, 2002). On the movement in general or other aspects of the movement see Carlos Muñoz, Jr., Youth, Identity, and Power: The Chicano Movement (London: Verso Press, 1989); Alma M. García, Chicana Feminist Thought: The Basic Historical Writings (New York: Routledge, 1997); Ignacio M. García, United We Win: The Rise and Fall of La Raza Unida Party (Tucson: Mexican American Studies & Research Center, Univ. of Arizona, 1989); José Angel Gutiérrez, The Making of a Chicano Militant: Lessons from Cristal (Madison: Univ. of Wisconsin Press, 1998); Richard Santillan, La Raza Unida (Los Angeles: Tlaquilo Publications, 1973); Jesús Salvador Trevino, Eyewitness: A Filmmaker's Memoir of the Chicano Movement (Houston: Arte Publico Press, 2001); Ernesto Vigil, The Crusade for Justice: Chicano Militancy and the Government's War on Dissent (Madison: Univ. of Wisconsin Press, 1999); Lorena Oropeza, Raza Si! Guerra No!: Chicano Protest and Patriotism during the Vietnam War Era (Berkeley and Los Angeles: University of California Press, 2005); George Mariscal, Brown-Eyed Children of the Sun: Lessons from the Chicano Movement, 1965-1975 (Albuquerque: University of New Mexico Press, 20050); Armando Navarro, Mexican American Youth Organization: Avant-Garde of the Chicano Movement in Texas (Austin: University of Texas Press, 1995); Navarro, The Cristal Experiment: A Chicano Struggle in Community Control (Madison: University of Wisconsin Press, 1998); Juan Gómez-Quiñones, Chicano Politics: Reality and Promise, 1940-1990 (Albuquerque: University of New Mexico Press, 1990); Richard Martínez, PADRES:The New Chicano Priest Movement (Austin: University of Texas Press, 2005); Lara Medina, Las Hermanas: Chicana/Latina Religious-Political Activism in the U.S. Catholic Church (Philadelphia: Temple University Press, 2004).

[4] Interview with Richard Martínez, Los Angeles, January 21, 1996.

[5] Interview with Ray Cruz, April 25, 2003. Richard Cruz attended Loyola University School of Law from 1967 to 1971; see document, Aug. 30, 1972 in Ricardo Cruz/Católicos Por La Raza Papers, California Ethnic and Multicultural Archives (CEMA 28) in Special Collections, Univ. of Calif., Santa Barbara. Hereinafter cited as Cruz/Católicos Col.

[6] Note from Ray Cruz to Mario T. García, April 24, 2003.

[7] Interview with Raul Ruiz, March 1, 1993.

[8] Los Angeles Times, April 5, 1968, Part II, p. 6.

[9] Martínez interview. Also see, Martínez, PADRES.

[10] Ray Cruz note.

[11] Ruiz interview and part of my unpublished manuscript entitled "Chicano Power: Testimonios of the Chicano Movement in Los Angeles," p. 107.

[12] Ray Cruz interview.

[13] Ibid. Also, "Católicos Por La Raza," undated document in possession of Pedro Arias.

[14] Richard Cruz interview, December 18, 1976 contained in private collection of his son, Camilo Cruz; hereinafter referred to as Camilo Cruz Collection. Also see Camilo Cruz, "Tribute to a Barrio Lawyer: Ricardo V. Cruz," in La Neta del 'border' y la frontera (April, 1994), pp. 17-19 in Camilo Cruz Collection.

[15] Cruz to Mom & Dad, n.d., 1974 in Box 1, Fld. 5 in Cruz/Católicos Col.

[16] Rosa Martínez interview, June 14, 2005.

[17] Ray Cruz interview and interview with Paloma Martínez-Cruz, April 25, 2003. Ray Cruz notes that SDS became a model for Chicano movement organizations including Católicos.

[18] Ray Cruz note.

[19] Interview with Miguel García, July 11, 2005.

[20] Garcia interview.

[21] Interview with Bob Gandara, Sept. 4, 2005.

[22] Ray Cruz interview and Ruiz interview.

[23] Ruiz interview

[24] Ray Cruz interview.

[25] Ibid. and Richard Cruz interview.

[26] Ibid. Also Muñoz, Jr., Youth, Identity, Power.

[27] See Alberto L. Pulido, "Are You Am Emissary of Jesus Christ?: Justice, The Catholic Church, and the Chicano Movement," *Explorations in Ethnic Studies*, Vol. 14, No.1 (January, 1991), pp. 17-34.

[28] Richard Cruz interview. Ruben Salazar was the leading Latino journalist of his time. He was the only Chicano writing for a mainstream English-language newspaper in the 1960s. On August 29th, 1970, Salazar was tragically killed covering the large National Chicano Anti-War Moratorium in East Los Angeles. On Salazar, see Mario T. García,ed., *Ruben Salazar, Border Correspondent: Selected Writings, 1955-1970* (Berkeley: Univ. of California Press, 1995).

[29] Undated press clipping in Cruz/Católicos Col.

[30] "Conference of Catholic Bishops," *La Raza*, p. 29.

[31] Católicos press release, Dec. 4, 1969 in Camilo Cruz Collection.

[32] Ibid., p. 392.

[33] Poem in compilation of *La Raza* articles on Católicos in Camilo Cruz Collection.

[34] "Catolicos Por La Raza and Mexican Americans," *La Raza* (Jan., 1970), p. 2.

[35] "Blessed Are the Poor," *La Raza*, Vol.I, no.2, pp. 55-65; Ruiz interview.

[36] Católicos press release, Dec. 4, 1969 in Camilo Cruz Collection.

[37] Católicos Public Letter, Nov. 29, 1969 in Camilo Cruz Collection.

[38] "The Catholic Church and La Raza," *La Raza* (Jan., 1970).

[39] "Catolicos" in Luis Valdez and Stan Steiner, eds., *Aztlán: An Anthology of Mexican American Literature* (New York: Vintage, 1972), pp. 393-94.

[40] "The Church: The Model of Hypocrisy," p. 9.

[41] *L.A. Free Press*, Jan. 16, 1970, p. 4.

[42] Interview with Fr. Patrick McNamara, April 13, 1996.

[43] Dolores del Grito, "Jesus Christ as a Revolutionist," in Valdez and Steiner, eds., *Aztlán*, pp. 393-94.

[44] Abelardo Delgado, "The New Christ," "The Organizer," and "A New Cross," poems in Valdez and Steiner, eds., *Aztlan*, pp. 394-97.

[45] Ruiz interview.

[46] Richard Cruz interview.

[47] McNamara interview. Rodolfo Acuña notes that McIntyre "single-handedly attempted to hold back the reforms of Pope John XXIII and Vatican II; Acuña, *Occupied America: A History of Chicanos*, (New York: Harper Collins, 3rd. ed., 1988), pp. 344-345.

[48] "The Catholic Church and La Raza," p. 8.

[49] See demands in La Raza, Vol. I, no. 1 (1970), p. 25; also Letter to Congress of Mexican-American Unity, no date, in Camilo Cruz Collection.

[50] Católicos press release, Dec. 4, 1969 in Camilo Cruz Collection.

[51] García interview.

[52] Rosa Martínez interview.

[53] Martínez interview. Some meetings were also held at the Church of the Epiphany; interview with Lydia López, October 24, 1996.

[54] See Cruz resume in Box 1, Fld. 11 in Cruz/Católicos Col.

[55] Ibid.

[56] Richard Martínez interview.

[57] Rosa Martínez interview.

[58] García interview.

[59] Martínez interview.

[60] Rosa Martínez interview.

[61] Ibid.

[62] García inteview.

[63] Martínez interview.

[64] García interview; also see Richard Cruz resume.

[65] Rosa Martínez interview.

[66] Martínez interview and Pulido, ""An Emissary of Jesus Christ," pp. 25-27.

[67] "Open Letter to Cardinal McIntyre, La Raza, Vol.I, no.2, p. 49; Martínez interview.

[68] Camilo Cruz class paper.

[69] Rosa Martínez interview.

[70] Ray Cruz interview.

[71] Martínez interview.

[72] Los Angeles Times clipping, no date, in Camilo Cruz Collection.

[73] Cruz to Rev. James Francis McIntyre, Dec. 26, 1969 in Camilo Cruz Collection.

[74] Gandara interview.

[75] García interview; interview with Rick Sánchez, May 30, 2006.

[76] See clipping, Los Angeles Herald-Examiner, March 3, 1970 in Box 5, Fld. 4 in Cruz/Católicos Col.

[77] Richard Cruz interview.

[78] García interview; Martinez interview; The People's World, Jan. 3, 1970, pp. 1 and 12; Los Angeles Times, Dec. 25, 1969 and Dec. 26, 1969, p. 3; L.A. Free Press, Jan. 9, 1970, p. 2 and Jan. 16, 1970, p. 4; The Militant, Jan. 23, 1970, p. 1; La Raza, Vol.I, no.1, p. 31.

[79] Martinez interview.

[80] Ibid.; Ruiz interview; Los Angeles Times, Dec. 26, 1969, p. 3. Also see clipping, no title, Feb. 6, 1970 in Box 5, Fld. 5, Cruz/Católicos Col.and Gandara interview.

[81] Ray Cruz interview.

[82] L.A. Free Press, Jan. 16, 1970, p. 4; undated Arias statement. Also, Gandara interview.

[83] Ray Cruz interview.

[84] Oscar Zeta Acosta, The Revolt of the Cockroach People (New York: Vintage, 1973), p. 17.

[85] Los Angeles Times, Dec. 26, 1969, p. 32; L.A. Free Press, Jan. 16, 1970, p. 4; The Tidings, no date, p. 1.

[86] In Los Angeles Times clipping, Dec. 29, 1969 in Camilo Cruz Collection.

[87] See clipping "Militants Mar Mass" from a compilation of articles by The Tidings, no date, in Pedro Arias Collection.

[88] Gandara interview.

[89] Martinez interview; Ruiz interview; Los Angeles Times, Dec. 25, 1969, p. 1 and Jan.1, 1970, p. 3; La Raza, Vol.I, no.1 (1970), pp. 31 and 69; The People's World, Jan.3, 1970, p. 12; L.A. Free Press, Jan. 16, 1970, p. 2; Gandara interview.

[90] "No Room at St. Basil's for Chicanos," undated document in Camilo Cruz Collection.

[91] Gandara interview.

[92] Clipping in Cruz/Católicos Collection; Lydia López interview; Gandara interview.

[93] Los Angeles Times, Dec. 26, 1969, p. 32.

[94] Acosta, Cockroach People, p. 21.

[95] Clipping from Los Angeles Times, Dec. 26, 1969 in Pedro Arias Collection.

[96] Ibid.; The People's World, Jan. 3, 1970, p. 12; Lydia López interview; Richard Martínez interview.

[97] García interview. García further notes that Gloria Chávez would crack up others at Católicos meeting by entering and saying to the men: "manos pa arriba, calzones pa bajo" [hands up, underpants down].

[98] Clipping from Herald-Examiner, Jan. 4, 1970 in Camilo Cruz Collection.

[99] L.A. Free Press, Jan.23, 1970, p. 4.

[100] García interview.

[101] The Tidings, Jan. 29, 1971; Los Angeles Times, Sept. 14, 1970, p. 18; Martínez interview; Ray Cruz interview.

[102] The Tidings, Jan. 29, 1971, p. 1; Los Angeles Times, Sept. 14, 1970, p. 18; Martínez interview.

[103] Los Angeles Times, July 28, 1974, Part II, p. 1; La Voz Catolica (Oakland), July, 1973. Also see, David Badillo, Latinos and the New Immigrant Church (Baltimore: Johns Hopkins University Press, 2006). Badillo, Latinos.

[104] See Acosta, Cockroach People, p. 137.

[105] Clipping from El Popo, n.d., Box 5, Fld. 4 in Cruz/Católicos Col.

[106] See Ian F. Haney López, Racism on Trial: The Chicano Fight for Justice (Cambridge: Harvard University Press, 2003). Although Haney López does not discuss the CPLR cases, he mistakenly notes that Acosta "secured the acquittal of a group of activists, Católicos Por La Raza," p. 39. While true that some were acquitted, others were not.

[107] Clipping from El Popo, March 10, 1970 in Cruz/Católicos Collection.

[108] Clipping from Herald-Examiner, May 22, 1970 in Pedro Arias Collection.

[109] García interview.

[110] Herald-Examiner, June 6, 1970, p. A-3.

[111] Ray Cruz interview. For the best study of the Chicano anti-war movement, see Oropeza, Raza Si! Guerra No!

[112] Ibid.; see obituary on Richard Cruz, "Richard Cruz: Chicano Rights Lawyer," in Los Angeles Times, July 24, 1993 in Camilo Cruz Collection. Miguel García, who like Cruz graduated from law school in 1971, received his certificate to practice law apparently a year before Cruz; see "The Fight for Miguel García and Richard Cruz," Box 1, Fld. 1 in Cruz/Católicos Col. A signature drive gathered five thousand signatures in support of Cruz and García to practice law; see clipping from Justicia . . . O?, Vol 1, No. 11, p. 6 in Box 1, Fld. 8 in Cruz/Católicos Col.

[113] Interview with Camilo Cruz, April 25, 1997.

[114] García interview.

[115] See Sillas obituary in Hispanic Link Weekly, Aug. 16, 1993, p. 3 in Box 1, Fld. 9, Cruz/Católicos Col. At its 1993 awards banquet, MALDEF awarded its Legal Service Award posthumously to Cruz. See program for Nineteenth Award, Los Angeles Award Dinner, MALDEF, Nov. 4, 1993 in Box 1, Fld. 9, Cruz/Católicos Col.

[116] Richard Cruz interview.

[117] Rosa Martínez interview.

[118] Ray Cruz interview.

[119] Camilo Cruz euology in Camilo Cruz Collection. Richard Cruz is buried at Forest Lawn Memorial Park in Los Angeles; see Certificate of Death, July 27, 1993 in Box 1, Fld. 9, Cruz/Católicos Col.

Part 1

Richard Cruz outside of St. Basil's Church, Los Angeles, Christmas Day, Dec. 25, 1969.
Courtesy of Special Collections, Davidson Library, Univ. of Calif. Santa Barbara

The Chicano Movement and the Catholic Church

The CHICANO y la IGLESIA [Church][1]

César Chávez

The place to begin is with our own experience with the [Catholic] Church in the strike which has gone on for 31 months in Delano. For in Delano the Church has been involved with the poor in a unique way which should stand as a symbol to other communities. Of course, when we refer to the Church we should define the word a little. We mean the whole Church, the Church as an ecumenical body spread around the world and not just its particular form in a parish in a local community.

The Church we are talking about is a tremendously powerfl [sic] institution in our society and in the world. That Church is one form of the Presence of God on Earth and so naturally, it is powerful. It is powerful by definition. It is a powerful moral and spiritual force which cannot be ignored by any movement. Furthermore, it is an organization with tremendous wealth. Since the Church is to be servant to the poor, it is our fault if that wealth is not channeled to help the poor in our world.

In a small way we have been able, in the Delano strike, to work together with the Church in such a way as to bring some of its moral and economic power to bear on those who want to maintain the status quo, keeping farm workers in virtual enslavement. In brief here is what happened in Delano.

Some years ago, when some of us were working with the Community Service Organization, we began to realize the powerful effect which the Church can have on the conscience of the opposition. In scattered instances, in San Jose, Sacramento, Oakland, Los Angeles and other places, priests would speak out loudly and clearly against specific instances of oppression, and in some cases, stand with the people who were being hurt. Furthermore, a small group of priests, Frs. McDonald, McCollough, Duggan and others, began to pinpoint attention on the terrible situation of the farm workers in our state.

[1] La Verdad (Dec., 1969) in Ricardo Cruz/Católicos Por La Raza Papers.

At about that same time, we began to run into the California Migrant Ministry in the camps and fields. They were about the only ones there, and a lot of us were very suspicious, since we were Catholics and they were Protestants. However, they had developed a very clear conception of the Church. It was called to serve, to be at the mercy of the poor, and not to try to use them. After a while, this made a lot of sense to us, and we began to find ourselves working side by side with them. In fact, it forced us to raise the question why OUR Church was not doing the same. We would ask, "Why do the Protestants come out here and help the people, demand nothing, and give all their time to serving farm workers, while our own parish priests stay in their Churches, where only a few people come, and usually feel uncomfortable?"

It was not until some of us moved to Delano and began working to build the National Farm Workers Association that we really saw how far removed from the people the Church's parish was. In fact, we could not get any help at all from the priests of Delano. When the strike began, they told us we could not even use the Church's auditorium for the meetings. The farm workers' money helped build that auditorium! But the Protestants were there again, in the form of the California Migrant Ministry, and they began to help in little ways, here and there.

When the strikes started in 1965, most of our "friends" forsook us for a while. They ran or were just too busy to help. But the California Migrant Ministry held a meeting with its staff and decided that the strike was a matter of life or death for farm workers everywhere, and that even if it meant the end of the Migrant Ministry, they would turn over their resources to the strikers. The political pressure on the Protestant churches was tremendous and the Migrant Ministry lost a lot of money. But they stuck it out and they began to point the way to the rest of the Church. In fact, when 30 of the strikers were arrested for shouting Huclga [strike], 11 ministers went to jail with them. They were in Delano that day at the request of Chris Hartmire, director of the California Migrant Ministry.

Then the workers began to raise th [sic] question: "Why ministers? Why not priests? What does the Bishop say?" But the Bishop said nothing. Slowly the pressure of the people grew and grew, until finally we have in Delano a priest sent by the new Bishop, Timothy Manning, who is there to help minister to the needs of farm workers. His name is Father Mark Day and he is the Union's Chaplain. Finally, our own Catholic Church has decided to recognize that we have our own particular needs, just as the growers have theirs.

Outside of the local diocese, the pressure built up on growers to negotiate was tremendous. Though we were not allowed to have our own priest, the power of the ecumenical body of the Church was tremendous on the Church. The work of the Church, for example, in the Schenley, DiGiorgio, Perelli-Minette strikes was fantastic. They applied pressure and they mediated.

When poor people get involved in a long conflict, such as a strike, or a civil rights drive, and the pressure increases each day, there is a deep need for spiritual advice. Without it we see families crumble, leadership weaken, and hard workers grow tired. And in such a situation the spiritual advice must be given by a friend, not by part of the opposition. Thus, what sense does it make to go to Mass on Sunday and reach out for spiritual help, and instead get sermons about the wickedness of your cause? That only drives one to question and to despair. The growers in Delano have their spiritual problems . . . we do not deny that. They have every right to have priests and ministers who serve their needs . . . BUT WE HAVE DIFFERENT NEEDS, AND SO WE NEEDED A FRIENDLY SPIRITUAL GUIDE. And this is true in every community in this state where the poor face tremendous problems.

But the opposition raises a tremendous howl about this. They don't want us to have our spiritual advisors, friendly to our needs. Why is this? Why indeed except that THERE IS TREMENDOUS SPIRITUAL AND ECONOMIC POWER IN THE CHURCH. The rich know it, and for that reason, they choose to keep it from the people.

The leadership of the Mexican American Community must admit that we have fallen far short in our task of helping provide spiritual guidance for our people. We may say, "I don't feel any such need. I can get along." But that is a poor excuse for not helping provide such help for others. For we can also say, "I don't need any welfare help. I can take care of my own problems." But we are all willing to fight like hell for welfare aid for those who truly need it, who would starve without it. Likewise, we may have gotten an education and not care about scholarship money for ourselves, or our children. But we would, we should, fight like hell to see to it that our state provides aid for any child needing it so that he can get the education he desires. LIKEWISE, WE CAN SAY WE DON'T NEED THE CHURCH. THAT IS OUR BUSINESS. BUT THERE ARE HUNDREDS OF THOUSANDS OF OUR PEOPLE WHO DESPERATELY NEED SOME HELP FROM THAT POWERFUL INSTITUTION, THE CHURCH, AND WE ARE FOOLISH NOT TO HELP THEM GET IT.

For example, the Catholic Charities agencies of the Catholic Church has millions of dollars earmarked for the poor. But often the money is spent for food baskets for the needy instead of for effective action to eradicate the cause of poverty. The men and women who administer this money sincerely want to help their brothers. It should be our duty to help direct the attention to the basic needs of the Mexican-Americans in our society . . . needs which cannot be satisfied with baskets of food but rather with effective organizing at the grass roots level.

Therefore, I am calling for the Mexican-American groups to stop ignoring this source of power. It is not just our right to appeal to the Church to use its power effectively for the poor, it is our duty to do so. It should be as natural as appealing to government. . . . And we do that often enough.

Furthermore, we should be prepared to come to the defense of that priest, rabbi, minister or layman of the Church, who out of commitment to truth and justice gets into a tight place with his pastor or bishop. It behooves us to stand with that man and help him see his trial through. It is our duty to see to it that his rights of conscience are respected and that no bishop, pastor or other higher body takes that God-given human right away.

Finally, in a nutshell, what do we want the Church to do? We don't ask for more cathedrals. We don't ask for bigger Churches or fine gifts. We ask for its presence with us, beside us, as Christ among us. We ask the Church to sacrifice with the people for justice, and for love of brother. We don't ask for words. We ask for deeds. We don't ask for paternalism. We ask for servanthood.

OF THE CHURCH[1]

Rodolfo Salinas

The role of the Holy Roman Catholic Church in the western hemisphere has consistently been identified with power interests, and history has shown that the Church's political position is all too often not in the better interest of the people. Thus, it is suggested that the established power of the Catholic Church on the right is juxtaposed against the powerless people on the left.

Since the Inquisition the church has supported the Spanish government's suppressive measures. This alliance of church and state was reaffirmed in and for the conquest of the New World, and continues to the present day.

The Church came to the new world as a conquering aristocracy to create a new empire for Rome and for Spain. It came for the salvation of the church, and not for the salvation of the indigenous people of the land. The Church State conquered these people, and then built its empire on their enslaved souls and bodies.

In Mexico, the Church denounced Los Padres Hidalgo and Morelos in support of the Spanish government. Although the Mexican revolution of 1810 was inspired by these two priests, the Church condemned their efforts. They were excommunicated and executed by arrangement of the Church State, Hidalgo in 1811 and Morelos in 1815.

Later, the Church supported the rule of Maximilian and the French in the 1860's against Benito Juárez, his *leyes de reforma* [reform laws], and the people.

And still again, the church supported the thirty year dictatorship of Porfirio Díaz against the people's revolution of 1910 which was represented by leaders such as Pancho Villa and Emiliano Zapata.

In recent times we have the Church blatantly defending dictators throughout the western hemisphere. There was Peron in Argentina, now deposed. There was Batista in Cuba, now deposed. Trujillo in La Republica Dominicana, also deposed; and Strausner in Paraguay. Thus, the Church has long identified with the ruling oligarchies of many Latin countries, and when members of the clergy attempt to initiate social and economic reform, they are suppressed. A case in point is that

[1] Con Safos (no date; circa late 1960s) in Ricardo Cruz/Católicos Por La Raza Col.

of Padre Camilio Torres of Colombia. He was one of Latin America's leading sociologists when the Catholic Church and the Colombian government forced him into exile for advocating social reform. He was eventually killed by government troops.

The Church in supporting the ruling oligarchies of most western hemisphere nations has acquired huge land holdings in these countries, including the United States. This assures the Church a significant role in the power structure of these countries, and impedes any sort of land or social reform for the people.

This historical purview indicates that the Church has failed to go to the people, but instead has forced the people to come submissively to it. And today, nuestra Raza of the Southwest United States is continuing this long tradition of humble and respectful servitude to their church; *pero hay señas de cambio* [but there are signs of change].

The need for educational reform is obvious, but the Church has done nothing. Rather, it has compounded the problems by excluding underachievers or youngsters presenting behavioral problems from its own schools. It has fostered bigotry to the point wherein a Catholic town, Cacerro, Wisconsin, turned with violence and hatred against Rev. Martin Luther King in his civil rights activities.

Our Catholic colleges have very few Chicanos, yet the penitentiaries have a large percentage of Chicanos. The Church has again remained silent on the need for any penal or law reform, or the need for more relevant college curriculum or the need for a *social outreach* to the barrios of the southwest.

La huelga struggle of César Chávez for the farm workers is a labor reform movement that has been ignored by the Church. Rather than supporting the people in this movement, the Cardinal of the Los Angeles Archdiocese has attempted vigorously to silence the Catholic clergy on this matter.

Thus the same struggle appears to continue in this day with our own people, the Church allied with the established powers against the people. And we suggest, therefore, that it is not the stereotyped Mexican who sleeps beneath the cactus, but the Church dreaming its high ideals which are seldom brought to earth. The Church, it seems, has unfortunately chosen to emulate Christ's words while conveniently forgetting his deeds. It is indeed a church of words and little action.

Christ was the best of revolutionaries and if he were walking the streets of Los Angeles today, the present cardinal would almost certainly not support his relevant and dynamic form of Christianity. This should not be the Catholic way.

Accordingly, the Church is going to have to change. It is going to have to awaken from its slumber beneath the cactus. It is going to have to start following the example of Christ, and start becoming *the living Christ*. It is going to have to show its people the *way* here on earth; it is going to have to stand firmly at the present day *Stations' of the Cross* and be willing to be crucified for the people. Not until it moves in this direction will there be any hope for the Church as a living institution. It needs meaningful relevance to the present lives of *the People* in order to exist.

THE CATHOLIC CHURCH AND LA RAZA[1]

Antonio J. Sclabassi, O.F.M.

Within the Catholic Church at the present time there is tension and turmoil unparalleled in her history. The Church is painfully trying to discover her place in the modern world; there are many hopeful signs of renewed life, dedication and commitment to the poor, and the oppressed.

One of these hopeful signs is the response of the Church to challenges given by various groups and individuals, such as the United Farm Workers and Católicos Por La Raza. The discourse between the Church and her fold has drawn fire from all quarters of the Chicano/Mexican community. And perhaps no one has challenged the American Catholic Church in the way that César Chávez has done.

Cesar writes: ". . . What do we want the Church to do? We don't ask for more cathedrals. We don't ask for bigger churches or fine gifts. We ask for its presence with us, besides us, as Christ among us.

"We ask the Church to sacrifice with the people for social change, for justice, and for love of brother. We don't ask for words. We ask for deeds. We don't ask for paternalism. We ask for servanthood."

The role of servant is what the Church is rediscovering more and more in modern American life. She can no longer lead and direct in a paternalistic way, but must put herself and all she is and has at the service of the poor and the oppressed.

GRASS-ROOT MOVEMENT NEEDED

A distinction must be made here between the Church as structure and the Church as people. The structure of the Church will only be moved and, where necessary, be changed, through the grassroot movement of the people who comprise the

[1] La Voz del Pueblo (Feb., 1970) in Ricardo Cruz/Católicos Por La Raza Papers.

Church. This process has already begun, and there is much evidence that it is quickly growing.

The Catholic Church, more than any other denomination, has the greater obligation to support La Raza in its endeavors because of the close historical ties of the members of La Raza to the Church. That support will and should depend on the circumstances of a particular time, place, and needs.

The concept of servanthood will be a painful one for many within the Church to assimilate, and yet that concept is an essential one given to the Church by Christ.

In this spirit of servanthood three weeks ago 57 priests met for three days at Los Gatos in order to form a California Chicano Priests' Coalition. This coalition is an action-oriented organization primarily for the collective support of these priest themselves in their work, but also to go on record as supporting the activities of La Raza.

CHANGES ASKED

Some of the changes within the structural Church which the coalition is asking for are:

- Formation of specialized pastoral teams of priests, sisters and laity to work exclusively with the Spanish-speaking without regard for parish boundaries.
- Redistribution of diocesan funds to support work among minority groups "without regard to ability to contribute."
- Participation of minority group members in determining Church expenditures.
- Direct Church funding of self-help programs controlled by the poor themselves rather than by other agencies.
- Train natural leaders for short-range service within particular communities, leaders the Spanish-speaking can identify with.

The Catholic Church has power and resources which can and must be put to the most effective use possible in the community. Our prayer is that the Church will respond effectively whenever a challenge to serve is given to it.

THE NEW CHICANO PRIESTS[1]

Agustín Garza

At a time when revolutionary movements hold nothing sacred, the Catholic Church finds itself fighting for its life alongside other more "worldly" institutions. Wounded most severely by both mild and militant dissent from within, the Church is dangling between ruin and reform, and everyone from the most pompous bishop to the most humble altar boy is suffering from an ecclesiastical identity crisis.

In the Americas especially, the Church is undergoing a phase of self-analysis and reflection. From the United Farmworkers in the Southwestern United States to the Movimiento de Sacerdotes para el Tercer Mundo en Argentina revolutionary groups have forced the Church to abandon its sanctimonious preaching in order to get it to go about the real business for which it was intended. The charitable acts of mercy which, according to many rebel priests, the multi-billion dollar Church has used to assuage the conscience of its bejeweled heirarchy, [sic] are being rejected as paternalistic gestures inconsistent with the true spirit of Christ.

Father Miguel Francisco Barragan, the free-lance Chicano priest who 3 years ago bolted the institution, puts it this way: "Our people are no longer asking for underwear, left-over bras and Christmas baskets. They need to build economic and political power."

Embittered and cynical about the Church's role in helping the Chicano people of the United States, the guitar-toting Father Barragan has gone about his own business, ever since Church officials took away his office, his car, and his salary.

In 1968, Father Barragan was asked to be the first Chicano priest to run the national office of the Bishop's Committee for the Spanish Speaking, a service-oriented Church agency set up 21 years ago in San Antonio, Texas.

Unsatisfied with the function of the committee which he claimed was used politically by the Church as a front to show that it was serving minorities, Father

[1] La Voz del Pueblo (Feb., 1970) in Ricardo Cruz/Católicos Por La Raza Papers.

Barragan fell out of good grace with his superiors when he tried to take the Committee away from the Church. His first step was to incorporate the agency in order to get funds from foundations and even Protestant Church groups. He felt that this would invest the Committee with some authentic power. He then opened a branch in Lansing, Michigan and another in San Francisco, California.

Boosted by $70,000 from Marlon Brando, Barragan began work on opening a Western flank for Chicanos of Dr. Martin Luther King's Poor People's Campaign. But San Antonio's Archbishop Lucey, who was a close friend of President Johnson, didn't go much for the idea and he gave Father Barragan an ultimatum: either he worked for the Bishop's Committee or he joined Dr. King's campaign. Not both.

Not to be upstaged, independent-minded Barragan held a march around the Alamo to publicize the conflict. "This is not a problem between Archbishop Lucey and Father Barragan. It is a problem between the Church and the poor," he said at that time.

That event marked the end of his formal association with the Church which in effect disinherited him but never sent him a formal letter of dismissal. Three years later Father Barragan prefers not to follow in the footsteps of the Prodigal Son: "I didn't have to leave. I could have crawled back and I'm sure I'd be playing golf twice a week and hearing confessions whenever I felt like it, and probably be a bishop some day. But that's not the solution to our problems."

While Father Barragan's rebellion against the Church was leading to the inevitable break with that institution, a close friend of his, Father Antonio Valdivia, was also soul-searching for a way to make his priesthood relate to the needs of Chicanos.

As a newly ordained priest, Father Valdivia had been sent to a predominantly Anglo parish in Castro Valley where in three years he heard at most 5 confessions in Spanish. According to Father Barragan, who was assigned for some time to an Irish-Italian parish, the policy of sending minorities to parishes where few of their own people live is a deliberate policy of the Church which doesn't want its priests to get involved in "the crisis of their people." Sending a Chicano priest to a Chicano parish forces the institution to change, says Barragan.

Father Valdivia, who grew up in Oakland, asked to be transferred to St. Barnard's Church in the middle of Oakland's Chicano district. There he picked up what he terms a social activist orientation.

"It was no longer just a question of saying mass on First Fridays. I became aware of the needs of my people."

Father Valdivia and Father Barragan became friends while they were both working with the city's anti-poverty programs. The more serious, no-nonsense Barragan, who at 36 is two years Valdivia's senior, had some influence on the more light-hearted Father Valdivia who remains within the Catholic Church.

Less articulate but probably more witty than Barragan, Father Valdivia didn't have the same bitter experience with his superiors. "I suppose that I could take more," he said. "Father Barragan scolded, criticized, and accused and I would say, "Bueno por el amor de Dios, todo se va arreglar." [For the love of God, everything will be okay]

Father Valdivia grew less naïve as he came into closer contact with Chicano life in the barrio. During the violent high school "blowouts" at Fremont High in 1968 and 1969, Father Valdivia was rudely awakened to the anger, frustration, and despair brewing among Chicanos.

Those were decisive years for Valdivia. He stood strong in defense of the Chicano students who were fighting for more Chicano teachers and counselors. Winning the respect and friendship of many students, he was asked to be a counselor himself. He needed little encouragement and is presently seeking a Masters Degree at Cal State Hayward so he can return to Fremont as a counselor.

Both Father Barragan and Father Valdivia are agreed that the Chicano priest must work more closely with his people in their fight against discrimination and injustice. And they both believe that technical training is an indispensible [sic] prerequisite if a priest is going to be effective.

"When I took over the national office I didn't know anything about education, politics, or economics where Christianity belongs. What the hell good am I for, I wondered," said Father Barragan.

When he left the Bishop's Committee he helped set up the Southwest Council of La Raza. He became director of the Economic Opportunity Section, training "barrio economic developers."

Much of Barragan's work, which involved setting up corporations to get money from federal agencies, required a knowledge of law which he didn't have. More and more he began to resent his dependence on Anglo lawyers and their technical skill.

Father Barragan left the council and is currently in law school to pick up the skills he needs "to help protect what we have and build economic power for La Raza."

The more the modern priest abandons his spiritual duties and immerses himself in secular life, the better he comes to understand the failures of his Church and the greater is the social responsibility he assumes.

"The real Chicano priest today has got to be a martyr," says Father Barragan. "If he's going to fight for his people, if he's going to develop their power, he's going to have to tear it away from the Church."

Much of the internal revolt within the Church started with the reforms brought about by Pope John XXIII who convened the historic Second Vatican Council. The changes, which at first involved minor alternations in Catholic ceremony and custom like the prohibition against eating meat on Friday, ended up a challenge to the Church's basic principles and deep-rooted traditions.

In Latin America, the spirit of self-analysis and reform was formalized at a Bishop's conference in Medellín, Colombia. The impact of that conference, and what is referred to among the Latin American clergy as the "spirit of Medellín," has changed the lives of priests throughout the continent. Revolutionary priests like Padre Gallego and Camilo Torres are admired by many young men and cursed by many reactionary bishops and cardinals who prefer to perpetuate the Church's role as supporter of unjust oligarchies and military dictatorships.

"We're getting theological help from the Theology of Liberation of Medellín. The theme of salvation is interpreted in terms of the dignity of man and his freedom from anything oppressive, be it poverty, illiteracy or domination by a foreign power," said Father Valdivia. "The conference at Medellín was the first-time Latin American bishops rubbed the nose of idealism in the mud of reality."

There are approximately 300 activist Chicano priests in the United States involved in the political and economic fight of Chicanos. They do not believe that a priest should not involve himself in politics and other worldly matters. They feel that the Church has actively and diliberately [sic] tried to pacify and tranquilize the Chicano in his poverty. As Father Barragan put it: "I'm convinced that the whole message of the Resurrection is preached to the middle class and the well-to-do while poor people are still getting the message of the Crucifixion, live with your poverty, carry your cross and all that nonsense."

Largely due to the efforts of these priests, the Church has begun to respond. It just granted Reies Tijerina $158,000 with the written stipulation that the money must be used to carry on the fight for the lands. It has set up an agency called The Human Development Fund which finances, among others, a group of Chicano priests called PADRES whose job it is to help the Church solve its racist problems and define the religious needs of Chicanos. The Church has even named the first Chicano Bishop, Bishop Flores of San Antonio, Texas.

But the more radical priests are not satisfied. Father Valdivia warns against accepting tokenism and Father Barragan, who outwardly labels the Church a racist institution, calls these "micky [sic] mouse" measures still part of the philosophy of minimum response.

Barragan estimates that Chicanos give the Church in Sunday donations at least 39 million dollars a year. He wants to see the poor boycott the Church and set up their own funds and their own banks. "Then we'll have more Chicano priests with power and authority, because the Church respects economic power like any pagan does."

Both in different ways, Fathers Barragan and Valdivia are Chicano priests turning the Church around, standing it on its head. Already suffering from a shortage of religious personnel, the Church can ill afford to lose these priests who are daily becoming more inpatient and who could easily find a more fulfilling life on the outside.

If they change anything, these priests would like to change the attitude of the Church which was summed up in this bitter statement on a Chicano poster:

"La Iglesia quiere mi dinero, pero no quiere mis problemas."

[The Church wants my money, but not my problems.]

Part 2

Supporters of Católicos Por La Raza, 1969.
Courtesy of Special Collections, Davidson Library, Univ. of Calif. Santa Barbara

The Origins of Católicos Por La Raza

CATÓLICOS POR LA RAZA AND MEXICAN-AMERICANS PART ONE[1]

Richard Cruz

We wish to share with you the feelings which gave rise to Católicos Por La Raza. As Mexican-Americans and as Catholics you have a right to know.

Members of Católicos Por La Raza (CPLR) are Catholics. We have gone to Catholic schools and understand the Catholic tradition. Because of our Catholic training we know that Christ, the founder of Catholicism was a genuinely poor man. We know that he was born in a manger because His compatriots refused Him better housing. We know that He not only washed and kissed the feet of the poor (Mary Magdalen) but did all in His power to feed and educate the poor. We also know that one day He rode through Jerusalem on a jackass and was laughed at, spat upon, and ridiculed. We remember, from our Catholic education, that Christ, our hero, did not have to identify with the poor but chose to do so. We also were taught that one day Christ went to the established church, a church which identified with the rich people, with people who were never ridiculed or laughed at or spat upon, and He took a whip and used it upon the money-changers of His day who, in the name of religion, would dare to gather money from the poor. And, finally, we know, as all Christians know, His love for the poor was so great that He chose to die for poor people.

We know these things because our Catholic education has taught us that these were the things Christ did, Christ who founded the Catholic Church. And we

[1] Special issue of La Raza on CPLR, 1969 in Ricardo Cruz/Católicos Por La Raza Papers.

know further that if you or I claim to be Christian we have the duty to not only love the poor but to be as Christlike as possible.

It is these feelings within us, as members of Católicos Por La Raza, which led us to look at our Catholic Church as it presently exists. A Church which, for example in Los Angeles, would dare to build a $3,5000,000 Church on Wilshire Boulevard when you and we know that because of our poverty our average education is 8.6 years and many, too many of our people live in projects. How many churches, let alone million dollar churches, did Christ build? We look further and found that, although as a matter of faith all of us are the Catholic Church, nonetheless no Chicanos are able to participate in decisions within the Church, which are not of purely religious nature. Would you have voted for a million-dollar Church?

So many other considerations led to the creation of Católicos Por La Raza. We do not have the time or the money to print them all. But we do ask you to remember, as Mexican-Americans, as Católicos, as Chicanos, that as members of the Catholic Church, it is our fault if the Catholic Church in the Southwest is no longer a Church of blood, a Church of struggle, a Church of sacrifice. It is our fault because we have not raised our voices as Catholics and as poor people for the love of Christ. We can't love our people without demanding better housing, education, health, and so many other needs we share in common.

In a word, we are demanding that the Catholic Church practice what it preaches. Remember Padre Hidalgo. And remember that the history of our people is the history of the Catholic Church in the Americas. We must return the Church to the poor. OR DID CHRIST DIE IN VAIN?

CATÓLICOS POR LA RAZA AND MEXICAN-AMERICANS PART TWO[1]

Richard Cruz

"I love going to Church," the viejita said, smiling. "It's so beautiful there, and my house is so ugly."

Her words and her smile tell more than a personal story. They reflect a tradition of attitudes and conditions that have long prevailed among Chicanos. And they indicate what the Católicos Por La Raza revolt is all about.

The Catholic Church gives the viejita a few hours of grace and beauty on Sundays. She is grateful, for it is a refuge from her living conditions on the other six days. But her gratitude and religious needs keep her from asking some crucial questions:

"Why must there be such contrast between the grandeur of the Church and the squalor of home?"

If the Church were made a little less grand, couldn't the homes of parishoners [sic] be made a little less squalid?

Should the Church just provide an escape from a rotting house, rather than a means of improving that house?

Católicos are asking such questions because there are few places where the Church is more entrenched than in East Los Angeles, and few places where so many Catholics suffer worse living conditions. Take housing as an indication of how most Chicanos live (when they're not in Church, of course):

Recently, the L.A. County Board of Supervisors took a survey of housing in the East L.A. barrio. It showed that 72 percent of dwellings in the target area violate the

[1] Ricardo Cruz/Católicos Por La Raza Papers.

County Building Code. The survey indicated that some 6,000 of the 8,200 homes covered require rehabilitation. Another study by the University of Southern California confirmed this finding; it described as sound only 15 percent of all housing units in East L.A.

What this means in terms of Chicano people's lives is large families crowded into small decaying houses and apartments. Home is a place of demoralization. So are most other buildings and facilities in the community . . . except, of course, for the Churches.

And how has the Los Angeles Archdiocese responded to Chicano housing needs? "We're not in the housing business," a Church spokesman said. And sure enough, the Archdiocese has not built a single unit of low-cost housing. When the chancery claims that their first responsibility is to serve the Mexican-American people, it apparently does not include their living conditions.

The Archdiocese seems to question whether housing is its concern. Católicos Por La Raza asks how a concerned Church can ignore these needs.

It's not as if the Archdiocese does not engage in building and property ownership. The fact that it controls about $1 billion in holdings is proof of that. And it's not as if there is no precedent for Church involvement in housing for the poor. The archdiocese in San Francisco and other areas of the county have participated in many low-cost housing projects.

Why not in East Los Angeles, where there is a major housing crisis among devout parishoners [sic]?

When the Church does build on the Eastside, it is rarely if ever with an eye to making basic improvements in social conditions. Little Chicano labor is employed in Church construction in the community; rarely does a Chicano builder or subcontractor participate in such construction.

The new Santa Marta hospital—which the Archdiocese has used as an example of concern for Chicanos—is a good case in point.

True, the Cardinal promoted the project and got president [sic] Nixon to help raise the funds. True, the hospital is badly needed in the Chicano community (provided the emphasis is on caring for the poor, regardless of their ability to pay). But an opportunity to help economic conditions in the community by means of hospital construction has not only been missed—it was vehemently opposed.

An organized group of Chicano builders was actively seeking work on the hospital and other Church projects. Last summer, the group was in line for a Church demolition job. The project would have given them the chance to prove their competency to the Church, and would have provided a number of jobs for Chicano workers. But the chancery of the Archdioses [sic] turned down their bid on the grounds that "these people can't dictate to us how we're going to spend Church money."

This attitude has carried over to selecting contractors for the hospital. The general contractor is, of course, a wealthy Anglo from outside the community. It is not certain as yet whether any Chicanos at all will be included in this $4 million project for the Chicano community.

The social attitudes of the Archdioses [sic] was beautifully summarized by a Church spokesman just after the Christmas demonstration by Católicos. "Jesus' revolution was spiritual," he said. "How arrogant these demonstrators are when they invoke Jesus in this social and political revolt of theirs."

In reply, let it suffice to remind the chancery how Jesus chased the money-lenders from that beautiful, beautiful temple.

THE CHURCH AND LA RAZA[1]

Richard Cruz

Chicanos throughout the United States are becoming aware that the Catholic Church must involve itself in their fight for self-determination. The Church must help lead the way, but in order to lead the way it must be truly "ecclesiastical" Church. The Catholic Church's credibility for the Chicanos that it seeks to Christianize is at an all time low and it can and will get lower unless the Church shows by example rather than just preach. Every phase of Church institutional life—parish, chancery, seminary, convent, social educational institutions, mass media, organizations, and affiliates—has to be mobilized to help Chicanos.

The basic issue for the Spanish-speaking barrios is representation throughout the structure of the Church. There are over 12 million Spanish speaking people in the United States, over 90% of whom are Catholic. The Spanish-speaking community is the largest ethnic minority group within the U.S. Catholic Church, representing approximately 23% of the total U.S. Catholic population and 67% of the Catholics in the five Southwestern states (California, Arizona, New Mexico, Colorado, and Texas).

The total population of La Raza in the U.S. numerically exceeds that of sixty nations. Eleven Latin American countries and Puerto Rico, all with smaller populations, have their own Hierarchy and have developed their own Catholic Institutions. Puerto Rico, with a population of 21/2 million, has 4 indigenous Bishops. La Raza has over 12 million of its people in this country (California and Texas each have over two million), but not one single indigenous Spanish surnamed person among the 270 Ordinaries who constitute the National Conference of Catholic Bishops. La Raza is almost totally unrepresented in official national and diocesan appointments. There are over 720 priests in the diocese of L.A., yet only 5% of them are of Spanish sur-name. Despite the desperate need for educa-

[1] Special issue of La Raza on CPLR, 1969 in Ricardo Cruz/Católicos Por La Raza Papers.

tional assistance, there is no aid program to La Raza's people. The pattern is the same throughout the Church. It has been a determining influence on the negative attitudes of our young people towards the pursuit of the religious life as a vocation and the Catholic laity's disenchantment with official social and apostolic groups.

It is not the Church or more specifically the religious views that are inadequate to meet the needs of today's poor, but some of the men who help run the Church. Cardinal McIntyre, who runs the diocese of Los Angeles has for a long time suppressed not only the laity but also his priests and nuns. The order of the Immaculate Heart sisters are still in disfavor with him despite the fact that many of them are relating to today's poor. Priests have relinquished their priesthood because they are not allowed to minister to the poor. Social action, to the Cardinal is regarded in the same vein as hell.

Last week, a delegation of Católicos Por La Raza paid a visit to the Cardinal. The purpose of the visit was to inform the Cardinal about the problems Chicanos face and to find out how the Church was involved in helping Chicanos.

The Cardinal responded by telling the delegation "we are aware of the militants and radicals in our society and we are prepared and trained to deal with them." Cardinal McIntyre apparently forgot that Jesus Christ was one of the most radical and militant men in his time. He threw out the merchants, money lenders and changers out of the holy temple. He chased them out with a whip. He chased them out because he cared enough about his religion and Church.

The Catholic Church is one form of the presence of God on earth. It is powerful moral and spiritual force which cannot be ignored by Chicanos. Furthermore, it is an organization with a tremendous amount of wealth. Since the Church is to be servant to the poor, it is our fault if that wealth is not channeled to help the poor in our barrios. We must work together with the Church in such a way as to bring some of its moral and economic power to bear in those who want to maintain the status quo, keeping Chicanos in virtual enslavement.

Chicanos can profit from César Chávez' experience in Delano. When the strike started in 1965, the California Migrant Ministry, a coalition of Protestant Churches was tremendous and the Migrant Ministry lost a lot of money. But they stuck it out, and they began to point the way to the rest of the Church. In fact, when 30 of the strikers were arrested for shouting Huelga, 11 ministers went to jail with them.

Soon the farmworkers [sic] began to raise the question, "Why ministers? Why not priests? What does the Bishop say?" But the Bishop said nothing. But slowly the pressure of the people grew and grew until finally a priest was assigned to Delano to help ministers to the needs of farmworkers [sic]. Finally the Church through pressure from the people, decided to recognize that farmworkers [sic] have their own peculiar needs.

When poor people get involved in a long conflict, such as a strike, or a civil rights drive, and the pressure increases everyday, there is a deep need for spiritual advice. Without it families crumble, leadership weakens, and hard workers grow tired. In such a situation the spiritual advice must be given by a friend, not by part of the opposition. What sense does it make to go to mass on Sunday and reach out for spiritual help, and instead get sermons about the wickedness of your cause? That only drives one to question and despair. We need a friendly spiritual guide. And this is true in every community where the poor face tremendous problems.

For example, the Catholic Charities agencies of the Catholic Church, has millions of dollars earmarked for the poor. But often the money is spent for food baskets for the needy instead of for effective action to eradicate the cause of poverty. The men and women who administer this money sincerely want to help. It should be our duty to help direct the attention to the basic needs of the Chicano in our society . . . needs which cannot be satisfied with baskets of food, but rather with effective organizing at the grass roots level.

Católicos Por La Raza is calling for all Mexican-American groups to stop ignoring this source of power. It is not just our right to appeal to the Church to use its power effectively for the poor, it is our duty to do so. It should be as natural as appealing to government . . . and we do that often enough.

Saint Thomas says that concrete attribution of an authority is made by the people. When there is an authority opposed to the people, this authority is illegitimate and tyrannical. As Christians and Catholics, we can and must fight against the mismanagement of OUR Church.

The leadership of the Chicano community must admit that we have fallen far short in our task of helping provide spiritual guidance for our people. We may say, "I don't feel any such need. I can get along." But that is a poor excuse for not helping provide such help for others. For we can also say, "I don't need any welfare help. I can take care of my own problems." But we are all willing to fight like hell for welfare aid for those who truly need it, who would starve without it. Likewise we may have gotten an education and not care about scholarship money for ourselves, or our children. But we would, we should, fight like hell to see that our state provides aid for any child needing it so that he can get the education he desires. Likewise we can say that we don't need the Church. That is our business. BUT THERE ARE HUNDREDS OF THOUSANDS OF OUR PEOPLE WHO DESPERATELY NEED SOME HELP FROM THAT POWERFUL INSTITUTION, THE CHURCH, AND WE ARE FOOLISH NOT TO HELP THEM GET IT.

THE CHURCH: the MODEL of HYPOCRISY[1]

Richard Cruz

As we hope you know by now, CPLR is a newly formed coalition of Chicano activists on many levels working within the framework of the Congress of Mexican-American Unity. We have committed ourselves to one goal: the return of the Catholic Church to the oppressed Chicano Community. In other words, we are demanding that the Catholic Church merely practices what it preaches and that it align itself economically and spiritually, with the Chicano movement.

After all, what people in the United States have been historically and at present more-faithful to the Catholic Church, the strongest and richest institution in the world. Do you really think that if the Catholic Church had all along demanded social and economic justice for our people that we would be in our present predicament? It has done the opposite because it has chosen to be silent although it knows we have been and continue to struggle for a place in the sun. Indeed, we know that Cardinals wine and dine with presidents. We know, for example, that the Catholic Church in Los Angeles alone has over one billion dollars in property and other assets (that's right, $1,000,000,000). And we can prove it! Compare such wealth further to the creator of Christianity, Jesus Christ, who was born in a manger, died for poor people, washed their feet—in short truly loved the poor—and you further realize that the Catholic Church is not even Christian.

We are not demanding Church money. We are demanding that the Catholic Church be Christian. For, you see, if it is Christian it cannot in conscience retain its fabulous wealth while Chicanos have to dance, beg, plead and steal for better housing, education, legal defense and other Chicano goals which you know so well.

[1] In Ricardo Cruz/Católicos Por La Raza Papers.

For these and so many other reasons, we need your Chicano bodies and spirit with us. Participation of all Chicanos and other socially concerned Catholics and community people is vital. Do not let us down! You see, we can expect politicians, judges, governmental officials, etc. to ignore our requests as they have always done. But we cannot function if our own people fail us at this time. Somos Católicos, somos pobres, somos Chicanos. Que Viva La Raza!!

DEMANDS OF CATÓLICOS POR LA RAZA[1]

Because we are Catholics . . . because we are Catholics who have in recent times repeatedly made private and public attempts for the attention of the Church, and because we are Catholics concerned about the social conditions of La Raza, we persist in our view that it is the responsibility of our Church to act upon the following demands:

Creation of a Commission on Mexican American Affairs within the hierarchy of the Church. This Commission will be composed of representatives from community organizations (elected from, among others, the general membership of the CONGRESS OF MEXICAN AMERICAN UNITY), priests and nuns. The Commission will research the problems facing the Chicano community. The initial task of the Commission shall be to:

1. Education
   a. Obtain a periodic accounting of Church assets and other holdings in order to determine the sources of funding the proposed programs.
   b. Establish a Chicano Educational Fund to meet the financial needs of our youth in education at all levels.
2. Housing
   a. Establish an agency, controlled by the community, with funds to approve loans or grants for building homes or asking repairs and improvements.
   b. Create a housing agency to build low cost housing for all persons presently residing in the housing projects.

[1] From news clipping in Ricardo Cruz/Católicos Por La Raza Papers.

3. Health
   a. Commission will administer and control those Church administered or controlled hospitals in the Mexican American Community, such as Santa Marta.
   b. Create a fund to provide free or low cost health insurance for lower-income Mexican Americans.
4. Democratically elected Chicanos serve, with full voting rights and obligations, with those whose duty is to administer the temporal affairs of the Church.
5. Leadership and Orientation Classes
   a. Leadership training classes shall be conducted throughout all parishes in East Los Angeles. Classes will be conducted by priests and personnel selected from within the Congress of Mexican American Unity.
   b. Orientation sessions shall be held for seminary students planning to enter the priesthood and for priests currently assigned to our barrios. Sessions shall consist of Mexican culture and thought, history, contemporary problems, etc. Sessions will be conducted by personnel selected from within the Congress of Mexican American Unity.
6. Parish priests currently do not have the time to be actively involved in the Chicano Civil Rights Movement. Presently much of our spiritual leadership in such matters comes from Protestants who cannot truly grant our Church's voice of conscience. Priests and nuns will be assigned on a full-time basis, to work actively with community projects and organizations.
7. Freedom of Speech for all Priests and Nuns

   Priests and nuns will be allowed freedom of speech without fear of retaliation from the Chancery. Specifically, no priest or nun will be removed from any position for advocating a position in the realm of secular affairs.
8. Use of Church Facilities.

   Many community organizations currently meet in either government owned buildings or Protestant churches. This anomaly contributes to the lack of communication between the Church and her people. It will serve both the needs of the community as well as those of the Church when those involved in social issues can use their own Church's facilities.
9. Public Commitments and Statements in Support of Issues Affecting the Chicano.

   The Church shall serve as the voice of conscience for the communities of poor people in their struggle for freedom and justice throughout the entire world. Specifically, it can and must make public statements of policy in areas other than those traditionally religious. The total power of the Church must be used to implement the aims and policies of Chicanos involved in their struggle for liberation against forces of repression, as for example:

a. the Farmworkers
b. the East Los Angeles Walkouts
c. Unrepresentative Grand Juries and other federal, state and local administrative and judicial bodies.
d. Inordinate (20%) number of Chicano war dead from the Southwest
e. The Viet Nam War in all its hideous aspects.
f. Hunger
g. Pollution

In conclusion we submit, THE CHURCH WILL REFLECT THE SOCIAL CONDITION OF THE PEOPLE IT SERVES!

Part 3

Richard Cruz, CPLR rally at Cal State, Northridge, 1969.
Courtesy of Special Collections, Davidson Library, Univ. of Calif. Santa Barbara

Católicos in Action

THE CAMP OLIVER TAKE OVER[1]

Editor's Note: The following is an interview with Vince de Vaca a student at UCSD who was one of the Chicanos who initiated the Liberation of Camp Oliver in Descanso [San Diego County] on November 30 and one of six Chicanos who were arrested for trespassing.

- How did you first become involved in this incident?

  It started Saturday, when a group of us were discussing the conference that was being held at the camp, and what we expected to come out of it; I and a friend decided to see what it was all about.

- Who were these people who decided to take over the camp?

  They were college administrators, community organizations chairmen; what you could call some of the pricipal [sic] people in specific organizations in San Diego.

- How did these individuals feel about the Catholic Church?

  They felt that they had been turned away by the Catholic Church, primarily because of the Racism of the Catholic Church. Racism manifested in many ways: like high school tuition costs: if you can't meet the tuition cost you don't go to school there anymore. You have to pay for all these things that the Catholic Church should be giving to the people, who have been paying their 10% every Sunday for the last 400 years.

[1] La Verdad (Dec., 1969) in Ricardo Cruz/Católicos Por La Raza Papers.

■ Who wrote up the 11 demands?

They were written by the people stayed at the camp and others who were going to coordinate activities outside the camp, nationwide.

■ What was the groups feelings after they had taken over the camp?

As far as we were concerned we were in there to stay, and if it came down to it we were ready to put our lives on the line to save that land.

When we first saw the police we really flashed. Here we are ready to die for this land, but where is our support? We realized that without the support we needed, to make this an issue, it was meaningless for us to lose our lives. We decided better that our going to jail would awaken the people to the realities of the Catholic Church as far as what is their main concern, saving souls of people or making money. These are the kind of things we wanted to demonstrate by our getting arrested.

■ When did the police arrest you?

The police were there for an hour and a half for two hours before we were arrested. During that time we were expecting all kinds of people to come down from the colleges for support They never came . . .

■ Who filed the complaints against you?

The caretaker was the man who signed the complaints that got us arrested. It was not the sisters.

■ Did you feel that your arrest and the rest of the group's did any good?

Yes, I think it did a lot of good. A first, when we were in jail, we were a bit disturbed. We rapped with a lot of Chicano brothers that we met inside the jail. A few of them felt that you can't count on Chicanos to back you up as far as the movement is concerned. They felt that they couldn't count on the support to back-them up when they needed it. This disturbed us for a while, but we were only in jail for three hours. We found-out, once we got out, how much support we did have from concerned people who helped us get out.

I think that community support now is excellent. At least now we're talking with the bishop. But I think that the bishop is going to have to receive another severe shock before he sees how really severe the problem is.

DEMANDS OF CATÓLICOS POR LA RAZA IN SAN DIEGO COUNTY[1]

1. The possession of CAMP OLIVER and that its transfer of title be done immediately to the Centro Cultural de LA RAZA.
2. That the Catholic Church via the Order of the Sisters of Social Service, continue to pay the upkeep costs of the Camp, including caretaker services, and that from now on the caretakers be Chicanos.
3. That the Catholic Church immediately cease exploitation practices of the Chicano community as manifested by employment at Camp Oliver of Chicanos at wages of $3.00 per day and the exploitative employment practices of Chicanos at other institutions.
4. That a rider be included in all legal transactions that the Catholic Church is not absolved of other responsibilities due the Chicano population and that the transfering [sic] of Camp Oliver to Chicanos be only the beginning step for further community control of its lands and other properties.
5. That the schools run by the different orders of Priests and Nuns as well as the Catholic Church as a whole announce:
   a. Open enrollment for all Chicano children.
   b. Free textbooks to all Chicano children enrolled in its schools.
   c. Free uniforms to all Chicano children enrolled in its schools.
   d. That immediate steps be taken for Catholic schools at all levels, to begin to plan for community control and that a time table be jointly prepared in which this can be implemented.

[1] In Ricardo Cruz/Católicos Por La Raza Papers.

6. That the Catholic Youth Organizations (CYO) respond to the needs of the Barrio residents particularly those who are socially and economically discriminated and that this organization immediately orient itself to social action work.
7. That the Catholic hospitals provide free medical and free hospitalization services to Chicano families and individuals who can pay SOME fees for the above mentioned services.
8. That the Catholic Church immediately release monies to develop a Chicano controlled development corporation to initiate:
   a. cooperatives
   b. credit unions
   c. housing projects
   d. communication enterprises such as radio stations
9. That Burial Services be given free to Chicanos that are not economically viable due to Institutional Racism.
10. That Chicano laymen and priests be considered for top decision making positions of present and future programs started by the Church.
11. That socially-oriented priests be jointly selected by the community and the Bishop for heirarchial [sic] positions, e.g. Monsignor and Auxilliary [sic] Bishops.
12. That the Catholic Church come out publically [sic] in support of the Delano Grape Boycott and that it begins an active campaign to support the efforts of the United Farm Workers Organizing Committee.
13. That the Catholic Church immediately fund the Drug Abuse project for the rehabilitation of addicts as developed by Henry Collins, member of the Chicano Community.

CONFRONTATION WITH THE CHURCH[1]

(Fall, 1969)

The seizure of Camp Oliver marked the beginning of a string of important events for the Chicano here in San Diego and throught [sic] the Southwest. Never had Chicanos come forth in a unified manner and openly challenged the Catholic Church's role in society.

The activities that took place during the final days of November on up to the present time were spearheaded by a group called Católicos Por La Raza (Catholics for the Race), but individuals and other groups supported and participated in the confrontation with the diocese of San Diego.

Unity and carnalismo were the key factors which helped in keeping the struggle strong.

Students and educators kept a week long vigil outside Camp Oliver in Descanso, sleeping through 25 degree temperatures. Parents from the barrios provided food for the "campers."

In San Diego candlelight vigils were held every night beginning on Monday, December 1 in front of the Bishop's "mansion," during which time, Bishop Maher never once showed his face.

At the University of San Diego, picket lines were set up in front of the Chancery building where the Bishop has an office. Organizations such as the Chicano Priests Association, and the Chicano Federation lent their support to the Católicos Por La Raza.

During all this, the church played a game of hide and go seek with the people. At first the Church denounced the Chicanos as "militants" and worse, called the 13 demands "illogical." As pressure from the community began to build the Church announced that the Católicos Por La Raza had "no real leadership" and that they would meet with the only legal voice of the Chicano community, the Chicano Federation.

[1] La Verdad (Dec., 1969) in Ricardo Cruz/Católicos Por La Raza Papers.

When the executive board of the Chicano Federation announced their support of the CPLR and advised the bishop to meet with representatives of the group, the diocese found itself with no more exuses [sic] to hand out to the public.

But the church continued to play its little game of evasion.

At a community meeting in the Logan Barrio, Chicanos confronted priests and nuns with the question: "If you are true Christians why don't you join us in Descanso or at the candlelight vigil?" They gave no reply.

On December 9, Bishop Maher visited a Catholic organization near San Diego State College, and was greeted by 120 Chicanos students from all over San Diego. Immediately Art Cazarez president of MECHA-MAYA at State, challenged the Bishop's refusal to meet with the CPLR.

"I didn't want to meet with a large group" was the bishop's excuse, although a committe [sic] had been selected before that time.

"Are you willing to meet with our committe [sic]?" asked Jim Salazar, member of CPLR.

The bishop agreed but only on his terms, which were at his office and when he would find the time.

"Meet with us tomorrow, in the barrio!" Chicanos shouted.

Rene Nuñez, administrative director of the Centro de Estudios Chicanos asked the bishop, "Are you an emissary of Jesus Christ?"

"I am," the bishop replied.

"Then I ask you," Rene continued, "did Jesus Christ ask the people to come to him? NO, CHRIST WENT TO THE PEOPLE!"

A meeting was finally held at Our Lady of Guadalupe Church in Logan Barrio on Wednesday, December 10.

Concerning the 1st meeting, members of the committee reported that the bishop would have to undergo a great deal of sensitizing before the talks would become more productive.

CATÓLICOS POR LA RAZA

November 29, 1969[1]

Hermanos y hermanas, [Brothers and sisters]

As we hope you know by now, CPLR is a newly formed coalition of Chicano activists on many levels working within the framework of the Congress of Mexican-American Unity. We have committed ourselves to one goal: the return of the Catholic Church to the oppressed Chicano community. In other words, we are demanding that the Catholic Church merely practices what it preaches and it align itself, economically and spiritually, with the Chicano movement.

After all, what people in the United States have been historically and at present more faithful to the Catholic faith than our people? The Catholic Church is the strongest and richest institution in the world. Do you really think that if the Catholic Church had all along demanded social and economic justice for our people that we would be in our present predicament? It has done the opposite because it has chosen to be silent although it knows we have been and continue to struggle for a place in the sun. Indeed, we know that Cardinals wine and dine with presidents. We know, for example, that the Catholic Church in Los Angeles alone has over one billion dollars in property and other assets (that's right, $1,000,000,000). And we prove it! Compare such wealth to the plight of our people and you begin to wonder, as CPLR has wondered, just who has taken the vow of property- the Chicanos or the Catholic Church. Compare such wealth further to the creator of Christianity, Jesus Christ, who was born in a manger, died for poor people, washed their feet- in short truly loved the poor- and you further realize that the Catholic Church is not even Christian.

We are not demanding Church money. We are demanding that the Catholic Church be Christian. For, you see, if it is Christian it cannot in conscience retain its fabu-

[1] Ricardo Cruz/Católicos Por La Raza Papers.

lous wealth while Chicanos have to dance, beg, plead and steal for better housing, education, legal defense and other Chicano goals which you know so well.

For these and so many other reasons, we want you and your association members to because members of CPLR. And believe us, we don't need your moral support. We need your Chicano bodies and spirit with us-NOW!!!

Specifically we need your presence on December 7, 1969, at 12:30 to 2:30 p.m. at a combination prayer vigil-demonstration to be held at St. Basil's Catholic Church, 637 So. Kingsley (corner of Wilshire and Kingsley). Do not let us down. You see, we can expect politicians, judges, governmental officials, etc. to ignore our requests as they have always done. But we cannot function if our own people fail us at this time. Somos Católicos, somos pobres, somos Chicanos. Que viva La Raza.

Sinceramente,
CATÓLICOS POR LA RAZA

[Richard Cruz]

CATÓLICOS POR LA RAZA PRESS RELEASE[1]

December 4, 1969

Católicos Por La Raza (CPLR) is a coalition of Mexican-American Catholics working within the framework of the Congress of Mexican-American unity. We have committed ourselves to one goal: the return of the Catholic Church to the oppressed Chicano community. We have today delivered the following message to the Roman Catholic Archdiocese of Los Angeles:

"Dear Cardinal McIntire [sic] and Members of the Catholic Clergy:"

"Mexican-Americans have been most faithful to Catholicism and its traditions. We have produced saints and martyrs; have given and continue to give truly sacrificial donations to our Catholic Church and for the most part have attempted to live up to Christ's mandate that we love our brother. We believe that you, our spiritual leaders, know these things to be true."

"We are confused, however, because while we have cherished Christ's words 'blessed are the poor', have lived in barrios and slums, have received on the average an eighth-grade education in the United States, and while we are treated as beasts of burden for the betterment of agribusiness, we know that, paradoxically, the Catholic Church is one of the richest and most powerful institutions in the world and the United States. We know, for example, that in Los Angeles County alone property owned by the Catholic Church is valued in excess of one billion dollars ($1,000,000,000). We know that the stained glass in Los Angeles' newest Catholic Church is worth approximately two hundred and fifty thousand dollars

[1] In Ricardo Cruz/Católicos Por La Raza Papers.

($250,000). We know of this wealth; yet Chicanitos [Chicano childen] are praying to La Virgen de Guadalupe as they go to bed hungry and will not be able to afford decent educations."

"We are confused our dear priests, nuns and brothers because when we have attempted to discuss our desperate needs at the Chancery Office, we were lied to and had the police called on us. Indeed, when we finally did obtain an audience with you, Cardinal McIntire [sic], our spiritual leader, you told us to 'Say what you have to say or get out.'"

"Thus, because we are Catholics, because we know that Christ was born in a manger, washed and kissed the feet of the poor and ultimately gave his life for the needs of poor people, and because we are Chicanos, we are left with no choice but to publicly demand that the Catholic Institution in Los Angeles practice what it preaches and channel its tremendous spiritual and economic power to meet the needs of its most faithful servants. After all, it is the Catholic priest, nun and brother, and not the Mexican-American, who have taken the vow of poverty."

"Understand that, unlike other peoples, we need not demand specific sums of money. Our demands are more basic. We are demanding that the Catholic Church be Christian. For you see, if it is Christian it cannot in conscience retain its fabulous wealth while Chicanos have to beg, plead, borrow, and steal for better housing, education, legal defense and other critical needs. Indeed, a Christian Catholic Church would not allow the Chicanito to go uneducated for lack of funds; it would channel its wealth through community-controlled housing agencies to rid our society of barrios and projects; and it would allow members of the Mexican-American community to participate in all Church activities which are not of a purely religious nature. Clearly, a Christian Catholic Church would publicly commit itself, its influence and wealth, to all social issues in which Chicanos are presently involved. The Farmworkers, the High School Walkouts, racist judges and grand juries and the fact that 20% of those dying in the immoral Vietnam War are Chicanos. These are but a few examples of the business of a Christian Catholic Church."

"Further understanding that we shall enforce our demands with whatever spiritual and physical powers we possess even if it means we must be jailed. Because as Catholics and Christians we cannot and will not anymore ignore the mockery the Church, as an institution and as the embodiment of Christ on Earth, has made of the words '. . . I come not to be served, but to serve.' (Matthew 20:28)."

Sinceramente,
Richard Cruz
Católicos Por La Raza
Euclid Heights Community Center
3045 E. Whittier Blvd, L.A.

On December 7, 1969, at the steps of St. Basil's Catholic Church, 637 South Kingsley Drive, Católicos Por La Raza will conduct a prayer vigil and religious demonstration to further indicate the sincerity of our demands. The Sunday activity will commence at 12:30 P.M. We urge Chicanos and all Christians and Catholics to unite with us in our cause and to celebrate with us the day when no members of the Catholic Clergy are wealthier than the poorest Mexican-American. The Church will be made relevant. So be it.

CONGRESS OF MEXICAN-AMERICAN UNITY[1]

December 15, 1969

Dear members,

A report on Católicos Por La Raza, its past, present and future activities, is in order.

On Sunday, December 7, 1969, approximately 350 Chicanos from almost all associations under the Congress (students - high school, college, law school, etc., Brown Berets, Welfare Rights people, SALUD social workers, La Raza staff, and many, many other representatives of our movement) gathered for a significant and successful demonstration at the multi-million dollar residence of Cardinal McYntire [sic], St. Basil's Catholic Church on Wilshire Blvd. A brave Catholic priest began our activity by blessing bread and reiterating our purpose—to return the Catholic Church to the Chicano community. Afterwards, several speakers proceeded to delineate the power of the Catholic Church, the nature of our demands and we then proceeded, accompanied by police at all times, of course, to attempt to see the Cardinal in the rear of the Church. Needless to say, he, nor for that matter any priest, would see or talk to us. We could only wonder what Christ would do if 350 Chicanos would want to see him. The spirits of the demonstration was such that many of us thought la revolución would begin that day. We wish you could have been with us to both feel and realize the historical aspect of our demonstration, the striking contrast in the brick and concrete structure and 350 angry Chicanos who were demanding no more than that the Church join us in our struggle for our gente [our people], nuestro movimiento [our movement]. By the way, there were approximately 12 priests, nuns and brothers in our demonstration. A

[1] Ricardo Cruz/Católicos Por La Raza Papers.

significant number considering it was CPLR's first public activity and the possible recriminations the Cardinal usually shows clergy who would dare be with and a part of poor people and the Chicano movement.

The Church, as you may have noticed, is reacting. The CPLR press conference of Dec. 5 (channels 2, 4, 5, 34, 13) was accompanied by the Church stating that it has been "active" in the barrios all along but just hasn't received publicity. They also showed the Cardinal dedicating an East L.A. hospital which, by the way, we know to have been financed by mainly non—Church funds. This was the first time the Church ever publicly acknowledged the existence of E.L.A. Also, it seems odd to us, as various members of the Congress, to not know that the Church has been "active" in the barrios all along. We know its churches are there. We know that it has truly Christian and color-blind individuals, such as Sister Campeon, who do what they can. But, unless we have been blind and stupid all along, we also know that its tremendous power—both economic and spiritual—has never changed a damn thing in E.L.A., nor do its schools let our Chicanitos learn in their own language. Please correct us if we are wrong. Let us know if the Catholic Church was with us at the walkouts, how much money it has contributed to our legal defense needs (p.s., the recent Chicano defense fund raiser put together by Oscar Acosta was held at the Council of Jewish Women headquarters), if it has said anything in its pulpits about grapes, etc. You may also have noticed that CPLR forced the Church to print in the L.A. Times that it was running its schools at a $9,000,000 deficit. That's history! It is significant because they feel our pressure but, predictably, have completely missed the point of our demands that the Church be Christian. In other words, the Church didn't, indeed couldn't say it is Christian (poor, etc.) but could only say it has a deficit. How many Chicanos know what a "deficit" is; we wonder if Christ would ever have put himself in a position to have a $9,000,000 deficit. The Church indeed knows CPLR exists, that it will not stop putting pressure, that, worst of all, it will continue to demand that the Church practice what it preaches for decades upon decades . . . We need your continued and increasing support. REMEMBER, NO MATTER WHAT ASSOCIATION YOU ARE IN, YOU AND YOUR MEMBERS CAN ACCOMPLISH YOUR IMMEDIATE GOALS MUCH QUICKER IF THE CATHOLIC CHURCH WOULD WAKE UP AND REALIZE THAT THE CHICANO MOVEMENT IS HERE TO STAY, IS A SPIRITUAL STRUGGLE OF AND FOR THE POOR, AND IS THE VERY BUSINESS FOR WHICH CHRIST DIED ON THE CROSS. THE SOONER WE CAN HAVE A CHURCH, THE SOONER WILL THE BONDS OF OPPRESSION UPON OUR PEOPLE BE LOOSENED FOR IT IS THE CHURCH THAT HAS MANIPULATED CHRISTIANITY TO TEACH OUR OWN POOR, NUESTRAS VIEJAS Y ABUELAS [our elderly and grandparents], TO FEAR THE VERY MOVEMENT THAT WILL LIBERATE, FEED AND EDUCATE NUESTRAS FAMILIAS MEXICANAS.

As usual, we can only fail if we are not united. We will sec you at the Chicano Moratorium. Remember and attend the following activities:

1. Sunday, December 21st, at 2:00 p.m., at Euclid Heights Comm. Center, 3045 Whittier Blvd, will be CPLR's next meeting. Attend along with members of your association.
2. At 11:00 p.m. we will have a Mass on the steps of St. Basil's, along with Chicano music and songs—CHRISTMAS EVE—BEFORE THE MIDNIGHT MASS OF ST. BASIL'S. That's December 25, 1969.

Sinceramente, Católicos Por La Raza . . .
[Richard Cruz]

CATÓLICOS POR LA RAZA REVISTED -THREE YEARS LATER (1972)[1]

Richard Cruz

Sometime toward the end of 1969, about 20 Chicano activists paid an unannounced visit to the main office of the Roman Catholic Archdiocese of Los Angeles. We were determined to see & talk to the Cardinal (McIntyre) himself, even though we know that his richly—decorated offices at the Chancery, 1540 West 9th St., downtown, had never seen the likes of us. Outside, as we began waiting for each other to arrive from various barrios (San Fer, Longo, East Los, etc.) and colleges (Valley State, ELA, L.B., CSCLA & LACC, among others), a Brinks armored truck pulled up & stationed itself directly in front of the Church's headquarters. "Mira no mas," wc mumbled to each other as two armed men hastily entered the offices with half a dozen or so empty money bags. Moments later they were to emerge & the bags would be full—in fact stuffed. Our emotions rose as some carnal said "Blessed are the poor!" This re-inspired most of our associates having arrived, we were more than ready to pay a visit to the official "Spiritual Leader" of countless thousands of Catholics from Orange County to state borderline at the east end of San Bernardino County. Vamonos, carnales! And within a few heartbeats we were beyond the marble entranceway & facing the elderly receptionist who greeted us on the second floor.

"I'm sorry," she said. "His Reverence is not in at the moment & you would simply have to have an appointment to see him even if he were." She was amazed at our bluntness when we informed her that we knew he was in because we had

[1] Unpublished document in Ricardo Cruz/Católicos Por La Raza Papers.

seen his black limousine parked in the back. Two nuns sitting patiently nearby (Looking like Saints I might add), began exchanging confused & disturbed glances with one another & with the grey-haired secretary as she demanded to know the nature of our visit.

"We're Chicanos from various parts of L.A.", we told her (todo proud), "and we've been trying to see the Cardinal for a long time to talk to him about the poverty of our people and what he & the Church are doing about it!" "And we're not going to leave until we see him!" someone insisted from the rear of our small, bold group. In the distressful look of this petite secretary, her hesitation & total bewilderment at our mere presence, could be seen a reflection of the tragic relationship of the Chicano and what is called "his" Holy Mother the Church. In her eyes an entire spectrum of history & emotion & drama unfolded—a people and their Church; and in our minds & hearts there paraded an avalanche of words: Missions, gold, Indians, Mestizos, exploitation, Tonántzín, La Virgen, Hidalgo, Juan Diego, education, milagros [miracles], sangre [blood], y revolución, poverty & hypocrisy, First Communion & Las Posadas, savages, civilization, Blessed are the Poor, wealth, Junipero Serra, jail chaplain, curanderas, brujos, sacrifice, cursillos, chancery, His Eminence the Cardinal . . .

She spoke again. "Now let me see if I have this straight, young men. You're from Chicago and . . ."

"No," we interrupted. And stumbled all over each other with comments. "You've never heard the word Chicano?" "There's barrios full of Chicanos & all kinds of Raza surrounding this area. . . ." "You know, Mexicans, Mexican-Americans!" "Orale—Chicago—chingou!" (We were sure good militants in those days, remember?).

JOIN US FOR A CHRISTMAS EVE CANDLELIGHT MARCH[1]

Our call is to you, our brothers and sisters, to march with us for PEACE and JUSTICE. We plan to celebrate CHRISTMAS EVE by showing that we are concerned about the problems that confront us on every side. More than ever before we need men and women who will not give up the struggle to help build a better world. The task of concerned persons today is to take the issues to other people-EVERYDAY. This Christmas Eve, why not join us as we take a message of PEACE to a few churches. These churches stand as silent symbols in a time when silence means continued war, hunger and poverty.

PLEASE BRING YOUR OWN CANDLES FOR THE MARCH.
(We will carry lighted candles rather than signs.)

9:30 Gather at Lafayette Park
Wilshire and Commonwealth entrance
10:00 March Begins
10:30 Leaflet at Immanuel Presbyterian Church
3300 Wilshire Blvd.
11:00 Leaflet at St. Basil's Catholic Church
Wilshire and Kingsley

COFFEE afterwards. 1027 S. Crenshaw

[1] Ricardo Cruz/Católicos Por La Raza Papers.

NO ROOM AT ST. BASIL'S FOR CHICANOS[1]

On Christmas Eve, in the lobby of St. Basil's, Church officials and policemen clubbed, maced, insulted and arrested numerous Chicanos when they demanded entry into Church during the televised midnight mass . . .

AFTER THEY HAD PROMISED FREE ENTRY IN EXCHANGE FOR A PROMISE BY THE CHICANO DEMONSTRATORS THAT THEY WOULD NOT TAKE THEIR PROTEST INTO THE CHURCH.

WOMEN, CHILDREN AND INNOCENT BYSTANDERS WERE CLUBBED WITHOUT MERCY FROM THE POLICE, THE CHURCH OFFICALS AND THE CARDINAL WHO ALLEGEDLY SPEAKS FOR THE POPE AND JESUS CHRIST.

The Chicano demonstrators, admittedly, are not

white

rich

and tuxedos they do not own.

CHRISTIAN, CATHOLIC AND RELENTLESSLY CONCERNED FOR THE POOR AND THE CHICANO . . . they are . . . raza, raza, raza!

[1] Ricardo Cruz/Católicos Por La Raza Papers.

CATÓLICOS POR LA RAZA
c/o Euclid Community Center
3045 Whittier Boulevard
Los Angeles, California

December 26, 1969[1]

Rev. James Francis McIntyre
Cardinal
Archdiocese of Los Angeles
1513 West Ninth Street
Los Angeles, California

Dear Cardinal:

I am the Co-Chairman for the group called Católicos Por La Raza. On Christmas Eve we planned to demonstrate, sing and worship in front of St. Basil's Church with the intent of calling attention to what we consider to be the irrelevancies and hypocrisies of our faith as symbolized by the multi-million dollar structure. . . . In the spirit of Christ and under the banner of our patron saint, La Virgen de Guadalupe.

Prior to the commencement of the Midnight Mass within St. Basil's, a Sergeant Domínguez from the East Los Angeles Police Department spoke with us concerning our intent to carry the demonstration within the church. We told him that we had no intention whatsoever of disrupting the services. He advised us that you had instructed him to inform us that so long as we did not carry our banners and candles within the sanctuary, that we would be welcome to participate in the celebration of the Mass, and that the doors would remain open.

Several of us did in fact enter the Church, through the lower, west side entrance which was swung open. We walked reverently through the side isle [sic] of the sanctuary into the front lobby. We asked the ushers for permission to open the main door leading into the sanctuary so that we could at least hear the sermon . . . it being a common practice, at least in our parishes, for allowing a standing audience in the rear.

While this brief verbal confrontation was going on, there were numerous persons standing outside the Church, on the steps pleading with the ushers to open

[1] Ricardo Cruz/Católicos Por La Raza Papers.

the doors. Nota bene: These potential worshipers were demonstrators and non-demonstrators.

When one of us merely reached for the door handle to the outside door, the usher struck the man in the back of the neck. Immediately, the usher in charge ordered the other ushers to throw us out, and in the twinkling of an eye, they viciously beat upon us and attempted to eject us.

Within minutes, the police arrived swinging long clubs at everyone in sight . . . including ushers, demonstrators and non-demonstrators alike:

1. If we were intent on disrupting the services why then did we not create such disruption when we were inside the sanctuary?
2. If we carried weapons, where are they, and why were none of the ushers injured?
3. If we had desired to carry our demonstration into the Church, why did we not do so when the front doors were open and seats available?
4. Why did the Police Department, through officer Domínguez, legally approve of our demonstration, invite us into the Church service and then beat us when we accepted the offer?

Father, what we seek is a reformation of our Church even as Our Savior sought to regenerate the Pharisees and the Scribes whose concern was not with the Kingdom of God . . . He is our Example, his methods of confrontation with the established authority is our strategy, even as he drove the money changers out of the Temple of God . . . And if we appear as rabble rousers crying for His death, "we recall that He too, was called a glutton and a winebibber because he lived with and championed the cause of the poor and the downtrodden."

You should know that the Chicano is not a demonstrative man, certainly not on Wilshire Boulevard. We find no personal satisfaction in calling attention to ourselves, our people and our culture on the streets of Hollywood. Our very own Catholic brothers, during the picketing, have insulted us, casting derogatory and racial epithets to our faces. These very children of God have enjoined us to Go Back To Mexico, have called us Communists . . . Once again pointing to our alleged differences, rather than our spiritual similarities as members of The Holy Faith.

We have no desire to return anywhere because in point of fact, this land is our land. We do not aspire to communist ideology because we know it to be as reactionary and godless as is the racist and inhumane government of this country.

Finally, and in good faith, we seek your forgiveness. And we seek to forgive those Catholic men and women who have condemned us without knowing us. During your sermon on Christmas Eve, you prayed to God that He should forgive us because of our innocence. God cannot forgive us unless you, personally forgive us first. We seek your forgiveness not only before God, but also before Man. Perhaps we might begin this Christian dialogue by your seeking to have charges against the demonstrators dismissed.

En Cristo,
Ricardo Cruz

Courtesy of Special Collections, Davidson Library, Univ. of Calif. Santa Barbara

Richard Cruz at St. Basil's Church, Dec. 25, 1969.

TESTIMONY OF PEDRO ARIAS[1]

My name is Pedro Arias. I was born in the year 1926 in Acatic, Jalisco, Mexico. Since 1952, I have lived in the U.S. I am married, both through a civil court and the church; and have seven children, six boys and one girl, the oldest being 15 years and the youngest 3 years old.

I have lived at my present address approximately five years and since then my family, as well as myself, have attended the religious service of the Catholic church, [sic] All Souls, which is the closest one to us.

To justify my presence the 24th day of December outside of the Church of Saint Basil, I should clarify that through the means of Baptism I became a Catholic even before I had a notion of it or of any thing else, since at the age of 45 days I was baptized. Afterwards, because of a custom and a family tradition, I continued attending church services. At the age of three years I received the Sacrament of Confirmation and at the age of six, with little notion of what religion was, I made my First Communion. Between the ages of 12 and 16 years, now being able to reason, I embraced the Catholic religion. I studied it within the religious organization, Catholic Association of Young Mexicans in Guadalajara, Jalisco.

At the age of 16 years I volunteered to enter the Mexican Army and within it I studied radiotelegraphy and everything connected with signals and communications.

While in the army, approximately in June 1944 I had my first reaction against the church, and when I say against the church I don't mean against my religion but rather against we humans who make-up the religion and specifically against those which we could call leaders of the church or, that is, the priests. The cause for my reaction was the assassination of a young couple and their young son of 8 or 10 years by people who were religiously incited and fanaticized by evil priests. This occurred in Tapachula, Chiapas, Mexico.

[1] In possession of editor.

Since then I have become aware of the corruption that exists among these elements and, also, I have understood and become closer to my Catholic faith, as I have come to the conclusion that if the Catholic Religion continues to exist and to increase despite its bad leaders, it is because it is a pure and true religion. At the same time, I have come to the realization that it is my duty and the duty of all Catholics to combat those bad elements because if they are not stopped, some day they shall destroy the Catholic Faith. They are gradually betraying the Christ and fooling themselves and deceiving their flock.

All those that have the least idea of what Christianism is, know that Jesus Christ, during his existence in this world, spent his time combating the hypocrisy and the riches, and at the same time he preached and set an example of humbleness and love towards his fellowman. He demonstrated his first example of humility by his having been born in a manger and he wanted to be worshipped in the same manner.

Therefore, my presence at the Saint Basil church was due to these sentiments which are so well rooted in me, and that is why I did not hear Mass inside the church which was built at the cost of several million of dollars, but rather under the heavens as it was originally done by man.

The above were, more or less, the words that I exchanged with Sergeant Domínguez about 11 P.M., on the night of the 24th of December when he suggested that I enter the church on that night. But, I assured him that on that night I would not enter the church for any reason. Sergeant Domínguez then asked me with whom he could speak to obtain more information in regard to the presence of the group, "Católicos Por La Raza". I suggested he speak to Father Bonpane, with Raul Ruiz, or Atty. Acosta.

Following that, I heard the open-air Mass, conducted by the priests from our group. When it finished, I gathered with several friends, and we talked of our satisfaction of what we had expressed. Then someone told us that some of the boys had decided to attend the Church Mass, following our open-air Mass; but that they had been shut out of the church. I wanted to find out what was going on, and went towards the main entrance. It appeared that ushers were struggling with some young men. One of the doors was partly open, and as I attempted to open it more, so that I could see inside, I felt a strong stream of something cold on my forehead and almost immediately I felt my eyes sting. Because of this, I could hardly see, and half-way down the stairs Mr. Martínez and Mrs. Aceves asked me what had happened. When I explained, someone handed me a moist handkerchief which helped to lessen the pain that I felt in my eyes.

CHURCH RESPONSE TO DEMANDS

-fraud wrapped around deceit and hypocrisy[1]

On January 22, 1970, the demands and grievances of Católicos Por La Raza (CPLR) with the institutional Catholic Church of Los Angeles were discussed personally with Archbishop Manning. On February 11, 1970, a response to the demands was issued by the Archbishop. This response is totally unsatisfactory for the following reasons:

1. The Committee which assisted the Archbishop in formulating his response is totally unrepresentative of the Mexican-American community. The Congress of Mexican-American Unity, comprised of over 220 Mexican American associations and organizations, is the official coalition of Mexican people in Los Angeles. Yet the congress was virtually ignored when Archbishop Manning formed the committee to study and pass upon the demands and grievances of CPLR. Nor have the priests on the committee ever involved themselves with grass-roots Chicano activities or organizations.
2. The response by the Archbishop in no way reflects new Church policy or procedure. On the contrary, the inter-parochial council presently being implemented within the Institutional Church is a year-old program begun by Cardinal McIntyre. As with other church programs, the Chicano people themselves had little, if any, say in its creation or implementation. It thus reflects neither the mood nor the needs of the Chicano people.
3. The response cites the participation of the clergy in such programs as the Model Cities Program, the Home Owners Modernization Effort and The Activities of the State Service Center as examples of Church involvement in "community endeavors." Had the Church been truly involved in community endeavors it would have known that at the recently terminated annual convention of the Congress of Mexican-American Unity a resolution was passed

[1] In La Raza, vol. 1, no. 1, p. 27 in Ricardo Cruz/Católicos Por La Raza Papers.

unanimously denouncing the Model Cities Programs as it is presently structured. The resolution was passed because as Model Cities presently exists there is little if any community participation. The same is true of the Home Owners Modernization effort. Yet the Church is proud of its participation in these programs, programs which the Mexican American people have officially denounced. Had there been a Catholic priest, nun or brother at the recent convention of the Congress of Mexican American Unity, the Church could have at least known of the aforementioned resolution. As to the so-called "clergy" involvement in the State Service Center, there is one single nun assigned to the center. And she has been sympathetic to the purpose and philosophy of CPLR.

4. The response completely ignores the specific demands and grievances of CPLR. There is no mention whatsoever of a commission on Mexican American affairs within the Church hierarchy itself; nor does the response address itself to an accounting by the Church, to its people, of its assets, holdings or liabilities.

The foregoing considerations are not intended to be an exhaustive analysis of the Archbishop's response to the demands of Católicos Por La Raza. They merely serve to point out that the Catholic Church in Los Angeles continues to completely ignore the desperate needs of the Chicano community in its struggle for self-determination. The Church is apparently ignorant of the fact that on February 14, 1970, the Congress of Mexican-American Unity unanimously passed this following resolution: "Be it resolved that the Congress of Mexican-American Unity officially endorses the goal and demands of Católicos Por La Raza. Be it further resolved that the recent response by Archbishop Manning to the demands of Católicos Por La Raza in no way approaches the letter or spirit of the demands of Católicos Por La Raza."

Thus, because we have the endorsement of our people, because the Church continues to ignore our just and Christian demands, has perpetrated violence upon us Christmas Eve and is presently treating 21 members of CPLR as criminals because we seek a more relevant Church, we will continue our struggle and will, if necessary in the not so distant future, send representatives to the Vatican to plead our cause before our holy father, the Pope.

We continue asking:

1. Why does the Catholic Church refuse to allow Chicanos to have an accounting of Church assets? If we are the Church, as they have preached to us for decades, and centuries, why can't we know of Church assets and liabilities?
2. Why can't Chicanos participate in Church decisions? Why has Bishop Manning refused to allow a commission on Mexican American affairs to exist

in the Chancery itself? We are considered good enough to donate constantly to the Church so why aren't we considered good enough to have a say in its policies and decisions?

3. Why can't the Church—-its priests, nuns and brothers—-sacrifice for nuestra gente, los pobres de los Angeles, as we do daily? Did not Christ love people so much that he was willing to sacrifice and die for them? Doesn't the Church claim to be Christ on earth. [sic]

WHERE IS THE CATHOLIC CHURCH?

OPEN LETTER TO THE CHURCH

May 26, 1970

Mr. James Francis Cardinal McIntyre[1]
Los Angeles, Calif.

Mr. Cardinal:

In Spanish, when one wants to discuss a subject or topic without wasting time and energies, we quote a popular saying "Get to the point."

I do not wish to waste my time, much less make you waste yours, therefore I shall disclose the main reason for this letter. Unfortunately it is necessary to give you a bit of personal history.

On Wednesday, December 24, 1969, approximately at 11 p.m. I attended and joined in a protest organized by "Católicos Por La Raza", against the waste of the monies of the Catholics of the Archdiocese of Los Angeles, at which time you were in charge of; monies which in all Christianity should have properly been utilized to help those fellowmen in need, and not on vainful luxuries, the latter being completely against the example doctrine and the law of God. I believe it would be useless to enumerate those vainful luxuries as they are well know and practiced by you, as also the final results of the protest organized by "Católicos Por La Raza" are known to you.

Very well, as a consequence of those final results, the 20th of January, 1970, I suffered the embarrassment of being affronted, arrested and handcuffed in the pres-

[1] As published in La Raza (Special Issue on CPLR, Fall, 1970) in Ricardo Cruz/Católicos Por La Raza Papers.

ence of my boss and fellow workers. I was accused of having violated 4 sections of the Penal Code, one of those on five separate counts, in other words 8 charges in all.

By the experience acquired in a number of cases of which I have had knowledge, or been a witness to, I know that Lady Justice in this nation is completely BLIND especially towards the Negroes and Mexicans; who, because of her blindness, she can not see. In spite of this, my conscience was and is so clean and charges so unreasonable, that I decided to take advantage of the "facilities" and "benefits" that the "Law" offers; in accord, naturally, with the money that one has to buy them with.

Time goes on . . . and the 15th of April of this year, a Deputy City Attorney supposedly representing the people of the State of California, presented before the presiding Judge, and to the popular jury, so that they should reach a verdict of guilty or not guilty; a police officer by the name of Armando Miranda, under oath to tell the truth and nothing but the truth. Miranda lied and gave false testimony against me!

After, on the 20th of April, an individual by the name of Thomas Vetter took the witness stand. He testified that he had been a Deputy Sheriff for 13 years and that he was a fervent practicing Catholic. This man, cynical, and shameless, with unconcealed racial hatred, exaggerated the statements, which had been agreed on beforehand almost to the point of being passwords; thus supporting them in their scheme against the defendants to get them convicted at any price, especially your servant, whom he said had attacked him on three occasions, encouraged the multitude to enter the church, had stated to kill all the "pigs", and had stated certain blasfemies [sic] against the Holy Pope.

As a result of all the aforementioned, the 8th of this month, the jury, which apparently listened only to the "official and aforehand [sic] agreed on" testimonies, came back with the verdict, which you are now aware of and which you expected.

Very well, as I am completely conviced [sic] that in spite of the "facilities and benefits" that the law puts at my disposal in accord with the money that I am ready to spend to defend myself, I have no recourse but to go to jail.

I am completely conviced [sic] that you and other members in the ecclesiastical hierarchy of this archdiocese in alliance with some of the so-called representatives of the law, are the ones responsible for having planned and carried out in your manner, the occurrences on the 24th and 25th of December at the Church of St. Basil, as well as the results of the criminal process of 21 of the defendants.

It is a fact, which has been proven publicly, that the Catholic Apostolic and Roman Church, of which I have been a member since at the age of 40 days, not function in the manner for which it was created; since in its womb people like you exist and have converted it into a financial business of institute which deals with religious sentiments, in which to receive the sacraments of Baptism, Communion, Confirmation, but most of all Matrimoney, [sic] it is necessary to pay for them. To the point of absurdity in the having to pay for Extreme Unction, literally having to pay for prayers to God asking Him to help save a soul. Even after death one must keep paying in order that these prayers "may reach God."

For the above stated reason and for a thousand more that I will later make known publicly, I want it made known to you that I along with my wife and our 7 children, as of this date we completely renounce our membership in the Catholic, Apostolic and Roman Church.

And listen carefully! We resign as members of the Church, and not as believers of the Christian faith, and the true principles of the Catholic, Apostolic and Roman Church, to which we will return when once again it becomes the church of the poor and the forsaken.

I would also, by means of this letter, make it known to you that I hold you, along with the other members of the Church and the pesudo [sic] representatives of the Law who have plotted to harm me, responsible for the vexations that I have suffered; of the possible loss of my job which I have kep [sic] for 14 consecutive years; and the encarceration [sic] which I most probably will have to undergo.

I hold you responsible (and may the accusation remain upon your consciousness until the hour of my death) for the consequences that my encarceration [sic] will bring upon my wife and 7 children. They may suffer hunger, a loss of the home that with a thousand sacrifices I had been paying, illnesses due to the lack of proper medical attention, and in short for all the sufferings and hardships that they will undergo during the time that I am imprisoned.

I repeat, Mr. Cardinal, that this letter should not be taken to be a rebellion against my Christian faith. I know that deep within the womb of the Church, there are thousands of priests that struggle to achieve that the Church become the humble wife of God Our Father, and that it become the protector of the poor. When this is achieved, even if it be only in part, I will again consider myself a member of that Church.

This letter should not be taken to be a plea of mercy, but rather as a call for justice for me and my companions, 3 of them sentenced already on one charge alone to three months in prison. My conscience is, I repeat, clean of all fault. Therefore, we smalltown [sic] folk say, what is done is done.

Lastly, Mr. Cardinal, I extend you an invitation to be present and witness (I'll give you the date later) the burning of the Baptismal certificates of myself, my wife, and our entire family on the stairs of the arrogant and vainful Church of St. Basil. This being the first act that will precede the struggle that I will undertake from that moment on against the exploitation, hypocrisy, arrogance and vanity that presently exist within the Church due to the stimulation by persons like you.

For social justice in all things; I remain your brother in spite of everything.

Pedro Arias
Alhambra, Calif.

PEDRO ARIAS TO CARDINAL FRANCIS McINTYRE[1]

On the 26th of May, this year, I sent Your Eminence a letter to which I have not received a reply. I expected you would do as others have to whom I have written (although these might be considered to be persons lower than yourself in education and dignity). Nevertheless they have replied even though I have attacked them in my letters, criticized them or manifested disagreement with their ideas or actions. Yet Your Eminence has made no acknowledgement after a period of over 90 days has elapsed. Since Your Eminence has available to him personnel to help him in the disposal of official and business duties, so that if a personal response is impossible, you may have someone else do so in your name. Therefore, if there is no justification or reason for your silence, I feel obligated to think that the education and dignity I was attributing to Your Eminence are qualities lacking in your personality.

While discussing with my friends your lack of reaction to my letter they speculated that your not replying might be due in part to the form in which I composed it, and for not addressing you with the proper adjective or title that in this letter I am using. Which is: Your EMINENCE

If the above is the reason, or one of the reasons, you can now see Your Eminence, I am correcting this fault and moreover, I apologize to you for the omission.

However, I do feel you should know that this error is due to my sincerity and custom in expressing myself, especially where religion is concerned. It is at this time

[1] As published in La Raza (Special Issue on CPLR, Fall, 1970) in Ricardo Cruz/Católicos Por La Raza Papers.

that I try to communicate in as straightforward a manner as possible. For example, when I direct myself to our Omnipotent God the Father, and I relate to him my most personal cares and sentiments, I call him simply Señor.

I use this same adjective when I speak to God the Son and further when I pray to the Mother of Jesus Christ, to our Mother, I call her "Mi Morenita" which translated is affectionately my little dark one.

So in my previous letter I did not address you with a little taking into consideration that since you are a representative of God, and my brother, it would be ridiculous to call you Your Eminence. But again, if I committed a mistake, I ask you to excuse me.

Other persons argued that the accusations contained in my last letter were the motives behind your silence. Perhaps because Your Eminence considers them false. But I doubt this could be so, and if it is Your Eminence should make known your observations or clarify this matter so that I in turn can remain silent. There is a common saying to the affected that silence is an admission of guilt.

Another possibility exists, that being that you might not have received my letter. If this occurred, I should point out that the letter has been published in various newspapers and it has also been distributed to people in the streets. This was done with the intention that in one way or another Your Eminence would be aware of the existence of this frequently mentioned letter.

Today, however, I am forwarding another copy so that you will know among other things, that it contained an invitation to which I had promised to send to you a precise date as I was unable to do so before.

With my present letter I renew the invitation and the day has been set for Sunday September 13, 1970, at twelve noon on the steps of what I call the vainglorious Cathedral dedicated to Saint Basil.

I pray that God give us all a long life and health and that Your Eminence will do everything possible to honor us with your presence.

Lastly, I want to place myself at your disposal for any clarification you might need for this or my previous letter. In other words, leaving aside the social amenities, Señor Cardinal, I am at your service for whatever you may wish, at whatever place and whatever time.

Wishing you health and prosperity and awaiting your reply I remain Your Eminence's attentive servant. For social justice on all levels,

Pedro Arias

P.S. Enclosed I am also sending a flyer relative to the above-mentioned invitation, and with Your Eminence's permission, I am sending copies of this letter also to the persons already mentioned that have received copies of my first letter to you.

DISTRICT ATTORNEY WELLIN REIDDER ON TRIAL OF THE ST. BASIL'S 21[1]

The People plan on calling approximately sixteen to eighteen witnesses. We have read the list to you. A good number of these are law enforcement personnel.

Basically, the situation as we intend to present it to you, ladies and gentlemen, is as follows:

On the evening of December 24th and the morning of December 25th, there was a Mass held at St. Basil's Catholic Church. This Mass was to be attended by Cardinal McIntyre, the then archbishop of the Archdiocese of Los Angeles.

The Mass was to begin at approximately 12:05. It was to be preceded by a procession with the Cardinal leading it in. There was to be a Mass upstairs, and there was to be a companion Mass downstairs for the overflow. The Masses were to be synchronized, and the Mass downstairs was to begin at approximately 12:05, so the procession upstairs could come in.

We believe our evidence will show that there were going to be microphones so that the ceremony could be at least synchronized through the preaching of the Mass, the gospel and the sermon, and then the services would separate. So there was this unity up to that point.

There had been considerable publicity as to this Mass. We believe the evidence will show that several members of the Anchor Club were contacted and asked to serve as ushers.

Now, the Anchor Club supposedly is a group of men in the government who serve as ushers and officials at these various functions.

[1] Transcript in Ricardo Cruz/Católicos Por La Raza Papers.

The evidence I believe will further show that the Anchor Club had been used at the dedication of the church sometime last summer, that it was in this light that a call was put forth to have members of the Anchor Club serve as ushers that evening.

The ushers in this case are deputy sheriffs. Some of them attended by themselves, some brought their families to the services at St. Basil's, and they were told they would have an opportunity to meet the Cardinal after the services.

At approximately 11:00 to 11:15 the church began to fill up, I believe the evidence will show that there was a demonstration on the sidewalk. This was for all intent and purpose [sic] a peaceful demonstration with persons parading back and forth in an official pattern with leaflets, carrying candles and banners.

There were also present some large Mardi Grass type figures on poles, the heads of figures. Mardi Grass figures I believe would be a sufficient descriptive term.

At approximately 11:30 or twenty to 12:00 the upstairs church was filled and persons were routed down to the vestibule through the doorway at the left corner of the vestibule, through the inside doorway, down to the lower church.

Now, this doorway apparently has two stairs well, one going down and one going up to the choir loft.

On both the center and the left photographs you will see the words, "choir loft" superimposed on the photographs. In this area here apparently there is a stairway that goes down here, one down to this lower church and one up to this choir left, which is perched above the back end of the congregation upstairs.

Sometime before midnight the lower church was filled and the ushers were instructed to close and lock the front doors. I believe the evidence will show that every seat was taken in the upstairs church, and there were approximately one hundred odd people standing, that every seat was taken in the lower church with somewhere in the area of one hundred people standing downstairs; that a Mass was held by the demonstrators on the sidewalk and on the stairs by three priests, Father Charles Coglan, Father Haun, and a Father Blase Bonpane; that at approximately 12:15 a woman stood up in the church and yelled: "Why don't you let the poor people in?"

At that point three males, two down the east aisle and one down the west aisle, proceeded from the upstairs church towards the back door leading from the sanctuary, which is the main church, into the vestibule.

One of the ushers, an Officer Vetter, saw this, and knowing that the doors had been locked in the vestibule area and knowing that the crowd was outside, followed this man back and had a tussle with him. The man succeeded in pushing the panic bar on the door and the crowd surged in.

The testimony I believe will further indicate that there ensued a pushing battle in the vestibule area for some five-odd minutes before the first unit of Los

Angeles Police Department responded, which consisted of some ten officers who had been on standby approximately half to one block away.

As I have told you before, most of this we allege occurred in the vestibule area. However, there were some persons standing at the bottom of the back stairs. If you will note, to the top left of the first diagram on the left of the board, there are some back stairs leading to this downstairs chapel, and it is our allegation that there were persons standing in the lower area at the bottom of those stairs.

When a party came down the stairs and informed them they were going upstairs, to go in, go in, and at that time Mr. Raul Ruiz and Mr. Jose Camarena allegedly walked in through that door, and paraded across the front of the church where the priest was engaged in prayer. One gentlemen [sic] had a club in his hand and approached to a point of two to three feet from the priest.

The group was carrying banners and were blocking the path of the parishioners and the alter area. Subsequently, these people moved up to the back end of the lower church, the stairs, and into the vestibule area.

Furthermore, we intend to show you that during the proceedings which lead up to the point that the group entered the vestibule area there were statements, there were urgings, and there were chants by several of the defendants, which in fact did incite the others to riot. They were chanting "get them. Kill the pigs. Get into the church." This sort of thing.

Furthermore, we believe we will establish that Alicia Escalante, specifically, with the aid of other of the defendants, hurled a cement canister used outside to deposit cigarette butts against the double doors—there is a wrought iron grating in front of these doors, then it is latched, and these are twelve-foot high doors—shattering one door and spewing sand inside.

We believe all of this will come to you, ladies and gentlemen, both from our witnesses and from film. We have films of a portion of the Mass, which I believe we will be able to show you.

OSCAR ZETA ACOSTA'S OPENING STATEMENT IN TRIAL OF ST. BASIL'S 21[1]

THE COURT: All right. Go ahead Mr. Acosta.

MR. ACOSTA:—that there has been a conflict, a controversy, between the defendants and other friends and members of an association to which they belong known as Catoligos [sic] Por LaRaza [sic] with the archdiocese, the Archdiocese of the Roman Catholic Church here in Los Angeles County, where each of the defendants reside.

The evidence will show that there were several attempts made to begin a dialogue and negotiations with Cardinal McIntyre, Monsignor Hawkes, and other members of the Catholic Archdiocese here in Los Angeles; that at least on one occasion there was a demonstration in the form of picketing in front of St. Basil's prior to this incident without any incident arising; that various members of our church, the priests and parishioners, criticized the demonstrators, criticized the defendants and members of CPLR for making these demands and having these demonstrations.

That there were two groups; that another group formed known as the Coalition of Concerned Catholics, which was basically an Anglo group as distinguished from the Mexican-American CPLR group, who joined CPLR on Christmas Eve.

[1] Trial proceedings in Ricardo Cruz/Católicos Por La Raza Papers.

That these arrangements had been made over a period of a couple of weeks at various community meetings open to the public in East Los Angeles.

That the intent of the defendants and their associates was to engage in what they would refer to as a Chicano Folk Mass on the steps of St. Basil's on Christmas Eve.

There will be testimony that will show that the customs and traditions of a Chicano Catholic are somewhat different from those of other Catholics. That is, that the Chicano uses a little different music and a few different means of expressing their religious convictions. Again, that is different from the Anglo Catholic.

That on Christmas Eve some three to four hundred members of CPLR—and I will use the term CCC as the Coalition of Concerned Catholics, the Anglo Group—that the two groups did meet at St. Basil's and did engage in a candlelight vigil on the sidewalk in front of St. Basil's; that there was singing with guitar Mexican songs, both religious and temporal among the group there.

That there was a meeting, actually a couple of meetings, between one of the defendants and the attorney for the group with a Sergeant Domínguez who was acting in the position of liaison between the church and the demonstrators; that as a result of the meeting it was agreed there was no objection to the Folk Mass on the steps, and furthermore that there would be no objection to any of the demonstrators entering the church when the regular Midnight Mass started so long as the demonstration was not carried into the church; that this agreement was communicated to the demonstrators prior to the beginning of the Folk Mass and at the conclusion of the Folk Mass by one of the defendants, Richard Cruz.

That the Folk Mass commenced and terminated without any incident; that it was a purely and strictly religious service.

That at the conclusion of the Folk Mass some of the persons who were gathered there entered the church or made attempts to enter the church and that the front doors had been locked, but the side doors still remained open, and that there were still persons going in and out of the church through those side doors.

That the two groups made two different entries; that there was one group that went downstairs into the lower chapel; that they did encounter Sergeant Domíngues [sic] but nevertheless proceeded through the chapel, seeking entry to the upstairs chapel; seeking entry to the upstairs chapel where the main service, the choir and Cardinal McIntyre would be participating.

That a second and smaller group entered through the side door directly into the lobby of the vestibule and requested of the ushers that they be allowed to enter as other persons had been entering; that this same smaller group of six, seven or eight persons could see through the windows that there was standing room only and that many persons were being allowed to stand along the aisles and towards the rear of the church, and they requested of the ushers in the vestibule that they also be allowed to enter and stand; that the ushers refused them entry into the church, and this small group of persons at that time requested of the ushers that they be allowed to remain in the vestibule, that the doors be opened, and that they be allowed to remain in the vestibule to participate in the Mass, standing there in the vestibule, and there will be evidence that this is customary, that late arrivals customarily in Catholic churches and particularly at St. Basil's are allowed to stand in the vestibule when there are no more seats inside or when they arrive late, and that they do in fact engage in their own worship there in the vestibule. There will be testimony that the vestibule is itself a part of the church, that it is a religious area, not unlike the pew area.

There will be testimony that the ushers at that point told this small group they could not remain in the vestibule, that they had been given orders not to allow any other persons to go in the main church; and that at that point one or two of the persons attempted to leave; that the group was basically attempting to leave; that they were going to go out the doors and go home, and that it was upon this attempt to exit the vestibule that the ushers began to beat upon the persons leaving.

There will be testimony that not only was there this fighting but that also there was the use of mace upon one of the persons in the vestibule in this smaller group; and that the crowd's response to the noise, the screaming, was the reaction to seeing the ushers beating upon the friends and associates of the crowd inside.

There will be testimony that this crowd on the doorsteps was not exclusively the crowd of the persons who had participated in a Folk Mass, but it in fact included persons who were presumably parishioners. In any event, they were not part of the demonstrating group.

That the ushers then pushed this small group outside through the front doors, and continued to beat upon them as they were pushing; that the crowd's response was a reaction to this; that a group of the persons standing there at the front doors did in fact enter the vestibule again to come to the assistance of those persons who were being beat upon.

There will be testimony that at approximately the same time, which was just within a matter of a couple of minutes after the initial scuffling there in the vestibule, that a group of uniformed officers arrived ready and immediately began beating upon anyone in the vestibule, including ushers, including parishioners, including women and including some of the demonstrators.

That the other group, which had been downstairs, at about this time came into the vestibule; that when they arrived there the vestibule was already crowded and packed and so forth with the scuffling that was going on; that they too reacted to seeing ushers and uniformed policemen beating upon friends and associates.

That the group of uniformed officers with their batons and the ushers with their mace did in fact clear the vestibule of all the persons, pushed them outside, down onto the doorsteps, and in fact continued to push them all the way down to the sidewalk, and at that approximate same time that all this was taking place, in this ten, 15 or 20 minute period at the most, numerous police vehicles arrived on the scene with their sirens and red lights; that there was heavy traffic right there on Wilshire Boulevard at that time; that the uniformed police and the sheriffs with the additional help then proceeded to clear the entire block, the entire area, not only in the front, not only from the church, but all the way down to either corner, of all the persons; that in their attempts to disperse the crowd there were again more repeated acts of violence upon the persons, including some of the defendants; that within a matter of another ten, 15 or 20 minutes the crowd did in fact leave the area and re-assembled at another location; that some of the persons had been arrested.

That the demonstration the following day was in protest of the brutality of that evening, of what the persons considered to be brutality in any event; that a smaller group, perhaps 50 to 100, did go to St. Basil's and engage in the picketing of St. Basil's in protest of the previous evening.

That one of the witnesses, a Mr. Sharkey, did make repeated attempts to clear the area of the demonstrators, despite the fact that there were officers and parishioners who did instruct and tell Mr. Sharkey to leave the persons alone, including a news reporter who questioned him about this; that he persisted in harassing and in some cases making derogatory remarks to the demonstrating group there, along with other persons who were presumably parishioners, and one lady in particular wearing a red dress who continued to insult the demonstrating group with racial epithets and racial derogatory remarks; that the only incident was that of a charge by Mr. Sharkey, John Sharkey, who did make an attempt to beat upon one of the persons demonstrating, but that it was immediately broken up by the demonstrators themselves; that they were separated and the police came and took Mr. Sharkey away from the area, again informing him that these persons demonstrating had a right to picket as they were doing.

That as a result of these incidents the Catholic church hierarchy has continued to negotiate with the group; that Cardinal McIntyre was fired partially as a result of this incident or retired, should I say, and that it will be testified that this caused an embarrassment to the church, and is the cause for the bias on the part of those witnesses who have testified against the defendants.

Thank you.

TRIAL OF ST.BASIL 21: TESTIMONY OF RICARD CRUZ[1]

BY MR. [OSCAR Zeta] ACOSTA:

Q Richard, will you give us your educational background and your present occupation.

MR. REIDDER [District Attorney]: Excuse me, Your Honor, but I don't see what relevance his educational background has to the charges pending in this case.

THE COURT: The objection is sustained.

MR. ACOSTA: Your Honor, every single witness for the City Attorney was allowed to tell the jury who they were and what they did.

THE COURT: That isn't what you asked him. You asked him what his educational background is, and the objection is sustained to that question because it is immaterial. If you want to ask him what his occupation is you certainly may.

MR. ACOSTA: Thank you, Judge.

BY MR. ACOSTA:

Q Richard, what do you do?

[1] Court Proceedings of trial of the 21 indicted members of Católicos Por La Raza including Richard Cruz and defended by activist attorney Oscar Zeta Acosta are contained in Ricardo Cruz/Católicos Por La Raza Papers.

A I am a law student at Loyola University School of Law, third year.

Q And are you familiar with an organization known as Católicos Por La Raza?

A Very much so. I am co-chairman of Católicos Por La Raza.

Q And can you very briefly and succinctly describe the character of that organization? What is that organization?

MR. REIDDER: Object as to the relevance.

THE COURT: Sustained.

MR. ACOSTA: Your Honor, that organization has been named here 100 times.

THE COURT: That is true.

MR. ACOSTA: And I think that the jury should know who it is we are talking about. It has been brought up by the City Attorney and by myself, Your Honor.

THE COURT: Mr. Acosta, he can identify the organization, but I am not going to permit testimony as to its purpose or anything along that line.

MR. ACOSTA: I didn't ask that.

THE COURT: That is the import of the question. Let's rephrase the question then.

BY MR. ACOSTA:

Q What is Católicos Por La Raza?

A It is a group of poor people, Chicano people, mostly from East Los Angeles who gather together starting with many different occasions that finally gathered all together to look at their church, the Catholic church, to protest what we consider unfair racist and otherwise detrimental activity by our own church towards our own people.

Q Did you at any time have any conversations or meetings with members of the Roman Catholic Archdiocese of Los Angeles within the past six months?

MR. REIDDER: Objection. Irrelevant.

THE COURT: Sustained.

MR. ACOSTA: Your Honor, several of the witnesses of the City Attorney have mentioned several meetings that they had with Monsignor Hawkes in particular with various defendants and their organization.

MR. REIDDER: Excuse me, Your Honor, this was brought out by the defense on cross-examination as to the reason for being at that church.

THE COURT: Well, if you are talking about any meeting that may have been had in connection with this evening I will permit you to go into that. If you will limit it to that, the Court will reverse its ruling.

MR. ACOSTA: Yes, sir, I will rephrase the question.

BY MR. ACOSTA:

Q Did you meet with any members of the Roman Catholic Archdiocese with respect to any issue to the incident at St. Basil's on December 24, 1969?

A Yes, personally. There were two meetings that I was personally involved with Cardinal McIntyre, Bishop Manning and many other hierarchy, and this was at the Chancery itself.

MR. REIDDER: I would object to the witness going any further. The question has been answered.

THE COURT: Mr. Cruz, I am going to ask you to listen to the question carefully and just answer what is asked in the question, rather than to go on an exposition, if you will.

THE WITNESS: Yes, Your Honor.

THE COURT: All right. Mr. Acosta.

BY MR. ACOSTA:

Q When did those meetings take place, approximately?

A One was on October 15th of last year, 1969. There were actually two meetings, but the other one for sure was somewhere around November, I believe, of 1969.

Q You were at St. Basil's on Christmas Eve?

A Yes.

Q Did the outcome of those meetings, the result of those meetings, have anything to do with your going to St. Basil's on Christmas Eve?

MR. REIDDER: Your Honor, I would object to the leading nature of counsel's questions.

THE COURT: Well, it is preliminary. It is leading, but I will overrule it.

Let's see if we can get to the substance of this. It is overruled.

THE WITNESS: Yes.

BY MR. ACOSTA:

Q What was your intent and your reason for going to St. Basil's on Christmas Eve?

A Because of the complete failure to have any meaningful exchanges of dialogue or anything resulting from the previous meetings by many people.

Q And did you go there as a group to St. Basil's?

A I don't understand the question.

Q Was the activity that occurred at St. Basil's pre-planned?

MR. REIDDER: Your Honor, I again would object to the leading nature of the question.

THE COURT: That calls for a conclusion in any event. I don't know what activity you are referring to.

MR. ACOSTA: The Folk Mass, Your Honor.

THE COURT: Let's rephrase it again so the witness can answer it.

BY MR. ACOSTA:

Q The Folk Mass that Father Bonpane was talking about, had that been prearranged, and, if so, when and where?

A Yes, informally by the community. Commencing approximately a week or two weeks before Christmas Eve, a general invitation was extended to the Chicano community, to many people and groups, to join with us on Christmas Eve in our Folk Mass.

Q Approximately what time did you arrive at St. Basil's on Christmas Eve?

A I believe at around 11:00 or 11:15, maybe.

Q You said you were one of the co-chairman of the group?

A Yes.

Q As a co-chairman of the group, what did you do when you got there?

A Well, I merely made sure that a lot of details were accomplished, that the candles were passed out and the song sheets. We had song sheets. We were trying to get our guitars together and the people who could sing. I had to make sure there was no blocking of any of the stairways or any of the entrances to the church since many of the parishioners were arriving. I was there just generally to invite and welcome our own people and the coalition people, and to talk to parishioners and invite them, and some did stay with us as we organized and began an official pattern to keep everyone moving. I did various things such as this.

Q Did you have any conversation prior to the Folk Mass with any member of the Police Department?

I don't think I did. I don't remember talking with them. I don't remember if there was anything about that; if I did, I don't remember. I was just talking to any people.

Q Did you speak during this service out on the steps? Did you speak to the group?

A Yes, right before and right after our Mass.

Q Can you tell us what the sum and substance of your talk to that group was?

A Before the Mass I was merely reiterating or reminding myself actually and all of us of why we were there, why we were on the street, and I explained that we were left out and of what we felt about the fact of being left outside by our own church; that we wanted to have our Mass on Christmas Eve outside on the steps to exhibit physically that the church had left us outside. So this was the first speech right before the Mass. I was inviting everyone to gather back here now, I said, "Over here away from the church entrance; let's go to Mass now, to come on in, and we will have our Mass."

Q You said you spoke to the group a second time after the Mass?

A After the Mass.

Q Will you tell us the sum and substance of what you told the crowd?

A That was a very short statement of—well, it was two things really—one quick statement about the Mass and what it meant to us. We had said our Mass more or less. I very quickly just mentioned the Mass is going on, and something to the effect that any of those who were Catholics and who wanted to go on in could go in: "I am going into St. Basil's to go to Mass."

Q Have you finished?

A No. I mean, I don't remember the exact words I used, because it was almost instantaneous. The Mass was going on. It was: Anyone could go home or come to Mass, that if anyone wanted to go to Mass they could, and that kind of statement.

Q Did you tell the people to go into the church?

A No.

Q Did you order them or anything of that nature?

A No, they were just told they could go.

Q Did you have the church's permission to enter the church?

A Yes. It was understood. I hate saying, yes, as if we talked about it. It was just understood. There was no problem. It was a church and the Midnight Mass.

Q I am sorry?

A Well, I mean, yes, several people, including yourself, we knew anyway that Sergeant Domínguez and the police were there.

Q Did you have a conversation with me prior to making that talk on the steps?

A Yes.

Q And what was my capacity there?

A Well, you are our lawyer. You have been our lawyer in many of the activities of Católicos Por La Raza, even before when we were exploring all the avenues of reaching the church, including, of course, the possibility of lawsuits and things, but you are our lawyer and a member.

Q Did you have a discussion with me that evening prior to your making your second speech to the group?

A Yes.

Q And what was the sum and substance of the statements, if any, that I made to you on this occasion?

A That you had had a discussion with Sergeant Domínguez. You mentioned to me to let it be known when I get on the microphone, I think you said something after the Mass or something, that if anyone wants to go in to the Mass inside to don't worry about going into the church in terms of the legality, that the doors would be open, and all these things. I don't remember exactly, but it was just something that I didn't even consider very important or especially relevant. It was assumed.

Q At any time did you ever believe or think or suspect that any sort of a special permit or permission would be required to enter the church?

A No. Many of us were Chicano law students and, of course, we made sure there was no problems, and we knew we were going to be within the law in what we were doing.

Q What did you do following your second statement to the crowd? Where did you go, if anywhere?

A I said goodbye to Father Bonpane and a few words, picked up a thing or two, and just started walking into the church, right at the steps.

Q Yes, go ahead. Continue.

A Well, I went up the steps with everyone else. There must have been 20 or 30, I don't remember, but there were a lot of people just going up to the steps, just going to church.

Q I am sorry?

A I am saying that I was just going to church. The people were walking up the steps from where we had been, and the crowd was all around going up the steps. Some people were blessing themselves, and just regular things, only now we were going into another church. That is the only difference. It was like people leaving one Mass and going into another.

Q Did you go into the church that evening; I mean, after the Folk Mass?

A Not the main church.

Q Where did you go?

A What happened was I noticed that the doors were closed.

MR. REIDDER: Objection. The question as worded is: Where did you go?

THE COURT: Sustained.

I am going to ask you again, if you will please, to listen to the question and to try to answer the question, rather than going off into something else. Listen carefully, and if you don't understand tell Mr. Acosta, and he will rephrase it.

Go ahead. Will you rephrase the question, Mr. Acosta.

BY MR. ACOSTA:

Q Did you go into the front doors?

A No.

Q Why not?

A Because the crowd wasn't. The doors appeared locked. The people were coming to the west side. This door over here on the west side was starting to swing around. I was towards the tail or side. I assumed they could go in through the west door. There was a crowd there, myself, a girl friend, and several people, and we just went down to the side of the church, in other words, to go in from that side.

Q Did you go in?

A We went in the downstairs one. I really still don't remember how that thing was structured. We were confused. We saw a downstairs type thing that looked like the church.

Q Did you see anybody push him out of the way?

A No.

Q Will you describe your entry, your manner of entry into that downstairs chapel and where, if any place, you went in that downstairs chapel?

A The manner of entry was just walking into church, just a footstep at a time, you know, just walking in. We knew that Mass was started, and we were late. At least I knew insofar as I was concerned, so I walked a little faster than normal. We just proceeded into the chapel area. I looked and saw the altar and the Mass and not everyone was standing. I could see that it was crowded, very crowded, so I just proceeded walking down the west aisle.

Q When you say everyone was standing who are you referring to?

A The celebrants and the people.

Q You have seen the witness here by the name of Mr. Gratz that was here last week?

A Yes.

Q Did you see that gentleman that evening in the lower church?

A No.

Q Approximately how long did it take you to get from the vestibule to the rear of the chapel?

A Ten or 15 seconds. It is a real rough assumption. We were just walking down more or less at a normal pace. Well, a little faster than normal, because we knew the Mass was started, and I was just looking to see where the seats were and everything, so it would have been 15 seconds or maybe ten seconds.

Q Then what did you do after walking that ten or 15 seconds?

A Well, I surmised that there were people in the aisles, that it was crowded, and that I was going to go into the vestibule, so I just kept walking to the end, to the lower part of this picture; in other words, to the end of the west aisle. I went up some stairs. I don't remember exactly where, but I went up some stairs which turned out to lead into the vestibule, the upstairs vestibule.

Q Why were you going up to the vestibule?

A I don't think I have ever been to Mass on time. It was just a matter of going back to the vestibule, which I have always done. I thought, "Well, the church is crowded. I'm going up to the vestibule." At least I thought it was going to be that, and it turned out to be the vestibule. I intended to stand there. And also one other reason is I assumed that is where my family would be. I had lost them. They were there that night—and my cousin—and I thought they probably were all up in the vestibule.

So after seeing that the crowd was still milling around, that it was crowded when I first started going back, I assumed everyone was going to be in the vestibule with the doors open.

Q Did you get to the vestibule?

A Yes.

Q Do you recall when you were walking up the stairs if any part of the group was walking in front of you or were you the first one?

A If I remember correctly I was the first one, but that is only because I didn't know anyone else. It wasn't a group. It was just people splitting up. It was my going to Mass and looking for my family and friends after awhile, but I didn't notice too well.

Q Did you see anybody running up the stairs around that time?

A No.

Q Did you see any sort of scuffling on the stairs?

A No.

Q Now, as you were walking through that lower chapel did you hear any unusual noises?

A Not really, no, I don't think so. There were just noises from a lot of people and, of course, all evening there had been singing on our part. They were singing in the choir, the church's regular choir, so I just don't know. There was a lot of music and noise and everything.

Q What did you see when you got to the top of the stairs and looked into the vestibule?

A I saw men beating men. That is what I saw. And women.

Q Can you briefly describe what you saw there in the vestibule when you got up there?

A Well, I saw some of these men—well, one person for sure—with an usher's thing and some other people near him, you know, various men and some with suits, and I saw I believe it was Tony or Richard, one of the two. I remember seeing one of them.

Q You are referring to—

A Salazar or Martínez, if I remember correctly, was one of the two, and several other people in the various stages of scuffling. I saw these ushers or whatever they were hitting people, and they were defending themselves by pushing back and some were yelling.

Q Then what did you do after you saw this?

A I remember I just stood there when I first got up to that thing, I just stood there, and I just was looking, because I had never seen an usher hit a man.

Then it is hard to remember it because it turned into a melee somehow with more people than there were police, but I remember this for sure: At one time I was knocked down. I wish I had done more things myself that I could remember, but I don't remember. All I remember is all the scuffling and seeing our people getting hit.

Q What did you do? I mean did you stay in the vestibule or did you go out or what happened?

A Sure, we left. I mean, the police did come. There was pushing. I think maybe I got knocked down again. I ended up outside. I don't remember exactly how I got to the west door. I remember being pushed, but I don't remember by whom or what. The reason is because I was behind when I actually came up the vestibule thing. I was more or less too far in from the west door, so I was out, but I don't know how. I saw police, but then I remember stepping outside. Several people were there, friends of mine, and I asked, "What's going on? What's happening?" You know how people will act: "What's going on?" I asked them: "What's going on? What happened? Whose hitting? Why are they hitting us? What's going on?"

At that time or shortly thereafter again there was a lot of confusion from people who apparently still thought they were going to go in that church, who were still standing around there. Everyone was talking, and I remember saying this, because some of them didn't know. I was the co-chairman and things had been going really nice. I remember saying, "Come on let's get away. Let's go to the front. Get everyone together and tell the people."

Q Now, of the people you said you saw still there at that west door entering were all of them to your knowledge members of Católicos Por La Raza or supporters thereof?

A I saw a lot of familiar faces, you know, but I can't remember which exact faces I saw, but there were other people there. I thought there were some parishioners there, you know, people in there that were parishioners, just people thinking they were going to open the vestibule or otherwise, so we could have our Mass.

Q After you were outside on the west side you said you had a discussion with some people. What did you next do? Where did you go?

A Well, as I am saying, I told Tom Varela, I told Bob Fernández, and I told other people: "Let's get the people out, get them out of the vestibule," or something to that effect. I said, "They are beating them."

When I told them this I myself started just pushing the crowd. I wanted the crowd to move back. I wanted to get some order to whatever was going on here, because I heard sirens and saw them coming. I saw them, and from previous work experience I knew it would be very well trained people who would be coming up the steps and things or otherwise coming, and I just wanted some order, so we went back to the front; at least, I did, and there were many people there, we brought many more, and we were up front again.

Q What did you do up front?

THE COURT: Excuse me. Mr. Acosta, we are going to have to recess at this time. Mr. Reidder is due in Division 18 for a few moments during the recess at 3:00 o'clock.

Ladies and gentlemen of the jury, we will take a recess at this time until 3:15. Please bear in mind my admonition to you.

(Recess taken, at the conclusion of which the following proceedings were had in open court, in the presence of the jury and the alternate jurors.)

THE COURT: You may proceed, Counsel.

BY MR. ACOSTA:

Q I think we had just gotten to the place where you had been kicked out the vestibule and you had gotten around to the front steps. Did you at that point make any statements to the crowd?

A Yes.

Q And what did you say to them?

A To tell you the truth, I don't remember the exact words, but the gist of it was something is wrong. I remember some people were bloodied. I said, "Let's go. The police are coming. Don't get hurt." And people were shouting, "We're trying to quit." We were trying to get order. This is basically what I was trying to do. Well, I was succeeding. At least I thought the people were getting together, you know, down from the steps, and I just don't know what the exact words were.

Q After you finished speaking to the crowd what, if anything, did you do?

A Some friends—José Pozo was one of them, I remember—said, "Let's go," you know, "Let's go." Because what I was thinking was to get them out, and I was saying, "Let's go. Go. Let's get out of here. We'll go to Euclid." I remember saying that, to go to Euclid Center, back where our meeting place was. Then I thought, "I had better go too instead of just saying it over and over," because we didn't want more police coming down and ushers.

Q Did the crowd or you engage in any form of chanting or sloganeering at that point?

A Everyone was angered, shocked and angered. There were parents and kids there. I was angry too. I remember saying "Viva La Raza" at least twice. I did say that, because it was the only way we could get people together. We could yell it and get people at least doing one thing in unison. The people heard it, they were scattered, and when they heard it they came in. We were together more or less, and then we said, "Go."

Q Did you then go?

A I did.

Q Where did you go?

A Well, again, some friends said, "Let's all go and you too. Go. Don't get hurt. Let's go." This just went through the crowd. Then some of the crowd started going west on Wilshire. I went down to the corner with several people.

Q Did you ultimately leave the scene, leave the area there?

A Well, not right away. What I did was several of us were walking. We didn't want to go back that way, in other words, back east. Yet, we wanted to make sure people left, so Tom Varela, Bob Fernández and myself—there was a cab right there—we got in the cab, and we drove. I told them to drive up there and to make sure the people were going, and I remember we yelled from the window even: "Go." There were still some people around, the police there, but I didn't see what subsequently happened.

Q Did you go to Euclid?

A Not right away. Yes, that night, maybe, that was more or less planned, but not right away.

Q Did you return to St. Basil's later on that day?

A Yes.

Q Was this Christmas Day?

A Christmas Day, yes.

Q What was the purpose or the reason for your returning to that church?

A Several reasons, of course, but we had to do it for our own people in the community. We knew because of the splash of the noise that occurred Christmas Eve we had to show that we were the disciplined ones, that we were not going to let this happen, that we had nothing to hide and no fear. This was the gist of the meeting at Euclid, and we went back at approximately 11:00 or 10:30 the next morning to protest, to demonstrate.

Q Did anything unusual—that is, unusual in the context of a demonstration—occur?

A Yes, something unusual occurred.

Q Tell us what happened, what you saw and heard?

A I arrived after it started. I arrived at approximately 11:00 or 11:30. I don't remember exactly. Sixty or 70 people from Católicos Por La Raza and the Coalition of Concerned Catholic people were in front of the church, some with picket signs, and they were saying "Cristo si—McIntyre no," you know, these type of grito shouts or comments were being made.

Fred López was on the steps saying, you know, "Keep this and don't get out of line." I went up there and continued instructing the disciplining, reminding them of Christmas Eve in words to the effect, "We are not going to let them do it again, but that means we have to be disciplined." The cameras were there, and we were very worried about the image that we might possibly project to the community, and we had to make sure once again that we were not going to provoke anything.

Q Excuse me. What cameras are you referring to?

A Well, the news. This is why I remember very well Mr. Sharkey, because I thought at the moment or at the time that he was one more of the so-called ushers and was going to come even down outside the church to continue what had occurred Christmas Eve. He was pushing people in the line. We were watching our people, young and old. I said, "Don't talk to them." I remember instructing them: "Don't talk to them. Don't do anything. Just keep your own business." He was running around, and we were just trying to ignore him completely. He tore up a sign, he did various things to agitate in my opinion, and then one of the persons in the line came up to me, who knows I am a law student, and he said, "Get rid of this man. He is messing us up. Some of the guys might get angry if he continues." Because everyone was very emotional about what they had done Christmas Eve.

I went around up to the steps where I was to the side of the church, the east side of the church, where there were three or four policemen. The police were all over. I instructed them that that man was violating our rights and to arrest him or remove him, I didn't care which. I remember saying that to them, to just leave us alone, and they did. They came down, and I don't know if you were with me. I think maybe you were around at the time, but they escorted Mr. Sharkey or whatever his name is across the street, and he was still yelling and all that.

Q Did you see any incident between Mr. Sharkey and Armando?

A Sure. Yes.

Q How far were you from where they were?

A Well, very close. All of us were trying to keep our people, all of them, away from Mr. Sharkey.

Q Did you hear anyone shouting any obscenities at that point?

A No.

Q Did you hear anybody shouting any obscenities of any kind of profane words from among the demonstrators?

A No.

Q After you saw them take Mr. Sharkey away did anything else unusual occur there at the demonstration?

A Well, this is before and after the Sharkey incident, but it wasn't unusual; at least, not insofar as church activity. This was that many of the parishioners were on the steps, apparently parishioners, or at least people who were yelling and cussing at us, and they said, "Communist, go back to Mexico." A lady came down the steps in a fur coat. I can only laugh, because I was telling them, "Don't do anything. Ignore everyone and just mind our business. Just show the public we are not here to make trouble but to demonstrate." and she pushed me down the steps, I remember some of them were laughing, and then I turned around because I thought, "Here we go again," or something, you know, and it was this lady. She was saying, "You dirty Mexican and you are just a bunch of Communists and take your pachucos, take them with you." It made me laugh, and she pushed me; as if I could take them with me or something. I just kept going down. She pushed me down two steps, and I just stood there and said, "Don't worry about her."

Q Since that day, Christmas Day, again in connection with Católicos Por La Raza, have there been any incidents of violence of any kind between Católicos Por La Raza and police and/or other citizens?

MR. REIDDER: Objection. Irrelevant.

THE COURT: Sustained.

BY MR. ACOSTA:

Q Has Católicos Por La Raza engaged in any other type of demonstration or protest at St. Basil's since Christmas Eve?

MR. REIDDER: Objection. Irrelevant.

THE COURT: Sustained.

MR. ACOSTA: No further questions, Your Honor.

THE COURT: Mr. Rosen [Second Attorney for Católicos].

MR. ROSEN: No questions.

THE COURT: Mr. Reidder.

MR. REIDDER: Yes, Your Honor.

MR. ACOSTA: Excuse me, Your Honor. I forgot one thing, if I may re-open.

THE COURT: All right.

MR. ACOSTA: I would like to have this photograph marked as Defendants' Exhibit next in order.

THE COURT: All right.

BY MR. ACOSTA:

Q First, I want to show you a photograph and ask you if you are familiar with that scene in the photograph?

A Yes, I am.

Q Do you recognize yourself in there?

A Yes.

Q Do you know approximately when and where this photograph was taken?

A This was taken Christmas Eve on the steps there. It was during either one of my little comments to the group, to ourselves, before or after, I don't know which one, but this is Abbott and some people and Father Haun, and, apparently it looks like Father Bonpane and some candles.

Q On the two occasions that you spoke to the crowd that you mentioned did you use that microphone that you have in your hand?

A Yes.

Q Are you right-handed or left-handed?

A Right-handed.

Q Is that a fair and accurate depiction of what you saw there that night at that time and place?

A Yes.

MR. ACOSTA: I have no further questions. Move to introduce this into evidence.

THE COURT: It will be received.

MR. ACOSTA: I would like to show it to the jury, if I may.

THE COURT: All right.

MR. ACOSTA: Thank you, Your Honor.

CHURCH VS CATÓLICOS[1]

A five week trial has ended for eleven persons who were accused of disrupting a religious service at St. Basil's Roman Catholic Church last Christmas Eve. Eight of the eleven persons were Chicanos who belong to a national religious organization called Católicos Por La Raza (CPLR). CPLR is seeking to right inequities in the Roman Catholic Church, including the failure of the Church to take care of the social needs of the poor. The other three persons included two Roman Catholic priests and a former Immaculate Heart Sister, all of whom were in sympathy with Católicos Por La Raza aims.

Oscar Zeta Acosta, a candidate for Sheriff of Los Angeles County, was selected as the group's attorney. Acosta is widely known as Chicano Movement lawyer throughout the Southwest. He had assistance from two other Anglo lawyers who stated their desire to enter the case.

The first week of the trial was spent in selecting the jury. The final composition of the jury included one Chicana, four blacks, and seven anglos. During that first week, the other two lawyers "expressed" their desire to leave the case because of the estimated length of the trial. They could not afford to spend that much time on any case. It is interesting to note that this is the general example that is followed by non-movement lawyers who initially give hope to defendents [sic] and then leave them holding the bag.

The case of Católicos Por La Raza illustrates the sincerity and insincerity of lawyers. The CPLR trial was clearly a political case in which the Roman Catholic Church, through Monsignor Hawkes and three other priests, filed the complaint against the defendents [sic]. Most lawyers will not get involved in political cases because of the ramifications that are involved. The Roman Catholic Church is a powerful institution that many fear. A lawyer's clientele can desert him if they disagree with his political motives, and thus his bread and butter are gone. It is only

[1] La Raza (vol.1, no. 1) in Ricardo Cruz/Católicos Por La Raza Papers.

movement oriented lawyers that try political case after case because they believe in what the defendents [sic] are fighting for. The desertion of the defendents [sic] by the other two lawyers gives more credence to what our people are not only stating, but feeling, "Dentro de mi Raza todo, fuera de mi Raza, nada! [Everything within my people, nothing outside of it!]

The second week of the trial began with the judge pulling a "Julie Hoffman" trick. Despite the fact that the trial had been quietly conducted, the judge ordered the bailiffs to seat the spectators one seat apart in the spectator section. His objective was to avoid any possible disruption in the courtroom. It appears that the judge was hoping for a "Chicano 8" trial. He further ordered more marshalls [sic] into the courtroom throughout the trial and ended his "Hoffman tactics" by finding Acosta in contempt of Court for objecting too strenuously.

As the trial continued, it became clear that the testimony as given by the priests and police officers was in conflict with the testimony as given by the defendants. The police officers testified that they had been "waiting" for possible trouble in the back of a house near the Church. They had been notified of the possible disturbance by Monsignor Hawkes a week before the Christmas Mass. It was also brought out that many of the Church's ushers that night were police officers from the Sheriff's Department who belong to the Church's Anchor Club. They were asked to usher Christmas Eve by Monsignor Hawkes, a member of the Roman Catholic chancery.

It became apparent that the Church had taken a dim view of the Chicano protests and that they were going to end them once and for all by calling in the police. The testimony brought out that some of the ushers (deputy Sheriffs in plain clothes) maced members of Católicos Por La Raza when they attempted to gain entrance. Other testimony from four metropolitan police officers distorted the picture. Some perjured themselves by stating that they were beaten up. One claimed that eight Chicanos jumped him but he fought them off with his elbows (a la James Bond style). Others made stereotypical racist comments by claming that they knew it was Mexicans that were involved because "those people were about five feet and two inches tall and weighed 140 pounds." They truly believed that that is a typical description of all Chicanos.

As the trial entered its final week, the prosecution attempted to further descredit [sic] the efforts of Católicos Por La Raza by calling Blase Bonpane, one of the defendants' witness, a "traveling revolutionary priest who was kicked out of Guatemala." An effort was also made to disbar Oscar Acosta because of the fact that he had not paid his lawyers fees for 1969. The judge charged Acosta with another contempt of court charge because his standing as a lawyer was questionable due to the fact that he had not paid $35 for his state bar membership. The following day, the judge later ate his words as close to twenty lawyers including the president of the National Lawyers Guild Association, came to Acosta's aid. Acosta was "re-instated" after paying his dues.

That same day the jury, which had deliberated for four days, came in with a verdict of not guilty for eight defendents [sic], guilty for two, and a hung jury on one. The prosecution was most unhappy.

The second trial consisting of 10 Chicanos is currently under way. Their charges are heavier and range from disrupting a religious service, to assault and battery and inciting to riot. Regardless of the outcome of the second trial, we cannot ignore the source of power that the Roman Catholic Church has.

It is not just our right to appeal to the Church to use its power effectively for the poor, it is our duty to do so.

NOTICIA

CATÓLICOS POR LA RAZA wishes to remind you:

1. We are located at Euclid Community Center, 3045 Whittier Blvd., L.A. California 90023. We invite your comments and contributions. Hopefully, with your financial assistance, we will soon be able to publish "Noticia." The last one (100,000 copies was distributed throughout Los Angeles and the Southwest). With your assistance, we will soon be able to prepare another updated edition. Remember, you are a member of CPLR if you say you are Chicano and are willing to sacrifice for the betterment of nuestra gente. We do not need your moral support, we need your ideas, talents and whatever else you can offer to el movimiento de Católicos Por La Raza. Please mail any articles (Spanish or English, preferably both) to us for possible publication in the next "Noticia."
2. We are extremely grateful for the $1500 in contributions which enabled us to bail out of jail after the Christmas Eve "ambush" and which also made our first "Noticia" possible. We wish to publicly thank all those who contributed and wish to let the Church and public know that the contributions range from pennies and nickels from Chicanitos [children], to several hundred of dollars from businessmen, professionals, priests, and nuns.

CATÓLICOS POR LA RAZA

A MORAL STRUGGLE[1]

Católicos Por La Raza (CPLR) is here to stay. On September 13, 1970, Pedro Arias and his family will burn baptism certificates to symbolically protest the Chicano disgust for the institution called the Catholic Church. As a member of CPLR, Pedro has made it clear that he is not renouncing the Catholic Faith or the Christian dogma. His act on that day is instead a renunciation of Catholic Church hypocrisy and racism as we in Los Angeles are only beginning to understand. We at first thought that the Church in Los Angeles was only hypocritical in that it built $4,000,000 churches for the rich and that it had at least a billion dollars in real property alone in Los Angeles. (Included in this edition of La Raza is a partial listing of such properties.) We believe this vast ownership of properties to be hypocritical because the Church has always preached "Blessed are the poor" and had Chicanitos selling Christmas seals, Tidings, Cookies, etc., for the economic betterment of the Catholic Institution. We also felt it was hypocritical because every Sunday countless millions of Mexicans, Mexican-Americans and Chicanos are asked to donate into the Sunday collection box. And donate our people do. Millions every Sunday throughout the Southwest. And so Católicos Por La Raza was angry because we couldn't stand to see our abuelitas [grandmothers] y los viejos [elderly] donating to a billion-dollar structure when we knew that the Chicano family was financially unable to afford half the food the Catholic priest in Los Angeles eats and was unable to afford decent education, housing, health services, etc. But this initial understanding of Catholic Church hypocrisy in Los Angeles, we soon found out, was only the surface hypocrisy. Because when we repeatedly attempted to talk to members of the Church hierarchy at the Chancery we were thrown out, insulted (Cardinal McIntyre once said: "I was here before there were even Mexicans. I came to Los Angeles 21 years ago."—(Ed's note: This statement by the Cardinal, and many similar statements by other members of the

[1] La Raza (Special Issue on CPLR, Fall, 1970) in Ricardo Cruz/Católicos Por La Raza Papers.

Church hierarchy in Los Angeles are on tape and available at La Raza office upon request.) It was at those times that we began to realize that the Catholic Church in Los Angeles was hypocritical in more ways than merely being rich while its most faithful of Catholics, the Chicano, remains poor. We began realizing that the Catholic Church in no way identified with the poor of the barrio. Not only was it economically unable to talk to the poor, because of its holdings and comforts, but also because its hierarchy, as good Irishmen, have simply no sympathy for the struggle of our people for basic needs. A few examples of this lack of sympathy are worth pointing out.

During the Roosevelt [High School]"blow-outs" Católicos Por La Raza sponsored a support demonstration and Mass in the downtown mall to call the Catholic Church's attention to its high school youngsters. Approximately 300 hundred [sic] high school Chicanos joined with us as we asked for the Catholic Church to use its tremendous influence and wealth in the solutiin [sic] of poor education for the barrio Chicanito. As you remember, over one-hundred high school Chicanos were beaten and arrested for merely demanding better education. Every single victim was Catholic, as were their families, yet when we went to St. Vibiana's Cathedral downtown, after our Mass, not one single priest would talk to the students. As the photo depicts, there were several squadrons of policemen waiting—the only representatives the Church felt was needed to talk to the Chicano when he is involved in a moral struggle.

We also found out, as published in the Tidings, that recently Bishop Manning celebrated a commemoration Mass for the Irish rebellion—which took place over one hundred years ago! The mass was celebrated at the Immaculate Conception Church in the Pico-Union barrio of Los Angeles. Apparently the Church of Los Angeles can prais [sic] movements and struggles for the liberation of peoples as long as the people are Irish. Twenty-one Chicanos and sympathisers [sic] were arrested Christmas Eve and jailed by the Church hierarchy. This apparently represents what the Irish Catholic Church of Los Angeles thinks of Chicanos who would dare struggle for their own independence and self-determination.

And so Católicos Por La Raza has only begun. We, and thousands of other Chicanos, will be at St. Basil's on September 13th [1970] to join with the Arias family. Our struggle is not only to pressure the Church in social action and commitment, but more importantly it is to educate our own poor in the barrios that the Catholic Church, as it is presently structured and as it presently thinks and feels, is merely robbing the poor. It is totally unsympathetic to the needs of the Chicano in the barrio. We ask that all the community realize that Católicos Por La Raza has been recognized by César Chávez as an extremely influential force in Church participation in the campesino struggle. With the continued support of the Chicano community and with continued pressure on the Catholic Church, there will someday soon be the day when our Catholic Church will realize the morality and beauty of the Chicano struggle. Black ministers throughout the United States have declared their allegiance to their people. Protestant Chicano and other ministers have openly declared to their hierarchies that they are Chicano first; i.e., La Raza Churchmen. We are Chicanos first and clergy, second. It is long overdue that the Catholic Church in Los Angeles and throughout the Southwest have the moral integrity to identify with el movimiento. Católicos Por La Raza will not rest until that day has come. The demands of CPLR . . . will someday be met. When that day arrives we can thank the many families within Católicos Por La Raza, such as the Arias family, for their dedication and love for the Chicano. Que Viva La Raza! Que viva Católicos Por La Raza! We will see you on the 13th. Bring your baptism certificates—and bring matches!

CATÓLICOS POR LA RAZA

BAUTISMO DE FUEGO [BAPTISM OF FIRE][1]

¡QUE VIVA LA RAZA!

On September 13th there will be a public burning at St. Basil's.

CPLR will declare invalid their baptism into the Catholic Church and they will baptize themselves into the true spirit of Christianity and Catholicism.

On that day the Arias family, along with thousands of other Chicano families from the barrio will burn their baptism certificates.

WHY ARE CPLR AND THEIR FAMILIES BURNING THEIR BAPTISM CERTIFICATES?

1. During the past year the Church has refused to help Chicano students in the barrio in their struggle to improve the quality of their schools and education.
2. The Church has silently accepted the fact that 40% of those in prison are Chicanos and does not even offer ministerial counseling service.
3. The Church is one of the greatest supporters of the war in Vietnam . . . 20% of all dead in Vietnam are Chicanos.
4. Over 60% of our Chicano families do not own their own homes. Yet the Church owns countless millions of real property in East Los Angeles.
5. The Church, through its racist policy does not allow Chicano clery [sic: clergy] to represent the Chicano community. Over 75% of all bishops and upper clery [sic] are Irish.

[1] Flier in Ricardo Cruz/Católicos Por La Raza Papers.

6. THE CHURCH THROUGH ITS SILENCE SUPPORTS AND CONDONES THE MURDER AND BRUTALIZATION OF CHICANOS BY THE LAW ENFORCEMENT AGENCY. WHERE WAS THE CHURCH WHEN THE SÁNCHEZ BROTHERS WERE MURDERED? AND WHERE WAS THE CHURCH WHEN THE PEOPLE PROTESTED THESE MURDERS AT THE MARCHA DE LOS MURTOS? [sic]

TIME-12 NOON	PLACE- ST. BASIL'S CATHEDRAL [sic] 637 South Kingsley Dr. Los Angeles	DATE- September 13 Sunday

Part 4

Richard Cruz, circa early 1970s.
Photo by Ray Cruz. Used with Permission.

Testimonios (Oral Histories)

RAY CRUZ AND PALOMA MARTÍNEZ-CRUZ ON RICHARD CRUZ AND CPLR

April 25, 2003

MG = Mario T. García
RC = Ray Cruz
PMC = Paloma Martínez-Cruz

MG: What is your parents' background?

RC: My mother was a legal secretary during most of our growing years in high school. She worked for the county council. And that really had an important impact on us and Richard because she would bring us as children, elementary grade, third, fourth grades, she would bring us once in a while to the administration hall in downtown LA and introduce us to her friends, the legal secretaries. When we were in high school Richard already had the goal of being an attorney. At Cathedral he was in the debating club. Boy did he love to debate. Richard was kind of argumentative anyway. When we were growing up in elementary and high school, we would argue all the time. It would drive our parents crazy.

RC: At Divine Savior we were altar boys. Of course it was always Latin. We didn't know what we were reciting, but that is the sound of David. I would go into "God the God that gives glory to my youth." Richard and I would talk about religion a lot and we would go into everything. We were always discussing, debating. To me, I was really talking to God, when I was speaking Latin, when I was there at the altar. Even though I know the movement, or whatever, the progress was to change the language to make it more secular or whatever, but to me, in those days, I thought I could communicate with God and this was his language. Even the old hymns in Latin, and I don't even know what they meant, but I still felt spiritually close.

MG: It's still impressive to hear the Latin occasionally in the service, or the music in Latin. It did have a very mystical . . . I don't know, intriguing flavor to it. In some ways you felt the solemnity, but you didn't fully understand it, but it was appealing I must say.

RC: I know even at one time I was thinking of being a priest. Richard and I were just very serious about everything, serious about religion, serious about philosophy. At Cathedral, we learned a lot more about St. Thomas Aquinas and what have you. Later after attending St. Mary's University in Moraga for one year, Richard went to Cal State LA and he majored in philosophy. There he was very much into philosophical issues. He identified himself as a Hegelian. I didn't even know who Hegel was at that time. So now my brother transformed to a Hegelian, whatever that was. Of course, that was a good topic for arguments. We talked about things, and we shared the same bedroom at home.

PMC: Even when he was at Cal State LA?

RC: Well, before that at Cathedral, and afterwards when he was a student, we didn't have the same room, but we were at the same place. We would always debate. It was like Plato. It was all semantics, what is the meaning of this? What is the meaning of that? And he was a natural debater, natural thinker. Being a lawyer was the perfect profession because you certainly have to debate in that profession.

MG: Were all of you good in school?

RC: Yeah. We all did well. Mark, our older brother, decided to go into the military and he never completed his college, he went one year to community college and went into the military, the army. He's the one who made more money then Richard and me combined, because he came out later and went into his own business as a mortgage broker. He was the most successful.

MG: Is he still alive?

RC: No unfortunately, he died in '91, of a head injury, he fell and hit his head.

MG: Is that before Richard?

RC: Yes, Richard died in '93. Unfortunately my parents had to bury two of their sons, which was very hard.

MG: Are your parents still alive?

RC: No, they died in '96. So I had to bury them. It's easier to bury your parents than to bury your brothers. I can't imagine what it's like to bury your son or daughter.

MG: And your dad? Tell me a little about him Ray.

RC: My dad is actually quite famous in his own way because he was an entrepreneur. He was a band leader in LA, he was well-known. A lot of people in the older generation remember my dad because he was Don Juan Cruz, the orchestra, it was a big band.

MG: When was this?

RC: This was in the forties. It was a big band.

MG: Were your parents born on this side of the border?

RC: My dad was born in Zacatecas. He came with his dad at the beginning of the last century, he was a merchant, my grandfather. He was concerned that Pancho Villa didn't think that he was working for him. He was concerned that Pancho Villa thought that he was selling products to the enemy. They had to migrate, they had to flee. My grandfather came over, my dad was already born, then they had more children, more of my uncles were born on this side of the border. My dad was fourteen years old when he started at Lincoln High School in Los Angeles. When he learned to play the saxophone, he recounted that they didn't allow anyone to speak Spanish. One time he was speaking Spanish and the saxophone teacher hit him in the mouth, which was a very shocking experience. For that reason my parents didn't speak Spanish to us, to Richard, myself, my brother Mark. I remember one time in 1960 I went to visit my relatives in Mexico, I went down south for a couple of months, and I came back speaking

Spanish. I told my dad and mom I wanted to speak Spanish at home. But they still spoke English. I guess they could not change their pattern.

MG: I've heard similar stories. People like that experienced discrimination and they somehow felt that it might spare their own kids from the discrimination. Maybe it did, maybe it didn't.

RC: In that book by Steven Lozo, *Barrio Rhythms* there's a reference to my dad's band and also to the fact that he was the first bilingual locotor in Los Angeles, KWKW. I remember listening to his radio program at home. He would tell jokes, it was bilingual, but I didn't realize, you need a historian to tell you the significance—my dad had the personality, he was an entrepreneur, he would do things that nobody trained him to do. He created the show because he was selling houses and used the show as his advertisement. He probably just went to KWKW and talked them into giving him a show. He would tell jokes and he would play music. His jokes were always really corny, he had the corniest jokes.

MG: This would be in what years?

RC: This was in the fifties, either late fifties or early sixties.

MG: How long did he have his band?

RC: He had his band until the late forties, early fifties, I don't know. I never really saw him in his band. I know he still had the band when we were born, but I never saw the band. But I did see him on TV. He was on TV, channel 5, playing maracas with these big sleeves, *mandero* sleeves. And he was doing this you know. We didn't have a TV, so we would have to go to the stores and look in the little TV in the window.

MG: Did he [father] pass on his musical genes to any of the three?

RC: I played the piano and we all studied piano and violin.

PMC: Grandma was a dancer and so the arts were very . . . Growing up in Arizona she was trilingual, she was classically trained as a dancer. Her mother didn't want her to become a dancer because the loose morals of the artists. She started as a roller-skating waitress in Los Angeles.

RC: At Carls Jrs., right in front of USC.

MG: Was your grandmother born in Arizona?

PMC: She was born in Arizona, the Arizona-Chihuahua border. She was born in Chihuahua.

RC: Grandma? I don't think she was born in Chihuahua, I'm not sure but I think she was born in Morenci, Arizona. But it's in her birth certificate.

MG: Were both your parents very religious?

RC: When we started going to Catholic schools, this was first grade, we were in Echo Park, and we went to Our Lady of Loretto School. They indoctrinated us to go to church every Sunday. Then we got our parents, who were of course very willing, but I remember that we were the ones who urged them to go to church every Sunday. All through those years we would go to church every Sunday, we would all go as a family. When my mother got older she became part of this very popular movement, Charismatic. We eventually had in our little church, Our Lady Divine Savior, we had a Spanish-speaking Charismatic priest. Most of the years when we were growing up, there were no Mexican-American priests. We had the Irish priests, but later that parish had Spanish-speaking priests.

MG: Did you have any sense of an ethnic consciousness, even in the early '60s?

RC: We did. I'm not sure where it began but we were much more tolerant, I don't know why, I'm trying to think if it was related to our college education, or even high school. In high school it was a mixed group, so I think we just got acquainted. I remember Jackson was one of Richard's closest friends and he was black. His other friends were white. Some of my friends were Latin, some were white, Asian, or German. David López Lee, he was Latin-Asian, he's now a professor at USC.

MG: Tell me more about Richard as a kid and through high school.

RC: Well, even in recreation he was a leader. He would take us to play sports. Here I am playing the piano at home and Richard says, "Come on Ray, let's go play basketball, let's go play football." He would organize little groups.

I think of Richard as an organizer, a natural leader, very sociable too. He was charismatic all the way through. He would bring people together. He would lead. He was the kind of person who wanted an audience and who wanted to be with people and to be sociable.

PMC: And bring people together.

RC: And bring people together. Because Richard and I debated all the time, we were just in each other's brains all the time.

PMC: Mark was the oldest brother by a few years?

RC: Yeah, Richard and I were closer in age and in our communications. Richard, from very early on, did well at school. At Cathedral at an early point was already planning to be an attorney.

MG: Did he play sports in high school?

RC: None of us went into the teams, but we just played in the park. We would play basketball.

MG: Was he a class officer?

PMC: Didn't he do choir?

RC: We did the Glee Club at Cathedral.

MG: Did you say that he was on the debate team?

RC: He was on the debate team. He did well in that. I remember him bringing home a plaque. It was some contest.

PMC: Or speech? I remember him reciting the first lines of his high school speech. It'd start out with a definition of a word, "To define this word."

MG: Did he ever think he had a vocation?

RC: A religious vocation?

MG: Yeah.

RC: I think he did. I'm pretty sure he did because I remember, all three of us did at one point, talk about being a priest, or a brother. None of us ever went to first base with it. We didn't apply to the seminaries or anything. Some of our friends did. I know we took the role of being a good Catholic, we took the role very seriously. We were indoctrinated, we believed that it was important to be a good Catholic. We learned St. Thomas Aquinas. These are some of the things Richard and I would argue about, we'd discuss, how to be a good Catholic. My parents were always arguing because my mother was a solid breadwinner and my dad was an entrepreneur who often didn't pay the rent. So we had all these arguments, constantly arguing. While they were arguing about money, Richard and I were arguing about God and about all the other social things in the world, right and wrong.

MG: Into college did both of you remain churchgoers, Catholics?

RC: Yeah, through college.

MG: Richard would still go to Mass?

RC: Yeah, at some point we stopped. I don't know at what point, probably mid-college. We stopped going on a regular basis.

MG: So Richard graduates from Cal State LA what year?

RC: 1966. He graduated with honors.

MG: Then he went to law school?

RC: Then he went to law school. He had to work while going to law school. He was also working for the county probation department in these youth camps.

MG: You both graduated the same year?

RC: Yeah, we graduated the same year.

MG: And both of you were still living at home?

RC: Right after that we both went to get a job with the probation department. It was the first job. Even in those days it was kind of difficult to get any professional jobs. There was still a lot of discrimination. We were still breaking a barrier in that most of the policemen were white, the sheriffs were white, everybody was white, but there was a little inroad in those days in the county. The County of Los Angeles was opening up from political pressure from Latinos to get jobs. This was one of the departments where there was initial penetration of Latino professionals. We were in the same training together. After a three month training I was assigned to juvenile hall. I worked there for a couple of years as a probation officer just to supervise the so-called delinquents, inmates, children. Richard was assigned as a court probation officer position. I don't remember exactly how long he did that. That was maybe for a year or so. He worked for the county doing these other camp supervision jobs for part of the year he was attending law school.

MG: He started at Loyola Law School in '67?

RC: It must've been right around then because he was just about finished in 1970. He was in the day program which was a three year program; the night program was a four year program. It took him four years.

MG: He was in the night program?

RC: Well he was in the day program but because during that time he did organizing of the law students, he did the Católicos, all of that, and we were involved in all of the other marches.

MG: When did he start organizing the Latino law students?

RC: Right away because he was the only Latino day student. Miguel García was the only Latino night student. There were only two in his class. There were more Jewish students enrolled there at a Catholic institution than Latinos. Richard told me that some of his friends were Jewish students and some of them were more of the progressive students who pushed him to organize. I remember he was telling me—of course he was ready—so right away; that was one of the very first things he did, him and Miguel.

MG: What did they call the group?

RC: Eventually it became the La Raza Law Student Association. Right now there's a La Raza Law Student Association, I don't know if they changed the name.

MG: But the origins go back to Richard's group.

RC: Yeah.

MG: What was the purpose?

RC: They pushed their way in because there was no intent by the Dean to cooperate without extra pressure. So they organized. I think the next year there were more students, Latinos. Eventually they were able to put pressure and they even had to make a heavy demonstration in the Dean's office. They actually went and forced their way in.

MG: In the Dean's office?

RC: The Dean's office in the chancery on 9th Street.

MG: Richard led this?

PMC: It was like practice for the MacIntyre, pushing the door in.

MG: That was within the first year. They did have confrontational . . .

RC: Yeah, they did have a confrontational problem with the Dean. I don't know if they acquiesced immediately, but this was led almost at the same time, the whole issue of the Church, the dioceses, having very little support, or no real—like the charities and things.

MG: So at the time Richard was a law student, you were also getting involved in La Raza newspaper?

RC: Yeah, because we all met. Once Richard got together with Richard Martínez and Raul Ruiz and started talking about the problems of the Church and then we would have meetings at the Euclid Community Center, and other meetings at the La Raza building. There was a long discussion, and I heard a lot of these discussions, who would be the leader. Who would be the outspoken front leader of the movement? I wasn't as much a leader myself, but I was a participant. It was Richard, Joe Razo, Raul Ruiz, and Richard Martínez. That was the main group. There were the other people who already had other leadership roles. I had probably more of a conservative position. I was just learning and being a part of it because it seemed an important thing to do. Richard and the others would bring out some of the numbers and statistics of Church's finances and wealth it had. Where was it going? How is it being applied to the needs of the Chicano community? But there was a discussion as to who should be the outspoken leader. Everybody agreed that it should be Richard, my brother. And I mention this also because Joe Razo, because he had a Lutheran background, did not want to be put in front. He wanted a back position. Raul was very much involved in La Raza. There was also a lot of discussion of whether we should use the term "Chicano" or "Latino" or "La Raza." Some of the things like Católicos Por La Raza, that's a Raza word. But again there was a lot of debate and everybody finally agreed that Chicano and Raza were the selected terms to use.

MG: So it was a relatively small group?

RC: Yes, it was.

MG: Somewhere in the fall of '69 it is organized . . .

RC: Yes, that is true. That's when it all occurred. I remember a lot of meetings. Also one thing that you didn't point out was the role of the Students for Democratic Society (SDS). They were very visible on the Cal state campus—I don't know about East LA College—that was kind of like the precursor to the peace movement. The peace movement was the campus organization. But the Students for a Democratic Society was very active when we attended. I remember Raul and my brother Richard and myself were going to some of these meetings at Cal State campuses. Then we started thinking we need our own group. That was kind of like a model.

MG: But you weren't members of SDS?

RC: Well we were in a sense of going to some of the meetings. There wasn't an official membership or dues. Later we started organizing UMAS (United Mexican American Students).

MG: Prior to Católicos Richard and you and the others were all involved in student politics at Cal State LA.

RC: That's right, the peace movement. This kind of predisposed us to the Chicano Moratorium march [Aug. 29, 1970] because we already had the orientation from the Students for a Democratic Society, we were already thinking that way. I know for myself that I was totally overwhelmed in a sense. We were going to these SDS meetings and they would give you the statistics of the world. And you compared that to what the conventional media gave you and they were two different worlds. To me it was kind of awesome for the first time to see. Before that time I was naïve like most people, you see only one point of view. I guess that's what college does right?

MG: What was your and Richard's draft status?

RC: We did have a student deferment.

MG: Were either of you ever called up?

RC: No, I know mine. I think Richard was exempted—I think his epilepsy got him out. He had epilepsy which really had very little impact on his life as an adult. But when he was a student he would have seizures and pass out in school. I remember at Divine Savior once in a while he would have that problem. All of a sudden he'd wake up at his desk and cry because he didn't know what happened. He never was hurt but he would talk about it when we got home. He went to some doctors and there was really nothing you could do. I think that's what got him out of the military.

MG: Was Richard at the time of organizing Católicos aware of liberation theology coming out of Latin America?

RC: I don't recall him using those terms, but I wouldn't be surprised because he was very interested in everything that had to do with the sociological issues of the day. He did major in philosophy and that direction was a very radical one, Hegelian and wherever it went from Hegel on. I wouldn't be surprised. Of course, he did name his son Camilo, so that was a good indication; he said that the name Camilo was a very important name of a revolutionary leader in Latin America. That's what I remember. To Richard, it was definitely a revolutionary statement.

MG: Did he mean Camilo Torres the Catholic priest in Colombia or Camilo Cienfuegos, the Cuban revolutionary?

PMC: The Cuban . . . Camilo says it's both, that's the info that he got, in the spirit of revolution embodied in both these figures. I remember being young and grandma introducing Camilo, my brother being tiny and young, grandma introducing him to the priest at Divine Savior and Camilo said something like "I'm named after a priest" so that was very much in Camilo's mindset growing up that he was named after an important priest.

MG: Maybe your dad had in mind both.

PMC: I know that my dad was always very versed in Communist philosophies around the world. He was very aware of different kinds of social movements.

MG: He must've been reading Marx too because he was in philosophy.

RC: Oh I would think so. There were some professed official Communists in our group.

PMC: I don't think our father was as much a professed Communist. I think our mom might've been at some point interested in professing Communism.

MG: Was Richard also involved in the farm worker movement?

RC: He did go to Delano, he did meet César Chávez. He went there more than one time. There were organized tours and trips that would go from campuses to Delano.

MG: Was this during your time at Cal State LA?

RC: Yes. He did talk to César Chávez at least a couple of times. Once he had already started organizing Católicos, he talked to César about the issues. I think whatever they talked about I know that César was a supporter of what Católicos was doing.

MG: When did you start using the term Chicano? Was it in high school?

RC: No, not really in high school. It was part of the moratorium and La Raza. All these people were deciding which word to use. We debated that quite a bit and finally came up with Chicano. It was just a handful of people. Raul had the press. Once you decide what you're going to call yourself now you have the press to kind of publicize it. We had to make those decisions because we were going to be organizing these rather massive marches. These same issues that anyone would talk about, is it going to be Mexican-American, or is it the more generic Latino. It was a concern that Mexican-Americans are large enough of an entity to have the right to claim their needs. So of course we were Mexican-Americans, it wasn't intended to exclude others. But Richard also preferred the word Raza in many cases, like Católicos Por La Raza because it was more open. It really means people.

MG: Why the use of the term Católicos?

RC: Yes, it was Católicos Por La Raza because it was the institution that belonged to the people. It was that philosophy. My brother Richard would say justice belongs to the people. He probably got that from that whole culture milieu and the Chicano movement at the time.

PMC: My mother was there during the McIntyre force-in. She was a good Catholic girl. She had become a novice Catholic nun, or she had taken steps to be a novitiate. I don't know what those steps are. She was very faithful growing up. When that happened that was a very big question for her. She said, "I thought I was going to hell forcing in the Cardinal's door."

MG: Did Richard have the same feelings or doubts about the strong confrontation with the Church after the Catholic education?

RC: Richard had this philosophical orientation. He was already going off into a different direction personally. But the movement was definitely for the institution and for those who owned the institution, which is the people. I think Richard himself was more philosophically oriented, above or beyond the Church as an important institution for him personally. I think he was philosophically way beyond being a devoted practicing Catholic at that point.

MG: So the confrontation with the Church was not an internal debate with himself?

RC: I don't think so. For me it might've been even more so. At one point I did burn my baptismal certificate. I thought I was going to hell. I was looking up in the sky to see if the lightning was going to come down. Because Richard was already so advanced in his philosophical studies—later on he would make statements of more of an atheist, years later. At that time, I think he was just more of a philosopher and less of a practicing Catholic and more concerned with this institution being important to the people. It was very important. I know Richard had, maybe it was antagonistic at that time, but we had feelings for the Church, we grew up with the Church. The Church was important to us; we went to the Catholic schools.

MG: How did your parents react to all this confrontation?

RC: My parents were concerned because they were more traditional. But Richard was very strong in his persuasion. He persuaded all of us in our family, my parents too, that this was a good cause, that the Church should be doing more for the people. Richard never asked anyone to stop being a Catholic or don't go to Church. He just felt that it was important to make the Church change. He had all the numbers. When you hear all the numbers, the majority of Catholics in the Southwest were Latino, and there's nobody to fight those numbers, and all the money—Richard and Raul had the numbers—huge, billions of dollars of the properties that the Church owned. Then the fact that Loyola, the school itself, there were hardly any Latinos, no visible charities—whatever charities they had at the time, we were not aware of them, or they were not focusing on the Chicano community.

MG: The objective was to go to the very top, to confront McIntyre on all these issues? Or was there some debate on strategy?

RC: There was some debate on strategy. I think this group, the leadership, four or five people, they wanted publicity. They were following a program of how do you get awareness in the community? It's a program in which you have to confront the issues, you have to articulate the issues, you have to confront the leaders, you expect a battle, you expect a conflict, you expect publicity, and you expect police brutality even, you expect that. That gives you more publicity. It's like this country going to Iraq. If you were on their side you would want to show the ugly American destroying innocent people. Then you prove how ugly the American side is, the war machine. It's the same thing in a sense; you're talking about the institutions, and how important it is to take ownership of these institutions, and in order to do that you have to confront them, you have to show them their bad side. It has to be dramatized and the publicity is very important. Firstly, I was more, do we have to disrupt the religious services, can we just demonstrate? So that was a debate and I was the one who was arguing let's just go in with the pickets and let's not disrupt anything or make any noise. They probably stopped listening to me early in the debate.

MG: How often were the meetings held?

RC: For a while we were meeting every month, even more frequently. Because then we were getting down to the actual demonstrations and planning every event.

MG: Were you there when they broke into McIntyre's office?

RC: I wasn't at that particular meeting.

MG: Was that planned all along to do that?

RC: I don't know if it was planned. Certainly it was part of the plan that it was a necessary step, definitely. I would go to meetings that were identified as meetings, but whenever talk went on without me, because all you really needed was for four people to agree. But the meetings I would go to there were sometimes, ten, fifteen people, sometimes twenty. So I wasn't in the foursome group, that inner circle.

MG: But you were there at St. Basil's Christmas Eve?

RC: Oh yes, I was there.

MG: What do you especially remember about that?

RC: It was a horrific experience. It was great up to the point, it was really fun to have a Mass celebrated on the steps of the church; that was radical but fun. Father Blase Bonpane, he gave out the host, which was the Communion. I was worried if it—this was an awesome thing too—when we were brought up you didn't touch the host.

PMC: It wasn't tortilla?

RC: It was tortilla, that was even one step beyond. Not only are you going to touch this thing but it's a tortilla.

MG: It's not the traditional wafer.

RC: Exactly.

MG: At St. Basil's, there were several hundred?

RC: Yes.

MG: How was that organized?

RC: That was what our meetings were about, to organize the publicity and there was a lot of organizing and getting the word out. We brought our family, we had quite a few people, my nephews, my dad was there too. My dad, my cousin Sylvia and other cousins.

MG: Was there a sense that there would be a confrontation?

RC: From what I could see, from the meetings I attended, there was not necessarily going to be a violent confrontation. But there was talk about this probably would occur because of the way they reacted. There was anticipation that they would react with violence.

MG: And that strategy was that they would march into the church itself during the Mass and Richard and maybe a couple of other people would face the congregation and read the demands.

RC: That was the plan.

MG: But that there had been no anticipation that there would be undercover cops there?

RC: No, the undercover cops, no. Certainly it was expected that they would call the police, but we were all surprised that the plainclothes officers, the ushers, had mace in their pockets.

PMC: That was a surprise?

RC: That was a surprise, we didn't know they were deputies.

MG: How far did you yourself go into the church?

RC: I didn't get into the church. I was in front, where the Mass was said. Then we approached the front doors and they were locked. These were huge doors. Have you seen St. Basil's?

MG: Yes,

RC: They're huge, these doors are like thirty or forty feet high. The whole front of the church. They open on motor, you push it, and it opens if they're unlocked, but it opens with a motor, an electric motor. When they're locked, they're locked, there's nothing you can do, it's all metal. The doors were locked. There was chanting, "Let the poor people in," a lot of people had the candles, they were small candles, not weaponized. Since the doors were locked, several people, including my brother went around to the side, to the side door, to see if there was a way to get in. At that point I was concerned, where is Richard going? I was kind of on the side. Then somebody was able to come through and open the door on the inside, just pushed it open, as soon as the door opened, mace was shot into the faces of the people. I was next to the doors at the time, but this was a testimony of the people who were even closer than me.

MG: Some people did get into the church itself?

RC: Oh yes, they got in from the side, but the big confrontation was at the main door. We couldn't get through that door. The few people that came in and opened it, they were on the inside, the people who went from the side were on the inside. It was this loud screaming. These were our parents, our children, it was not the kind of group that you would want to be exposed to mace. An instant later there were police with riot gear and huge big sticks and they started pounding people and there was screaming and yelling.

MG: You saw people getting hit?

RC: Oh yeah, I saw people getting hit. I don't know if you've ever seen the face of an angry policeman but with the clubs, it hurts. When you see that look, I guess it's military training or whatever it is, but when they're ready to fight it's quite ugly, you can see it in their eyes.

MG: Where was Richard all this time?

RC: Richard was already on the other side. He wasn't at the front, he was probably in the building.

MG: How long did the confrontation last?

RC: It was probably just a few minutes. These [police] buses were in the back of the church all along, the police with riot gear. As soon as they gave the word, as soon as the doors opened, the mace and the police, there was no time in between. People were getting hit with the sticks. We weren't really trying to fight the police. There was no battle there. People were getting hit and getting maced. It was just chaos.

MG: Did people start getting arrested?

RC: The only concern was you're going to want to protect your own people. You're close to the scene helping people who are getting hit, you're not really assaulting police.

MG: Did they try to arrest you?

RC: They arrested a few people that night.

MG: Including Richard?

RC: I don't think they arrested Richard that night. They did arrest a few people. I don't remember who was arrested that night. Later on there were twenty-one [arrested].

MG: Can you also answer the $64,000 question? Where was Oscar Zeta Acosta? He claims in his Revolt of the Cockroach People that he was on the inside in the confrontation. People like Richard Martínez and Raul Ruiz don't remember Oscar being inside at all. They said he had to be outside because he was our lawyer. They needed him outside in case we were arrested.

RC: I can't contribute because I know he was there somewhere, but where he was I don't know. My main concern was my brother, I was just trying to protect my brother, that was what I was doing, I was trying to find him.

MG: Where did you see Richard later after the confrontation?

RC: It was maybe fifteen minutes later where the people were kind of away from the church, the police had already done what they were doing, and we were going around trying to find people on the street, Wilshire Boulevard. That's when I was able to see that Richard was ok. Some people were arrested and we were trying to figure out who got arrested. There were people hurt, beat up and bleeding, we were concerned about these people.

PMC: Was my dad beaten in any way?

RC: I don't think so because he wasn't around the doors, he was on the side. I don't think he got maced.

MG: What were his thoughts about what had happened?

RC: For the leaders that expected violence—and Richard was one of them—it was what they expected. In a sense this was more like the revolutionary perspective. By the Cardinal doing what he did it made it real clear that there was a need for change. It was really what they expected and wanted, in a sense. You push a button, an institution does what you think it'll do, and it proves that you were right all along. Certainly they could've handled it a lot differently if they wanted to. If they wanted to keep people out of the church they could've just put their guards just in front of the church. Just make it real clear that you can't go in.

MG: Were there political differences in *Catolicos?* Was pretty much everyone in tune with what needed to be done?

RC: With what we were doing? I would say so. There were people like me who perhaps wanted to avoid confrontation, avoid the more dramatic types of scenes or the conflicts with the police. For the most part, everybody expected that this would happen. It's going to happen whether you want it to happen or not. You cannot make change unless you confront the institutions. When you do confront them they're going to react with violence.

MG: Was there any discussion, then or even later, that the possibility of confrontation would alienate other Latino Catholics?

RC: Yes, yes. There was quite a bit of discussion as to that possibility of alienating the majority of conservative people because again like our parents as well, you cannot really go too far to discredit the Church without offending people. I think that was an acknowledged risk, and yet at the same time, I think that was one of the reasons why the effort was made to show the numbers, to show the injustice, to show that this is important. And then the people would participate—again, there was never any effort to overthrow the Church; it was just to make the Church more sensitive. I think most of the people might not want to participate in some of the demonstrations, but they would at least acknowledge that this is a valuable issue and this was a change that needed to be made.

MG: But there was this recognition prior to the St. Basil's confrontation that these kinds of actions might alienate . . .

RC: . . . could alienate, yes we had that discussion. We debated that whole thing quite a bit, in terms of the impact it would have. The social ramifications of all of that.

MG: What do you remember of the later arrests and trials that included your brother?

RC: There were two groups. I was in the group that had lesser offenses.

MG: You were then charged?

RC: Yes, I was charged, I was one of the eleven. That's why I say I remember two groups, one of ten and one of eleven.

MG: How were you notified that you were being charged? Did they arrest you?

RC: They arrested us, the detective came to our house one day and said he had a warrant for our arrest. He was very polite, I think it was Sergeant Domínguez.

MG: This was where your family lived?

RC: Yeah, at home, where my parents lived, the house I'm in now.

MG: Did they arrest both of you at the same time?

RC: Yes, they came and they agreed not to put cuffs on us if we went peacefully. We did and my parents were there and it was kind of a dramatic scene.

MG: Were you expecting it?

RC: Yeah, we knew they were actually investigating. We knew they were going to come up with charges. Of course we didn't know when they were going to come or who was going to be included. Of course, Richard would've been expected because he was the most prominent leader. I'm his brother and I was there, so I wasn't that surprised.

MG: Where did they take you?

RC: They took us down, there's a jail in San Fernando in the northeast, the northeast precinct. We spent one night there. The next day we got released on our own recognizance. We did call Zeta Acosta. It was not a problem getting out on our own recognizance the next day.

MG: When were you arrested? January?

RC: It must've been January sometime. I don't remember the exact date. There was about a month of time. It wasn't right away. It was maybe even more than a month before they actually started the prosecution. Then when we went to trial that was already months later. There was quite a lengthy trial for our group because there were eleven defendants. We each had our own little mini-thing. There was also a meeting with Zeta where we discussed the question whether we would be tried in one group or individual trials or two groups. Eventually they decided, but this was a discussion, and we were all there trying to come up with the best plan. There was still an intent to make a political statement, so it would be a political trial. I again am more conservative saying well, if I'm innocent, I want to be tried, I want a defense to prove I'm innocent, I don't just want to be there to accept the fate of whatever they want to give me, just to make a political statement; if I'm innocent, I want to be defended as an innocent. So that's probably why I was in the second group and not in the first group where Richard and the other leaders were.

MG: Zeta Acosta only dealt with Richard's group?

RC: With both groups.

MG: In the end were both groups defended as a whole?

RC: Yes, eleven in one group and ten in the other.

MG: And you and your group were charged with what?

RC: I was charged with assaulting police officers with a candle. And these were big, strong officers with sticks. I allegedly approached them with a big candle and they didn't say I battered them, it was assault; I threatened them with a big stick in the church and they told me to go back and I refused or whatever. I was shocked. I was in the area, I was at the foot of the church, but I had a small candle. I went into some detail. I actually spoke on my defense as my only witness. I explained that my main concern was the welfare of my brother, I was trying to look for him and find him and help him if he needed my help. So I had a small candle because of the Mass service in my hand. I put it down because I could already see this confrontation in front of the church and the mace and the billy sticks. I put my little candle down and then I walked around to the side to see where my brother was. I said I never assaulted the police or threatened with any weapon. The police, when they testified, Zeta asked them the obvious question, is this the one you identify , is this the one who did this assault? They said yes. One of the police officers admitted that because I was wearing a suit, I looked a little different than during the confrontation. The jury believed me and not the two officers. I had told Sergeant Domínguez earlier that I was innocent. I told him if I'm convicted, you're never going to forget this if I'm convicted. In my way I was trying to threaten him.

We had a lengthy trial. That was part of kind of a sense of being together and being part of a movement. We would go down to the Grand Central market every day for lunch, downtown. I guess as a student it didn't have an economic impact it would have if you had a regular job, you would have to go every day. It was over a month, just our group, going back and forth.

MG: In your group, were you all acquitted?

RC: We were all acquitted in my group.

MG: Was Richard's group?

RC: In Richard's group there were quite a few convictions.

MG: They weren't held simultaneously?

MG: Richard was convicted of some charges?

RC: Yes, Richard was convicted of disrupting a religious service. He did sixty or ninety days, I don't remember exactly.

MG: Did he serve it?

RC: Yes, he served at least half. Even then they didn't give you the full sentence.

MG: What did Richard feel about the whole trial and the sentencing?

RC: He was kind of brave about it. He was rather philosophical about the whole thing. He just took it in stride. He felt that he accomplished something and that this was the price to pay. Although I didn't attend his trial, at least in our discussion, the intent was to make it a political trial. I think they did make that important point during the whole process.

MG: What do you recall about Zeta Acosta's defense in your group?

RC: Well, Zeta was a very colorful person, very strong character. I felt Zeta was a strong person, he was articulate, I thought he was persuasive in convincing the jury, this was a jury trial. So I felt that I was being defended in a good manner. Looking back on it now I think maybe we should've had more of a defense instead of me speaking as my own witness. At the time we were still very much a part of this movement and we felt that this was important to just go through the process and prevail as we could.

MG: Did the fact that the leaders such as Richard were on trial spell the end of Católicos with the distraction of having to deal with the defense?

RC: In a sense yes. I'm pretty sure Richard's trial was the second one, the more serious ten was after our group of eleven. After that period, what happened to Richard was that he had to finish law school and he was already being delayed by a year. The next time we got together as a group was when there was a hearing to discuss his acceptance to the bar. They denied him the bar based on moral turpitude.

RC: This would be later. Cardinal Manning also was a witness on behalf of Richard.

MG: He did do that?

RC: Yes he did. I was there.

MG: What do you remember about that visit?

RC: It was awesome. At any time to be in the company of the Cardinal in your own home is awesome, as a Catholic we have the highest regard for the institution, even though we're protesting the institution, though that was a different target, McIntyre. For Manning to come to our home, we were very impressed and very much, my dad and mom were there, they were also in awe of his presence. I know that dad kissed his ring. We all didn't kiss his ring but my dad and mom did. It was a very conciliatory type of meeting. I guess from our family perspective it kind of showed a really positive sense of appreciation that the Church can change. Here is a good sign. I guess in the sense of having faith right? It's not necessarily faith in God, but faith in an institution that has the welfare of the people at heart. It was a very positive experience.

MG: Manning had initiated the meeting?

RC: I'm pretty sure he did. I don't think Richard would've invited him over to the house. Who would've thought of that? Exactly who did I'm not sure.

MG: Richard was prepared to be conciliatory himself?

RC: Yeah, Richard was. At this meeting it was just a very low-key meeting. There wasn't really any great debate going on. It was just the fact that he came to our house and met with us and was gracious and we were gracious with him. Everyone was very diplomatic. We were trying not to appear to be too much in awe. Especially Richard the leader of the movement.

MG: Was it just your family and the cardinal?

RC: There were a couple of other people, I can't remember, but it was a very small group.

MG: What did Richard think at the time of the resignation of McIntyre?

RC: That was good. We all felt like that was an accomplishment.

MG: You felt like you had actually forced him to step down?

RC: Yes, that's the way we looked at it. Whether or not it happened that way who knows.

MG: So Richard finished law school when?

RC: Shortly after that. It must've been within a year.

MG: Then he takes the bar exam?

RC: Yes, he passes the bar the first time. Then they deny him acceptance to the bar based on moral turpitude?

MG: Based on what?

RC: Based on the misdemeanor, disrupting a religious service. Richard filed a protest, a hearing to review that decision. Art Goldberg, as a matter of fact, was the main attorney that helped Richard's defense. You have a confrontational hearing with the attorneys. As I said Cardinal Manning was willing to speak on behalf of my brother.

MG: He actually appeared?

RC: Yes he actually appeared as a witness

MG: They overturned it?

RC: They did overturn it. It was all about his moral character and what he stood for. I think the way moral turpitude can be used, this is just my analysis, it doesn't mean necessarily that a crime was committed, moral turpitude is just a general term for moral standards that would not be appropriate for somebody who practiced law in the state of California. There are many attorneys who have misdemeanors. If you have a felony you can't practice law in California.

MG: For Richard, what was the extent of his political activism after Católicos? You mentioned the Moratorium, was Richard part of that?

RC: Yes. I would say he wasn't the top figure but he certainly was involved along with Rosalio Muñoz and the other leaders, Richard was one of the main organizers because of his networks. Actually everybody who had any leadership role at the time everybody was involved.

MG: There wasn't a specific Católicos contingent in the march?

RC: No, not really, not a Católicos contigent. It was just leaders and community all melded together.

MG: You were there?

RC: I was there.

MG: It must've been quite a scene.

RC: It was. I was in the park [Laguna Park] where again, another over-policing situation. After the march, I was also driving around and . . . there were scenes where there were police cars on fire. Someone had turned over a police car and ignited it, so there was that kind of thing going on. But in this park, I guess we had planned to convene in this park, that was probably the end of the march that they later named Ruben Salazar Park. I was there. I remember all of a sudden there was an assault by the police and tear gas on the people. That was again a very horrible thing because there were so many children and people that were defenseless and frightened and running.

MG: Were you and Richard together?

RC: I wasn't exactly with Richard, but we were all there, I don't know where he was in the group, but I was kind of by myself in the park.

MG: How did he feel about what happened that day [August 29, 1970]?

RC: It was another scene with over-policing. We were all outraged because we knew what happened to Ruben Salazar and in that context it was just a horrible thing. Many people really wanted to rebel. What could you do? It was very horrible, even just seeing children and mothers, when I was running I saw a lady that had fallen and I had to pick her up. We were running from the mace and the police and the clubs. That was quite sad and frightening. In those days, we really didn't have much faith or confidence in our police in general. You know the term "pigs" was used quite frequently.

MG: Just one final question. Over time how did your brother put the *Católicos* into perspective, or did he ever talk about looking back years later did he feel that it had been something worthwhile? Was he disillusioned?

RC: I don't think he was disillusioned. He lived many years. There weren't any other movements or demonstrations of those kind afterwards. But he felt that it was an accomplishment. Certainly changing the guard as far as getting Cardinal McIntyre out was something he credited his group and the movement. Also the increased charity activities [for Latinos] by the Church. Richard went on to do other things in court, the civil rights things, and other important issues that he worked on as an attorney. In a way that changed his focus, and his mode of operandi. The reason why he became an attorney, he wanted to be a civil rights attorney, a constitutional attorney. He did not want to participate in day-to-day trials, defending somebody for being drunk or whatever. He wanted to participate in the appellate type of hearings, trials, cases. He wanted the constitutional issues, civil rights, that was his main interest. That's what put him in another track. After that there weren't really any other issues that came up that we were still fighting about. The same issues came up for some time but there wasn't really any focal point that would require more demonstrations. Católicos was a statement that we made as a community that Richard felt was articulated well, and the point was made. It wasn't like we expected to be at a negotiating point. I know personally that Richard wouldn't be the kind of person who would want to be in a committee to advise the Church on how to spend their money. That wouldn't be fun. I'm sure there are other well-meaning people who would. I would be that kind of person. I would say put me on a committee and I would debate how much money we would spend on this and that. From Richard's standpoint it was to make a change in the direction of the way the Church was going and to make the Church more sensitive to our needs, the people. I think he felt he accomplished that. I think we all felt that way. I felt there was quite a bit of progress in that way.

MG: You mention that he became an atheist. All along he's already been moving away from the Church anyways.

RC: Right, he's becoming more of a philosophical person. Like I said the Church belongs to the people. Even if he's trying to improve the Church whether he needs it for his own day-to-day life needs is not the question he sees, but the people need it. The institution should be doing what it can for the people. I'm sure that would summarize the way he felt about the Church. I think he always felt good. He was a debater all the way through his life on all the issues. He would constantly bring up, in the same circle of people, mostly the lawyers who graduated from that generation, he was still very much, up until he died, articulating the issues, reminding people—a lot of his friends began working for the same institutions. One of his closest friends is a public defender. At least he's not a prosecutor, but he is still working for the state and county. Another guy worked for the federal bureaucracy as an attorney and he would tell me, he could get Richard a job as a federal attorney, and Richard didn't want it. Richard wanted to be in a position where he could take on or address the issues of any institution and he didn't want to be employed by any institution that would compromise his freedom of speaking and ability to proceed objectively and analyze what's going on in the society. He never really changed in that sense. He was always an analyst and always bringing up issues and telling people. Even his friends he would confront. We all knew that if we were going to have a beer with Richard, we're going to hear something that maybe we don't want to hear.

ROSA MARTÍNEZ ON RICHARD CRUZ AND CPLR

June 14, 2005

RM = Rosa Martínez
MG = Mario T. García

MG: What's your sense of the origins of Católicos. People talk about it that it originated with Ricardo Cruz. But what do you know in terms of whose idea was it? Was it Ricardo that really brought it together? What do you know about the origins of the group?

RM: When I got together with Richard, I was going to Cal State Northridge. He and some other people were organizing the campuses in demonstrations against the Church. What I remember, it was Ricardo, Raul Ruiz, Richard Martínez. Those were the people I saw initially. Pedro Arias. Those were the people who came out, who articulated the vision and the mission of CPLR.

MG: When you encountered this, it was already basically formed?

RM: Yeah, it was forming. There may have been manifestations before I got involved. It had already kind of taken some shape already, maybe about half a year already.

MG: When you first were exposed to this, in terms of a time frame, it surfaces in '69, but later in '69, in the fall, when do you think you first encountered the group?

RM: It was before the midnight Mass at St. Basil's. Ricardo had been going to different campuses and organized campus representatives to go to the main meetings, to get the information and bring it to the campuses and spread the word like that. Maybe about six months, I'm not really clear. I'd been involved in the organizing meeting prior to the Mass at St. Basil's as a representative from Cal State Northridge. We had been brought to the MEChA meetings and that's what they were doing, they'd go to MEChA meetings, present, ask for volunteers who would go to the meetings and get the information and keep organizing on the campuses.

MG: This would've been into the fall semester [of 1969]?

RM: Yeah, probably.

MG: So you were involved with MEChA at the time?

RM: Yes.

MG: They would come to meetings?

RM: They would go to campus meetings and present the concept and the politics of it, the rationale, they were seeking support. At that time there was a lot of activity on the campuses, Chicanos wanted action. It was a cause that brought a lot of people, stimulated and excited a lot of people.

MG: They received, for the most part, a positive reaction? Do you remember any reservations?

RM: There was discussion. It wasn't unanimously supported. There was debate. Basically, I went [to Católicos meetings] as a volunteer, not necessarily as an official delegate from MEChA.

MG: Did Richard and the others ask for MEChA to endorse their actions?

RM: They were looking for MEChA's support. He came to campus to talk once, maybe a couple of times in the Free Speech area. He had been invited. It was a very dynamic talk, hundreds of students came to listen to him.

MG: And he spoke about Católicos and what they were doing about the Church?

RM: He spoke about the Church and what was going to be the response from the community. He spoke about the closure of the Catholic parochial schools.

MG: Getting back to the discussion about MEChA, some had reservations?

RM: There were reservations.

MG: Do you recall along what lines?

RM: It was two camps, the conservatives, and then the really progressive activists. There was debate on whether MEChA should support the demonstration against the Church.

MG: Did they think it was too much to take on the Church, or too sensitive, for those with a Catholic background maybe a little too much?

RM: A little bit of all that. The Catholic upbringing that we all endured, other politics, whether we were ready to do that as a group, and how much of that energy would go towards that.

MG: Was this discussion held while Richard and the others were present or after?

RM: If I remember it was afterwards.

MG: From all indications, Richard was a really dynamic speaker.

RM: That's true, absolutely. He was a great speaker. He was committed, he was passionate, he was bright and articulate and convincing. He presented a good position.

MG: So then you went as a volunteer to some of the Católicos meetings. What do you recall about them? Where were they held? Was it at the Euclid Center?

RM: I'm trying to remember, it might've been at the Euclid Center.

MG: I've seen references to that. What kind of meetings do you recall that they had and how many people?

RM: There were a lot of people which was evident in the hundreds and hundreds that showed up for Midnight Mass. There were a lot of campuses, East LA College, LACC [Los Angeles City College], Northridge, the other campuses. So there were representatives and the discussion was educating us about the Catholic Church, what was going on with the school closures, the resources of the Church, how much the Latino community gave to the Church and how little was received from the Church.

MG: You went to more than one meeting?

RM: Yes, I went to several meetings.

MG: Thinking back, ball park figure of how many people attended these meetings? 50, 60, 100?

RM: These were just the campus meetings, I'm sure other meetings that were being held. Maybe 30 to 40.

MG: The meetings that were under the auspices of Católicos, how many people would go to those meetings?

RM: You mean from the different campuses? 15, 20, 30, it depended. It varied.

MG: Was it mostly Richard who would speak for Católicos at these meetings?

RM: Richard, but also Pedro, he spoke, Richard Martinez, a few other people. Raul Ruiz, it seemed that Richard was the most visible.

MG: Did you then begin to participate? There were some earlier actions prior to Midnight Mass, they had vigils, they had some picketing of either the chancery office or Cardinal McIntyre's office over at St. Basils.

RM: I wasn't at the vigil, I was at McIntyre's office when we walked in there, and the Midnight Mass at St. Basils. It was a whole weekend thing when we did the Mass at St. Basil's.

MG: Were you at the meeting where Católicos essentially burst into McIntyre's office?

RM: Yeah I was there.

MG: Give me your recollection of that because that is so incredible.

RM: It was, it was incredible for me. I think Patricia Borjon, myself, Raul Ruiz, maybe Pedro Arias were there, Richard, a handful of people.

MG: Take me through what you remember.

RM: I remember they had asked us to wait in the front office. We stood there for a while. Richard never waited for anything. We're standing there strategizing about what to do next. Richard said let's just go in. We all walked in there and McIntyre was noticeably upset. He was ashen. Of course, Richard presented, and Raul and others presented, what Católicos was asking the Church. He listened. The thing we had noticed, if I remember correctly, someone, Raul, someone was looking out the window and saw the Brink's truck coming and taking away money, something like that. I think they were afraid of our purpose, it was misunderstood or something. It was a pretty tense moment. Not so much from Católicos I don't think, because our intention was communication, I think it was seen as intimidating by us. I was looking up at the heavens and thinking the Holy Ghost was going to come down. All my Catholic upbringing came to me at that moment. I was in terror of being struck down. I got over that.

MG: McIntyre was quite distraught. Did he react in any way? How did he respond?

RM: He was taken off his guard. He was very very nervous. You could see he was visibly shaking. He didn't quite know what to do. He was at a loss for words. It was unexpected.

MG: Some other priests were there?

RM: Some priest came in, I don't know who it was. I do believe someone called the police. It was fun.

MG: This was at his office at St. Basil's?

RM: It was at the archdiocese.

MG: It was at the chancery office?

RM: Yes.

MG: That's right, that's right. Some of the other protests had been at St. Basil's vigils. This particular incident was at the chancery office.

RM: Which is no longer.

MG: Then of course, the big event was the Midnight Mass protest. What do you remember about the strategizing for that event? Was there much discussion about doing the protest at the Midnight Mass? What was the intent of the protests? What was the strategy that evening?

RM: In the informational meetings that I had attended, the strategy was to hold a Mass there and to have a speaker in there, and celebrate the Communion. I wasn't in any other strategy meeting. The intention was of course to get noticed and to have the Church respond to the demands of Católicos. It was a high visibility event because they said that the Pope always watched that Mass. That Mass was always broadcast to the Vatican.

MG: Oh. I knew it was a televised Mass but I had no idea that it would actually be seen at the Vatican. Richard knew about that?

RM: Yeah.

MG: What's your estimate of how many people supporting Católicos showed up that evening?

RM: Hundreds.

MG: There was an alternative Mass that Father Blase Bonpane said?

RM: Right. The Mass outside.

MG: They were said at the same time?

RM: Exactly.

MG: It was right there at the stairs?

RM: Right in the front. There was an effort by some people to go inside and join in the Mass. There was the whole thing "Let the poor people in."

MG: That's, of course, when they discovered that the doors had been locked on them.

RM: That's right.

MG: So Richard and a few others are able to get in through the side and try to comc up and open the doors and meet the ushers. Where were you at this point, still outside?

RM: I was still outside.

MG: When are you aware that there is a conflict taking place in the vestibule? When does it begin to spill over outside?

RM: At some point before that even happened I had to leave because I wasn't feeling well. Just before anyone went in I had left.

MG: So you weren't there for the actual altercation and struggle that took place and the cops came in.

RM: No I wasn't.

MG: So you found out about it later that evening?

RM: Yes I did.

MG: Did Richard expect conflict to take place?

RM: I don't think they expected what happened. It was a surprise. I don't know, I don't remember anyone talking about expectations except to have CPLR's voices heard and responded to.

MG: What was Richard's reaction or assessment about what happened that evening? Did he feel that it was a success or that it was less than what he expected?

RM: Let me think for a second. He might've seen that the media coverage, that in some way it was successful because the media focused in on the organization and the purpose of it. In that sense it was successful because when there's conflict like that there's always more media, you know, breaking into churches, celebrating Mass, what is that you know? The irony is that I don't live too far from there now. There's Masses in Korean, it's such a trip to go by there, there's a Thai Mass, Korean Mass, Spanish Mass, all day long. It pales in light of the new cathedral.

MG: I had never visited St. Basil's and I was in LA on some other research in May and I had to go through that part of Wilshire, and I stopped by to see the Church, I'd never seen it. Those stairs leading up to the church, it's a very small space. With a few hundred people, everyone must've been really congested.

RM: It kind of spilled out onto the street.

MG: A month later in January, Cardinal McIntyre announced his retirement. Do you know the reaction of Richard and the others to that? How did they feel about that?

RM: I think people were generally pleased and hoping that the next person that would come in would be more responsive to the Spanish-Speaking community and recognize the needs and the specific situations and conditions of that community that needed to be addressed. In a sense, the change of leadership, the Católicos felt that they had some influence, somehow they had impacted the Church enough to replace someone that was insensitive and so conservative. He was old; he needed to retire.

MG: A little bit later, Richard and 21 are arrested. What are your memories of that? Richard's reaction? What did you do? Were you part of the support group to deal with that?

RM: I had Camilo with me during the trials.

MG: You were pregnant with him?

RM: Yeah. Camilo was born December 27 . . . I remember because the day they all got taken into custody, after the trial, for the final sentencing, I had a big huge breakfast at my house, and we went to court.

MG: Did they arrest Richard at his place? At your place?

RM: At his mother's house.

MG: How did you feel about it? It must've been scary.

RM: It was traumatic for me, of course. It was traumatic.

MG: Had Richard expected to be arrested?

RM: Yeah. Anyone who was really active in the movement, an activist at his level, who could organize and bring people together. There was phone tapping, people followed him, we talked about that, so it wasn't a surprise that he got arrested. There was a feeling that there were people who were spies, who infiltrated meetings.

MG: Did Richard ever receive death threats?

RM: I would say probably. Not necessarily for CPLR, but in general as an organizer. Maybe he wouldn't tell me about it. We all sort of felt that when we organized and had demonstrations we were in a sense taking a risk on our safety. I wasn't surprised if my phone was tapped or if I was followed.

MG: Did Richard feel threatened? How did he deal with those kind of situations?

RM: I don't think anything like that stopped Richard, or inhibited him in any way of what he was doing. It didn't bother us in our life, it didn't alter anything we were doing.

MG: Let me ask you this, but you don't have to answer, was Richard or other Católicos armed?

RM: I don't know.

MG: Did Richard serve some time?

RM: Yes, he served five months.

MG: That's right. How did you deal with that?

RM: That was hard because Camilo was an infant at the time. I used to see Richard at the jail. He had an accident in the kitchen when he cut his finger, they took him to the hospital, the medical ward, and then they lost him. One time I went there I had Camilo and his dad and Ray with me, and we couldn't find him. They couldn't locate him at that jail. They couldn't locate him. It was hard times because you never knew, how many people have strangled themselves in their cells. I remember that incident really clearly.

MG: What happened? They had transferred him to another jail?

RM: They had transferred him and they didn't know where he was.

MG: Where was the jail he was transferred to?

RM: I think it was in unincorporated East LA.

MG: You obviously located him.

RM: Yeah, we found him. That was awful, that was scary.

MG: Later in August in 1970, was Richard out already? When they have the burning of the baptismal certificates, had Richard already served his time?

RM: No, I don't think so.

MG: Yeah, the time frame wouldn't be right. There was a lag of time between when he was sentenced and when he goes to jail.

RM: They went through the trial and found him guilty one day in summer and we went to court for the sentencing, they took him into custody.

MG: Did you go to most of the trial? What do you remember, especially about Zeta Acosta's defense?

RM: Zeta was amusing. The jurors loved him I think. He wore these outrageous ties. He was good. He did the best he could. We had fun. We'd go out to lunch every day together. It was an interesting trial. It was an unusual and interesting case in terms of Chicano activism and especially the Church. It did turn attention to the Latino community, the relationship with the Church, and made a number of changes in terms of how the Church operated in the *barrio.*

MG: During the trial, Richard and the others were out on bail, correct?

RM: Yes.

MG: Would Oscar ever come to your place to have strategy sessions with Richard or the others?

RM: Yes, they would all meet together. Antonio Rodríguez and the others who helped out would meet.

MG: Is Oscar as outrageous as he comes out in the books?

RM: Yeah, he's quite a character.

MG: What was your sense, and what was Richard's sense, especially after the Christmas Eve demonstration that got so much media attention, was there any sense that elements in the Mexican-American community had not looked upon these actions in a favorable way?

RM: I'm sure there were people. Even his parents at first, who were devout Catholics, were skeptical. Eventually they came out and supported and were at the demonstrations. That happened to a number, not just his family, it wasn't just the radicals out there, it wasn't just a Chicano movement, it was also community people who had an understanding of what was going on and supported it. I'm sure there were a lot of people who felt it wasn't right. What were we doing? A lot of people felt that way. A lot of people also felt it was right.

MG: During this period, when Richard is organizing Católicos, does he stop his law school classes at Loyola? Is he still taking classes?

RM: I think he had finished them.

MG: He finished his law degree in '71.

RM: I don't think he stopped taking classes. I know he went to take the bar along with all the other guys he was studying with. I don't remember stopping classes.

MG: He was still enrolled?

RM: Yes. Anyways he was very bright, he didn't have to put in all the work that others did. I remember seeing him studying for the bar lying down, taking a nap, that's how he did it.

MG: During this time, when he's organizing Católicos, how does he sustain himself economically, and into 1970 with the trial and all of that?

RM: When he went to jail, I got some welfare checks, I got about six months. I got some social service help.

MG: But Richard didn't have a job at this time?

RM: I don't remember, he might've had a grant.

MG: Maybe he was on financial aid?

RM: Yeah, I think he was on financial aid, like I was too for a while, because I was still going to Northridge. When I stopped I was able to get some social support for a while. I think that's what it was.

MG: Yeah, probably, that makes some sense that he was on some financial assistance. So you finished your degree at Northridge?

RM: Yes I did.

MG: When did you finish?

RM: '71.

MG: The same year he finished his law degree?

RM: Yes. I didn't know I had finished. I said I had to go back and finish some classes. After Camilo was six months I called and asked what I needed to do and I had all my credits.

MG: Speaking of Camilo, can you substantiate that you and Richard named him after Father Camilo Torres, the Colombian revolutionary priest?

RM: Yes.

MG: Is that true?

RM: Yeah. There's actually two, Camilo Cienfuegos.

MG: Did you have in mind the two?

RM: Yeah. I have a book somewhere that had stories on them.

MG: Whose idea was it, Richard's or yours to name him Camilo?

RM: I think it was my idea.

MG: Ah really? You had been reading up on this and studying?

RM: Yes.

MG: Latin American movements and so forth?

RM: Yes.

MG: What was your major at Northridge?

RM: Chicano Studies.

MG: So you were encountering these types of discussions and so forth?

RM: Yes.

MG: Richard felt ok with naming him Camilo?

RM: Yeah.

MG: So it's really both Cienfuegos [the Cuban revolutionary] and Father Camilo Torres.

RM: It's not the singer, there's a singer Camilo something or other.

MG: What's your impression of why, after about a year, into the fall of 1970, and certainly by the time of the moratorium of that year on August 29, Católicos doesn't really function much more. What's your sense of why it didn't continue beyond that short period of time?

RM: I think after everybody went to jail it started becoming kind of static. There was no energy behind it because people were that involved in the trials, there were 21 people, the leading people who articulated it. A lot of people went to jail. After that Richard had the hearings, the state bar hearings, if he had moral turpitude. And then the Church got involved in the community, things started changing.

MG: Richard, he was there on August 29 at the moratorium?

RM: Yeah, we were both there.

MG: What are your memories of that day?

RM: We got gassed. We were at the park. We went to the march at the park. Then the sheriffs came in and started gassing people.

MG: By this time you already had Camilo?

RM: Yes.

MG: But he wasn't there?

RM: No.

MG: Fortunately. Had Richard served as a monitor at the march?

RM: I don't remember that, no, I don't think so.

MG: Did you guys march with any particular contingent?

RM: We were with CPLR.

MG: Was there a Católicos contingent?

RM: There might've been.

MG: What was Richard's thoughts about what happened on that day?

RM: He was very angry, we all were. It was an abuse of power and an effort to suppress the Latino voice. That was a big demonstration against the Vietnam War. It was really significant the number of people that came out. It was just a really bizarre thing the way it turned out, that they came down like that. And so many people were hurt like Ruben Salazar.

MG: Richard hadn't been scheduled as a speaker that day?

RM: I don't remember.

MG: I've never seen his name in reference to that day. But not many people got the chance. During this period with Católicos, did people refer to Richard as Richard or Ricardo?

RM: I think it was Ricardo. I started calling him Richard when we first met. It was Ricardo.

MG: But the others in Católicos would refer to him as Ricardo?

RM: Yes.

MG: What's your sense of Richard's own evolving religious views? Does this whole struggle, what does it do to his own sense of faith or religion? What kind of change did you see him undergo along those lines?

RM: He grew up in a very religious family. They went to church as a unit all dressed up in suits. They were the model family. Why he went this way, it was so different from his upbringing, is a good question. He felt the injustices, not just the Church, but in general, in society, against Latinos, against Chicanos, against mexicanos. He was such a spiritual person, very much so, but not religious.

MG: At the time of Católicos, he's not a practicing Catholic?

RM: No. He became very adamant against the Catholic practice, the traditions of the Church. He was very articulate and had studied the oppression, and how the people were held down by the Church, were held back. He also worked with César Chávez and the farmworkers and trying to get the Church to support the farm workers also, that was important, they needed that.

MG: But he basically leaves the church?

RM: Yes.

MG: When you say that he retained some sense of spirituality, does he become an agnostic?

RM: No, I wouldn't put a label on how he evolved or what he evolved into in terms of his practice. Did he believe in God? I don't know. Maybe not. I think he was kind of bitter about the Church. But that doesn't mean that he couldn't have a deep sense of the spiritual.

MG: Were your children baptized?

RM: Yes, they were baptized after I broke up with Richard.

MG: But you don't go through the same changes that he went through in terms of faith?

RM: After we broke up, I went back to the Church, I did go back, I went because he and his mother and I remained close, and she asked me to. It was through her initiative that the children got baptized, they were already big, they were coming down the aisle and the priest said, are they getting married? Camilo had a Christian name, but my daughter Paloma didn't.

MG: Did Richard attend their baptisms?

RM: No.

MG: Did they make their First Communions?

RM: No.

MG: Thank you so much, this was very useful to me.

CAMILO CRUZ ON RICHARD CRUZ AND CPLR

April 25, 1997

Mario T. García (MG): Do you know where your father's parents were from?

Camilo Cruz (CC): My grandfather was from Zacatecas City, Mexico and he came to the United States around 1910 and 1912 during the mass immigration from Mexico after the revolution. He ended up in East Los Angeles. My grandmother is from Arizona and her side of the family was from Chihuahua, Mexico.

MG: They both came around the same period of time?

MG: They met in the LA area?

CC: Yes, my grandfather was a band leader. He played mariachi music orchestra style and my grandmother liked to dance and they met in one of the dances.

MG: Do you know in terms of your grandfather's own family what social class were they in Mexico?

CC: I'm not sure in Mexico but they were poor, my grandfather was the oldest son so he had to take care of the family and they were very poor in LA.

MG: Were your grandparents children when they came to this country with their parents or where they already adults?

CC: My grandmother was actually born in Arizona and my grandfather was already an adolescent when he came.

MG: What was the name of your grandfather?

CC: Ramón Cruz Magallanes, or Ramón Magallanes Cruz one way or the other.

MG: What about your grandmother's?

CC: Celia Duran Cruz.

MG: Your father was the youngest of three do you know the date he was born?

CC: July 1st 1943.

MG: What do you know about your dad's early history, childhood?

CC: He was brought up in a very Catholic house. He went to Divine Savior Elementary School in northeast Los Angeles and then he went to Cathedral High School which is right near China Town also northeast Los Angeles.

MG: Did all his siblings go to the same school and were your grandparents particularly religious?

CC: They all had the same education, they all went to the same school and my grandparents were very religious. My father was trained as an alter boy so was my uncle.

MG: What church did your grandparents go to?

CC: Divine Savior.

MG: Does it still exist?

CC: Yes it still exists that's were they had both my grandparents' funeral.

MG: Did your grandfather make a living as a musician?

CC: Early on I think he did. He used to say he was involved in international business. It was my grandmother's earnings that bought the house; she bought the house.

MG: When did they buy the house do you have any idea?

CC: I have no idea.

MG: Is the house in Highland Park? Is it mostly a Mexican area?

CC: Yes the house was in Highland Park area. It is one of the older Mexican areas. It is in the northeast area.

MG: What else do you know about your father's childhood? Was it a happy childhood?

CC: He said they had their troubles. He wasn't necessarily unhappy but I think it was stressful for my dad to grow up. They would do the normal teenage thing. They would go out drinking and partying, carousing. I don't know if he was that happy with the strict religion, I think he felt kind of enclosed.

MG: Did he ever talk about whether if he enjoyed or didn't enjoy spending time in school?

CC: From what I remember he used to say that to a certain extent he liked it. He was getting a good education but then again, he didn't like the fact that he was receiving these strict rules, a strict structure of a Catholic upbringing in the house or in school. He didn't like rules I think. He was given rules all his life and when the 60's came I think that's when he found a way to break all of them.

MG: Was it mostly a Spanish speaking family?

CC: My grandparents, his parents were against Spanish in the house. They were assimilationists I think.

MG: So they were both bilingual?

CC: Yes they both were very bilingual. I never spoke Spanish to my grandparents. They spoke Spanish and English very well. My father never knew Spanish really. My father was a Pocho, he didn't know Spanish here.

MG: Your father graduated from high school in 1961?

CC: Yes in 1961.

MG: Then he went directly to college?

CC: Then he went to Saint Mary's College for a year and a half up north.

MG: Do you know the circumstances of why he went all the way up there?

CC: It was Catholic college. I'm sure he wanted to get away for a while but it was probably a good opportunity. He said he partied too much and fought too much, got into trouble too much over there so he decided to leave. I would love to know the real reason he left Saint Mary's.

MG: It sounds that even as a young boy he was spirited.

CC: He's extremely spirited, extremely emotional. He was run by his emotions. There was one time when he was an alter boy, he just started crying. He had a breakdown as an alter boy. He was disturbed I think by all the rules by the Church.

MG: Was he involved in actual fist fights do you know if as a young boy he engaged in that?

CC: I think in college he did. In college he did in Saint Mary's because he said he partied and fought too much. That's why he left. He got into fights in his college years. He was a fighter. He was into overpowering people who he felt were oppressing him. He went through mental means, professional means, and physical means. He felt it was his right and his obligation to overpower someone who is going to oppress him. Eventually down the road in his life he fought the Church off in his mind and in his opinion he fought off cops, lawyers, he fought in the courtrooms.

MG: Ramón was older, how much older?

CC: He was about a year and a half.

MG: Then there is a sister?

CC: It was an older brother, Mark. He passed away in 1990.

MG: How much older?

CC: He's about 5 years older than my dad.

MG: Ramón and the other brother had gone to the same Catholic school as your dad, did they go to college?

CC: My uncle Ray went to Saint Mary's as well. He may have graduated from there. I'm not sure. Mark the oldest brother he didn't go to college, he was in Korea.

MG: So your father was in Saint Mary's for a year and then he came back to LA?

CC: He came back and went to LA City College. He was there for about a year. And then he transferred to Cal State Los Angeles.

MG: He graduated from Cal State LA, what year do you know?

CC: No, I don't know.

MG: Do you know what he majored in?

CC: He majored in philosophy.

MG: Did he ever talk to you about those experiences he had at Cal State LA?

CC: Those were the years he started working with philosophy and became aware about the Chicano experience and the struggles. He saw movements there. I think Cal State LA represented for him the Chicano consciousness. He always had problems with authority and the establishment and Cal State LA mixed in philosophy and all these people and what he saw on the streets and he started to become like every Chicano at that time, very conscious of the bad situations.

MG: When he was an undergraduate was he still a practicing Catholic?

CC: Yes.

MG: Did he go to Mass?

CC: I don't know if he still went to Mass but he was still calling himself a Catholic.

MG: When he was at Cal State LA do you know when he started getting involved with the farm workers cause?

CC: I don't know about that necessarily. I do know that he did work with César Chávez, he was an intern in Salinas, he did work up there. He did farm worker work.

MG: Would it have been around this period?

CC: Possibly.

MG: So he graduates around 1966 and 1967 and does he go directly to law school?

CC: No he takes some time off and he goes to New York as a probation officer for the summer. People needed him to come back to Los Angeles from New York to help or start organize for Católicos I think. A major factor for my dad coming back from New York I think was to help run Católicos Por La Raza.

MG: How long after does he go to law school?

CC: About a year I think.

MG: Do you know how he decided to go to law school at Loyola?

CC: I think he wanted to stay Catholic. I think he was still Catholic all this time and he wanted to go to Catholic law school and it was a good law school at that time and so he decided to become a lawyer. It fit his ideas of justice that were forming at that time, and he knew that he wanted to fight for justice some how. He was into philosophers and he used these philosophers as a consciousness to see that things are wrong. I don't think he knew specifically what he was going to fight for at that time maybe Catholic Church or justice I don't know.

MG: When he was attending Loyola Law School was he still living at home?

CC: I think so. I think he lived at home for a while and I think he went on his own and found his own apartment.

MG: Tell me what you know about the organization of Católicos Por La Raza.

CC: What I know about Católicos is that there were several leaders and my father was the organizer of those leaders. There were several different people in Católicos that made up the co- group and my father was called the co-chairman. He was like the leader of Católicos from what I remember. The funeral you can see that and when people mentioned Católicos, they had memories of my father, they had specific memories of what my dad did in jail, or what he did on the streets. They had memories of him as the main leader and you can see it in the papers as well from the way they cover it, as my father being the leader of Católicos. There were several other key figures as well like Richard Martínez, Raul Ruiz, Pedro Arias, and a couple of others.

MG: Did he ever tell you why they were organized?

CC: He never told me why. I wish I could have asked him. He died a total angry atheist; he did not like the church. And I felt asking him then why he was into the Church movement. I think the Church was his instrument to involve the community. It was the only way to get Chicanos involved. The Church was such a big part of community that he felt that that was going to be the way for him to reach out to the community and let the community know that they are feeling injustice. People won't feel injustice if you give them numbers about immigration or politics but if you show them what the church in their block is doing, was what he felt was going to make the people angry and be involved.

MG: Unlike other movement activist at that time, he obviously understood the power of religion, the importance of religion.

CC: My thing is, if he started questioning religion at this time, that to me shows how powerful he felt the Church was. He wasn't going to leave the Church even though he was questioning it. He knew he had all these people involved, he knew the Church was going to be his way of getting these people to start questioning authority. He needed to utilize something to get the people active.

MG: This transformed the church into a way in which it should have been all along, working for the poor. If they could get the Church or transform the Church to be an institution to be on the side of Chicanos, then that would be a powerful ally. They understood that if the Church could be transformed to be a Church for the poor, that it would be a tremendous force for organizing people. I think he understood the importance of religion and the importance of the Church as an institution and if it could reach out to the poor and organize, then they wouldn't need to bring an outside source. The bases were already there for organization.

CC: Definitely. And again, it is the Mexican relationship with the Church that is deep. You can't remove that relationship. I know my dad was struggling with that in his later years.

MG: And they felt that the hierarchy in the Church under the Cardinal McIntyre years was unresponsive and insensitive to the poor Chicanos and it was therefore McIntyre and the church authority that were not allowing the church to be on the side of the poor. So they had to take it on.

CC: They had to take it on.

MG: They are radicals because they are rejecting the authority of the church.

CC: They were radicals and they started realizing it.

MG: What else do you recall that he told you about Católicos? Their activities?

CC: He would talk about how radical they were. They were a very serious group he said. He would tell me that they would carry guns. He just said that the reason they were so radical was because they honestly believed they were going to take things over. I think he felt that they were going to become some hierarchy in the Church because they were going to actively take it over. They actually thought they were going to remove people and place themselves in power. They thought they were going to start Aztlán. They actually thought that their movement was going to take over.

MG: At the time that Católicos was organized, would he have been living at home or alone?

CC: I think he would have been living on his own.

MG: Tell me again how your mother comes into the picture?

CC: They met at a Católicos rally at LA City College. They were talking to a different number of schools, to Brown Berets. They met at a rally and then they started going out and she was inspired by his speaking. My dad was a very good speaker. He was very good. At the funeral, people would talk about my dad's speaking abilities. He would start going up there and he would start laughing and then he would start getting really angry. He was very dynamic, a very animated speaker, he was excellent.

MG: You said your mother is of Puerto Rican background?

CC: Yes she is Puerto Rican.

MG: How did she get into Los Angeles?

CC: She was born in New York and she came to LA when she was 19 or 20.

MG: What were the reasons?

CC: She wanted to leave home. She had a terrible home life. She had a strict Catholic upbringing as well. She just left; she wanted to escape her family. The Hollywood scene at that time was to just come and check it out. She wasn't political at all. The hippy movement was first her thing and then she saw black power and at around the same time she saw brown power.

MG: What year were they married?

CC: I don't know, I think it was 1969 or 1970.

MG: Did they marry in the Church?

CC: I don't know. That is a good question. I know she had a wedding shower because she was telling me how they partied. A lot of people were partying all the time.

MG: Your uncle Ray was also part of Católicos?

CC: He helped with Católicos. He was conscious of the community and he wanted to help and he was helping my dad.

MG: We have mentioned Martínez, Ruiz, and Arias. What other names would have been important in terms of Católicos Por La Raza? Some of the key people.

CC: Key people are Tony Salazar, he was very important. He got arrested and he did a lot of time. Bob Gandara, my mom. The twenty one people who got arrested would be key figures.

MG: Do you know what year your father got his law degree from Loyola?

CC: I think he got it in 1971 or 1972.

MG: And then what did he do?

CC: Well, they wouldn't certify him. He passed the bar exam the first time and studied with Antonio Rodríguez and Miguel García.

Photo by Ray Cruz. Used with Permission.

Richard Cruz, Rosa Martínez, Ramón Cruz Sr., Sept. 13, 1972 at Richard Cruz's Hearing before the California BAR.

MG: And they wouldn't certify him because of his political activities?

CC: Because of his political activities and his moral conduct during the sixties.

MG: And he challenged that? Did he appeal it?

CC: Yes. It was a big case. A lot of press covered it.

MG: They went to court?

CC: They went to court. And he won in court. He got certified.

MG: And this was?

CC: Maybe 1973.

MG: And in those intervening years what was he doing?

CC: He was organizing at all times. He was organizing La Raza Law Student Association, he was doing a lot of work with Abogados de Aztlán, which was a group getting Chicano lawyers together to do Chicano work. He was always active. Católicos had already disbanded I think.

MG: What did he do as a lawyer?

CC: As a lawyer, he stuck to work with the community for Chicanos only. His first big case was a labor law case involving Chicano union members. He was right away into discrimination. His second big case had to do with sterilization. He worked with Gloria Molina and Kent Russell and they helped eliminate forced sterilization on Latinas in USC Medical Center in the mid 70's.

MG: Did he have his own law office at that time?

CC: Yes he did. He had his own law office with other Chicano lawyers, Rudy Díaz, Percy Duran.

MG: So he would take on these kinds of cases?

CC: He would take on discrimination cases, civil rights cases, and criminal cases. He was always Chicano.

MG: The case Gordon Castillo Hall Case when did that develop?

CC: That was around 1977 or 1978. It was in the late 70's early 80's. That was my dad's biggest case.

MG: Can you tell me what you know about that case?

CC: A young guy named Gordon Castillo Hall was arrested and put in prison for 3 to 4 years for a crime he did not commit.

MG: For what crime?

CC: It was a murder crime. It was at a party and a postman off duty he was going to his home and he got shot by some gang members. And they framed Gordon. But it wasn't Gordon it was some other guy.

MG: And he got sentenced to life in prison?

CC: Yes. He was sentenced to life in prison and my dad got him out after three or four years on appeal.

MG: How did he come on that case?

CC: The original lawyers were giving the family poor counsel and the family got word of my dad and the sterilization case he did and they approached him. That case really involved the community.

MG: And he worked on it how many years?

CC: Four or five years.

MG: And these cases were the kind that would not bring much income.

CC: He didn't make income in this case. All the money went to his fees to just live and for lawyer fees, to hire his assistants. He never made any money. We lived in a small apartment in East Los Angeles. He was very poor. We didn't live with him but we would spend weekends with him even though he was working on the case.

MG: So your mother was the main bread winner?

CC: Definitely. She brought us up. My dad didn't really bring us up. She was responsible for everything.

MG: You said she was working at UCLA?

CC: At that time she was at the Chicano Studies Research Center editing books for people.

MG: This was full time?

CC: This was full time.

MG: Into the 80's was your dad still taking on these kinds of cases?

CC: He was taking on criminal cases, criminal defense cases, and some other labor law cases.

MG: So these cases didn't bring much income?

CC: He didn't bring in income. He made money here and there but it was never to make his life a semi-normal life. He was always struggling.

MG: Was he active in MALDEF?

CC: He was active. He was also active in La Raza Unida Party and in a lot of lawyer stuff, a lot of law committees. He was involved in the Mexican American Bar Association.

MG: When did he become to get ill?

CC: He got ill late 1992 early 1993. He found out he had cancer and then he died in the summer of 1993. He found out half a year before he died that he was sick. He had lung cancer.

MG: He was a heavy smoker throughout his life?

CC: Yes. He smoked for 30 years about 2 to 3 packs a day.

MG: What day did he die?

CC: He died July 21st, 1993.

MG: Did he die in a hospital?

CC: He died at USC hospital of all places. Where he fought sterilization. He died a poor man. He didn't have insurance.

MG: During that time did he talk more about his life?

CC: He mentioned some things but he was very prideful. He didn't want to show that he was giving up a fight. Everyone knew him as a fighter. At his birthday celebration we had for him two weeks before he died he said that the biggest fight of his life was the cancer. That he has had many fights; Católicos, the cops everybody but that this was going to be his biggest one. He didn't want to tell people that he was capable of losing a fight. To him this was just another fight. People wanted to hear that from him. That's what they were used to hearing from Richard Cruz was that this was just another fight. And what made him such a tremendous man was that he was a fighter. If anyone could win this fight, it was my dad. Richard Martínez said in a letter for us to read at the funeral that my dad's death showed people, Chicanos, how human we are. We are not super beings and that we are all going to die. When he was dying he said he had a good life. No matter how poor he was he said he did good things in life and that's all that mattered. Although he didn't get credit. He got credit from people but he didn't get credit from the history books I think he deserves. Rudy Acuña's book was the only one who gave a couple of paragraphs to my father. I think more work needs to be done on him and Católicos.

MG: So you think that he himself believed that this was just another fight and that he would overcome it?

CC: He did not want to write a will because he saw that as giving up. I don't know how mortal he thought he was. I think he thought he could fight and win this. On the exterior anyways. On the interior he must have been going through something weird. In the hospital he wouldn't let go and die. We had to put him on life support. After life support he kept fighting he tried fighting his way out of the bed. He literally tried fist fighting me but he couldn't because he was immobile but he just didn't want to stop fighting.

MG: Was his family at his bedside?

CC: My uncle had already died. My grandfather was there. My grandmother was already ill with Alzheimer. To me his death bed experience was the most symbolic of his whole life. He was laughing and crying and he kissed my mom and he was fighting. He was struggling. He was a very passionate man. As much as he was a fighter he was also some one who was loving, passionate about his emotions. That's what people loved about him. Fighting and partying. That's what he did. People really appreciate him for that.

MG: What point did he really separate himself from religion?

CC: The mid seventies. He wrote a letter where he says he was divorcing his parents and another letter where he tells my mom he is going to divorce her. This was around 1974 or 1975. He was divorcing a lot of things at that time and the one thing he divorced himself from I think is God. I think he felt God had betrayed him and that the Church was just a big betrayal. Even though he was a big part of it. He used to tell Chicanos that they shouldn't be too into religion. That religion is good and that we can give ourselves a voice, to channel our anger and be positive about it and to do it for a good cause. But in a way, the Church was also taking away our power. That we can start our own movement without a Church. We can start a Chicano Movement and we can be back to the land without any need of the morals, without any need of Christ and God.

MG: How do you remember him as a father?

CC: As a father, he was good at times and bad at times. He wasn't ready for children, he was so involved in the movement. He loved my sister and me very much though. He was a great father in terms of his creativity. He was a funny man; he made us laugh. He was very entertaining. But he had his addictions as well. He had alcoholism, drug abuse; he hurt my mom and us. My sister got a lot of the male anger and she really resents that.

MG: Did your parents divorce?

CC: Yes they did, in 1975 I think.

MG: So you would see your father only on weekends?

CC: I would see him on weekends. He would take us out to his parties.

MG: Did your father ever re-marry?

CC: No he didn't. He had another child. My half brother's name is Carlos Cruz.

MG: So your father's personality would be described as what?

CC: He had a lot of different personalities. I think his personality was one of giving. He gave; he loved to give. He was one of justice and he loved to help people get things, acquire things, knowledge. He was extremely intellectual. He had ideas that blew people away. He was a very giving, funny man. My father's sense of humor was the most serious sense of humor you would ever see. It was very funny but humor that was not superficial, humor that meant something somehow. He was serious, happy, he was very emotional. If he felt an emotion he felt it one hundred percent. He was very passionate.

MG: At the funeral you mentioned that a number of people got up and spoke. What do you recall about some of the ways that he was remembered by his colleagues?

CC: As a powerful man, as a speaker, a leader. He was definitely a leader. He was a Chicano's Chicano. A man's man. That's what people said. Chicanos loved him. Lawyers loved him. He was very deep and he made people feel things. That's why they made him leader of Católicos. He was very dynamic; he showed leadership qualities. He was a friend and leader to people. My dad believed people are born leaders and people got that from him.

MG: How many people came to the funeral?

CC: I would say about 350 to 450.

MG: How many spoke?

CC: It was supposed to be an hour and a half but it went for three hours. Everyone spoke. All kinds of Católico members came.

MG: Was it videotaped?

CC: It was. There were good comments on him.

MG: Did Raul Ruiz take photographs at the funeral?

CC: Not at the funeral but he did speak at the funeral. A lot of key people in the community that have gotten recognition were at the funeral.

MG: The funeral was held where?

CC: It was held in Forest Hills in Hollywood.

MG: Was he cremated?

CC: Yes he was.

MG: So his remains are in a vault?

CC: We got a marker for him. We put in the marker that he loved his people.

MG: You're the oldest you were born when?

CC: December 27, 1971.

MG: And your sister?

CC: April 18, 1973 or 1974.

MG: When you would visit him, did it seem like he read a lot? Did he have a library?

CC: Yes, he was an intellectual. He loved reading. The biggest thing about my dad was that he brought in things to the Movement that people wouldn't understand. He talked about dinosaurs, he talked about apes, about astronomy. He related all to Chicanismo somehow.

MG: So his interest varied?

CC: Yes. He listened to classical music and to jazz; he was into reading philosophy, western philosophy. He prided himself in the fact that he utilized western philosophy to overthrow certain institutions.

MG: Was he ever into Marxism?

CC: No. He despised the Marxist movement. He eventually felt that ideologies all together are wrong. He felt the Chicanos who desired to put a label on him and herself was our downfall. He said so many people could have been lawyers or doctors right now but they went for the Marxist party, the Communist Party. He was very mad at the philosophers and people he knew who turned Marxist. He said that we could have started our own businesses, medical institutions for Chicanos.

MG: He felt there should have been more of an effort in people becoming professionals.

CC: Yes and using that power for Chicanismo, for the Chicano nation. He was a nationalist at that time and to the day he died I think he was as well in the old sense of the term Mexican-American; we got to stick to our own and we can't be talking or listening to Karl Marx.

MG: Did he use the term Chicano to identify himself?

CC: Yes, he was very proud of it. He was sad before he died that the term Chicano is not used so much anymore.

MG: You said earlier that your mother without his knowledge baptized both of you.

CC: He ended up finding out; he got very angry.

MG: Did your mother continue to be a Catholic?

CC: She continued to be a Catholic and to this day I think she feels a sense of relationship to the Catholic Church.

MIGUEL GARCÍA ON CPLR

(July 11, 2005)

GAR = Miguel García
MG = Professor Mario T. García

MG: I've been doing research on Católicos Por La Raza. I wanted to talk with you about your involvement. Why don't we start with you giving me a little bit of background leading up to your involvement with Católicos.

GAR: How far back do you want me to go?

MG: I don't want to get too much into it, but are you a Cathedral High School product?

GAR: No I am not. I first met Richard Cruz at the end of my third year, I was an evening law school student at thc Loyola University School of Law and Richard was a daytime student. He had just finished his second year. In the summer he went up and did an internship with California Rural Legal Assistance, also known as CRLA. Apparently that had an impactful meaning and significance to Richard. When I first met him I was leaving an evening class. I had already been told by another fellow student, "did you know there's a Mexican student in the daytime? No I didn't. Well, you guys should meet each other." He had told Richard, did you know there's an evening Mexican student? He didn't know that either.

MG: You were the only Chicano in the evening?

GAR: We were the two.

MG: That was it?

GAR: That was it. I was coming out of evening school. I was a commuter. I really just went to school to get the education I needed so I could qualify to take the bar.

MG: Where had you done your undergraduate work?

GAR: I went to Cal State Los Angeles. I was already married. I was married in 1965. I graduated from Cal State LA in '67, February. I was admitted to Loyola Law School to start in September '67 now jump to 1968 after the summer. That's when I met Richard, because he's there waiting at the doorway. I see this skinny kid with a cowboy hat, and that's Richard.

MG: Cowboy hat?

GAR: Yeah, cowboy. He spent the summer over in Salinas. So I think he brought the hat back. He introduced himself to me. We started a relationship which was primarily regarding his interest to know more about the Chicano movement in East Los Angeles. By this time, which was 1968, I had already been involved, I was a social worker in East LA. I had been one of the founders of a group called SALUD, an acronym for Social Action Latinos for Unity Development. It was Chicano social workers that had joined with welfare rights organizations, Alicia Escalante, Irene Villalobos, Bob Gandara, and others, who were very active in their advocacy for our clients, which were welfare recipients, recipients of our services. Bob Gandara and Alicia Escalante were very well-connected with other people in the community and through my involvement with SALUD and WRO, Welfare Rights Organization, we formed a coalition of community organizations to advocate for better services for our clients as well as an increased representation of Mexican-American Chicanos within the department of public social services. There were no supervisors or directors that were of Mexican descent or Chicanos. Therefore we were advocating for more representation from people in our community in positions of authority as well as better services for our clients. Through that coalition I got to meet and know leaders in the Chicano movement and Richard, when we met, he found out that I already was acquainted with people that he wanted to get to meet. He asked me to introduce him to those persons and to also invite them to meetings which I did. He very quickly became acquainted. He was an individual who was quite intelligent and personable. Very soon he was part of that Chicano movement group. Of course we were at the university, at the law school, but I was also part of that movement through my involvement with the Department of Public Social Services and my involvement with SALUD and that coalition.

MG: He just wanted to become involved, or when you met him, did he already have the idea for Católicos?

GAR: No, whether he had the idea for Católicos only he can answer that. Probably so, because I think soon after he started getting people. I think that was his primary focus. I think he already had the idea.

MG: But he didn't initially broach that with you?

GAR: Not that I remember, not that I think so. What he broached with me was he introduced himself. By this time, there had already been a small group of law students, Chicanos, that had organized Chicano Law Students Association. He informed me of that and, of course, I was interested and I became part of that organization. Soon thereafter six Mexican-American Chicano students were admitted to Loyola Law School, so within a matter of weeks, I think it was just beginning that semester, we went from two and we increased it by 300% and we became eight.

MG: Did you form a specific chapter there at Loyola, of the Chicano Law Students Association?

GAR: Yes we did.

MG: Even though it was just the two of you?

GAR: I think by this time the other six had come in, so it was no longer just me and Richard. Richard had been there for two years, I had been there for three years. At the beginning of my fourth year, then six others came in. so we became eight instead of two, and we had enough numbers so we formed a chapter of Chicano Law Students and it was quite an active chapter. There were several focuses. The two that I can really remember was one, to increase the number of slots as we called them, dedicated or set aside for incoming Chicano law students that would be there with a full scholarship or a partial scholarship. We also pushed for our group, Chicano Law Students, to be involved with in the interviewing and selection process. So increasing the number of Chicano law students within the law school plus becoming involved in the selection process, making recommendations, getting people to apply for these slots because, you may be surprised to know that we couldn't fill all these slots after we got the university, the law school to set aside 15 of them. The competition was so great for the number of students that were graduating. UCLA wanted them, USC wanted them, Loyola wanted them, other universities wanted them. There weren't enough graduates to go around, especially graduate students with the orientation or inclination for community involvement and advocacy for the community versus just students who wanted to become lawyers. We really focused on those individuals that we believed had a higher probability that they would come back and contribute to the community in some fashion.

MG: So you had had a series of meetings with the law school administration over these issues?

GAR: We did and not only with the law school's administration but also with the university's administration, mainly with Father Merrifield, who was quite a progressive individual. One of the years our strategy was to try to get fifteen slots. We went over to the university; we had an appointment to meet with Father Merrifield, and whenever we had these appointments and we were pushing for a greater number of slots, we would always call upon our fellow students at the chapters of USC and UCLA and they would in turn, when they had something going on they would call us, and USC, UCLA and us were the three chapters that worked very closely together and we developed friendships that remain to this day.

MG: They would attend the meetings at Loyola?

GAR: Yes, because we believed that in numbers, greater numbers, more impressive the visit would be.

MG: Did Richard emerge right there already as the key spokesperson?

GAR: Oh definitely, he was the first president of Chicano Law Students. He definitely was the one pushing. After all he was a full-time student and he was a community-oriented organizer, especially around the Catholic Church.

MG: He was full-time in the day school?

GAR: Yes.

MG: What was your initial impression after first meeting Richard?

GAR: First impressions, a skinny kid with a big hat. We were about the same age, it's just that I was already married, I had a child, I was a homeowner, I had a day time job, so my orientation was a bit different than Richard's. He was a full-time student, devoting himself to his studies, having time to play around, to party, he was quite a party guy. If you partied with Richard you started Friday, it went through Saturday, and it would go to Sunday, and then most of the people would be gone by Monday. So in his fifty years he lived a good seventy-five.

MG: Out of all of this when does Católicos begin to emerge?

GAR: I couldn't give you a date, but I would say within a matter of months from the time, let's see, well we had Christmas Eve . . .

MG: That's in 1969.

GAR: That's 1969.

MG: So you must've been organizing earlier in '69?

GAR: Well, if that was in 1969 . . . let me get my dates.

MG: The Christmas day protest is December 25, '69.

GAR: Then it was earlier.

MG: Yes, it must've been earlier in '69,

GAR: We must've met in '68 then. So I started '67, I finished the first year, I must've met him in my second year. Yes, I met him in my second year.

MG: Into the '68—'69 academic year.

GAR: Maybe the early part of '69. We worked together, we met and organized the entire year. It had been a good amount of time before we had that Christmas Eve demonstration.

MG: Going back to the Law Students Association at Loyola, would it have been into the '68-'69 year? It would've had to have been, because it was after you met Richard.

GAR: We already had the additional number of students, in fact we had even more than the additional six, so I must've met him at the beginning of my second year. We worked a good six months to a year before St. Basil's.

MG: So sometime in that academic year, into '69, was when Católicos begins to surface?

GAR: Yes, a good full year before the Christmas Eve demonstration. What will give you the correct time period and dates is the La Raza and Justicia O! publications. It was before the St. Basil's demonstration; we had already published a lot of LA County's Assessors' records, showing all the property that was owned by the Catholic Church. To the best of my memory, we confronted the Church for a good number of months before the St. Basil's demonstration.

MG: Was it Richard's idea to form Católicos?

GAR: Yes.

MG: What was his argument to put together an organization like this?

GAR: That the Church was not sufficiently involved in the needs of the Mexican-American community, even though the Catholic Church was overwhelmingly Mexican and Latin. Therefore, they should have a higher level of responsibility in terms of returning some of the wealth that had been contributed by the community, especially those who had passed and left their property to the Church, or just that even though Mexicans and Mexican-Americans were mostly at the lower income level they would always be there at Church on Sundays contributing. The Church needed to reciprocate and do more for those who needed help in our community. Definitely, that was Richard's brain child and he was the one that kept pushing on those issues.

MG: Who were the initial members? The same group from the Law Students?

GAR: It started at the law school, but then it expanded to the community in general. There were other people that became involved in Católicos Por La Raza. It was more than just the law students. It started at Loyola, at the chapter of Chicano Law Students, but then it became a broader base, including people in the movement in East Los Angeles, in the Chicano movement in East LA, because the Chicano movement really consisted of several hundred people, that knew each other, that would be very dedicated and committed. It was not unusual to attend two or three demonstrations a day. It was mostly the same people who would be attending all those demonstrations.

MG: People wore different hats. You could be a member of Católicos and be a member of MEChA.

GAR: Oh gee, I was a member of SALUD, I was a member of Católicos Por La Raza, Chicano Law Students, I was part of the staff of Justicia O!, we published it out of La Raza magazine headquarters, so we had a very close working relationship with Joe Razo and with Raul Ruiz, who were the co-editors of La Raza.

MG: They became involved with Católicos right?

GAR: Exactly, Raul Ruiz was one of the ones arrested on that evening. He was hit over the head. I believe Joe was arrested that day as well.

MG: I think so. You reach out also to the student movement?

GAR: Definitely, MEChA.

MG: Would you go speak to campuses? Or would Richard?

GAR: There were several persons who would go and speak at campuses and try to make it a broader-based organization. We had Long Beach State, people from Cal State LA, Northridge. MEChA and the Chicano Law Students worked very closely together.

MG: How many core members of Católicos would you say there were that would meet on a more regular basis?

GAR: Core members, oh gee, I would say about a dozen or so, the ones that were really committed, the leadership core of the organization. Most of it was at Loyola Law School because of Richard.

MG: The meetings were held at the law school?

GAR: I don't remember that, not necessarily, a lot of the meetings took place at Euclid Heights Community Center. A lot of the meetings took place at La Raza magazine headquarters, or at the law school, people's homes. We jumped around, there was not an office for Católicos Por La Raza, or even for Chicano Law Students. We might've had a telephone at the law school where we received calls, but I don't remember that we had an office per se.

MG: Do you remember the term "Cathedral Mafia" used to describe Richard and his brother and a couple of other guys in Católicos from Cathedral?

GAR: No I don't remember the term.

MG: I got that term from Richard Martínez, he used that term, that Richard and others were referred to as the "Cathedral Mafia."

GAR: Richard Martínez?

MG: Yes.

GAR: Richard Martínez, he was very much involved. What was his primary organization?

MG: At that time he was at LA City College, I believe.

GAR: In terms of the Chicano movement Richard Martínez was an important individual.

MG: But I think at the time of Católicos he was at City College in LA.

GAR: I don't see that much Cathedral influence other than of course Richard.

MG: Yeah I don't know where Richard came up with that term but he used it.

GAR: It was mostly law students and other Chicano movement people. I don't see Cathedral playing a key role other than Richard.

MG: At what point does it become clear or you began to focus on addressing or confronting Church authorities?

GAR: Confronting Church authorities . . .

MG: Somewhere into the fall of '69 you began to try to get meetings with McIntyre.

GAR: That was I think the focus. We saw that the power was at the archdiocese and that Cardinal McIntyre was much too conservative and much too old and he really was an obstacle to the Church becoming more responsive and progressive. Yet we had to deal with him, once we saw him we saw that he was really way beyond being lucid and of much use to anybody. I was as close to McIntyre as three feet away when we went into the rectory, and they wouldn't allow us to have an audience with him. I think it was Joe Razo and he was the first through those doors, a priest tried to stop him and he threw him a body block, that allowed me to keep going into the inner offices. As I was going to where McIntyre was they closed the doors on me but I managed to get my arm in. I feigned that it was really hurting my arm and when they let a little bit of the pressure off I pushed my way in and there was McIntyre and there he was standing, very nervous, and he kept on saying, "Call the police, call the police, call the police." He didn't seem to be all there.

MG: You and Joe led the charge in?

GAR: It was more than just me and Joe, it was everybody. It was just that I happened to be right behind Joe, and as he threw the body block and took the first priest down, then that allowed me to keep going. I don't even remember how exactly I got to where McIntyre was.

MG: When everyone gets into his office, what happens then?

GAR: We stated our demands. You need to get the Church more involved in our community. We want more positions open for law students, for students in our community to become lawyers. It was a very short meeting. It wasn't even a meeting, it was just a statement of demands. Then we got out of there because we knew the police were coming.

MG: You guys gave him a copy of the demands?

GAR: I don't remember, I would think so.

MG: Did McIntyre say anything?

GAR: No, just [in a stammering manner] "Call the police, call the police."

MG: And there were others of his staff there?

GAR: Yes.

MG: Priests?

GAR: There were three others.

MG: Did they actually call the police?

GAR: I have no idea, because we left, we didn't stay there long. They never did come afterwards.

MG: How many of you?

GAR: There were a good six or eight.

MG: Who went in there?

GAR: Yes. Actually into the inner office, where McIntyre, there were three or four, but the entire group was about a dozen.

MG: Not everybody went into his office?

GAR: No, most of them didn't make it that far.

MG: Because of what?

GAR: Other priests who were there who interposed . . .

MG: They got in the way?

GAR: They got in the way. Or maybe the students weren't willing to go all the way in.

MG: And this was at the chancery's office?

GAR: Exactly. We walked from the law school over to the chancellery. It was like two, three, four blocks. It was very close by.

MG: The law school downtown is on what street?

GAR: 1440 West and 9th. The chancellery was on 8th street, around there. It was very close by, we walked.

MG: Is it after that confrontation with McIntyre that the decision was made to do the protest at St. Basil's or had that already been planned?

GAR: It was after. I don't think it had been planned. Do you have the date of the chancellery visit?

MG: It's November.

GAR: Oh, so it's very close to the protest. We realized that we needed to keep things going, Christmas was coming. I'm not sure, it wasn't my idea, about the Christmas Eve demonstrations, it was either Richard's or somebody else's.

MG: How much planning and organizing went into that event?

GAR: Quite a bit, to spread the word, to let people know about it, we had a good turnout, we had about 300 people, I'm sure we had to do some organizing, spreading the word, make some phone calls, we might've put an article in Justicia O!, there might've been an article in La Raza. We did the usual, spreading the word, making phone calls. As I say, there were a good three or four hundred people in the Chicano movement. Word would spread pretty quickly.

MG: What do you remember about the protest at St. Basil?

GAR: What I remember is being there, getting there, there was a Mass being said outside, and there were tortillas being given instead of the Eucharist. I had some time on my hands so I cased the place out and I went to the parking lot and I noticed that there was a door and I was curious about that door and I happened to go in, I'm not sure why. I went in and I was surprised to see an entire separate service going on down below the main street level service. Why I did this I don't know. I went inside. I didn't sit but I walked along the west side of the downstairs service. It led to some stairs and I went up the stairs. There I was in the street-level vestibule. I went and hung around for a minute or two. I went outside and rejoined the crowd. When later on in the demonstration, when we decided we wanted to go in and the doors were closed on us, then I let some people know that there was another way to get in. There was a group of us that went in through that door, which included a fellow that always wore all black, we called him "Karate," he wore a hat with a lot of buttons.

MG: How many followed you?

GAR: It was a good dozen or fifteen, it included Oscar Zeta Acosta, Joe Razo, "Karate," who else . . .

MG: Did Richard go?

GAR: I don't think Richard was part of that group. I think he was too busy being the leader outside. We went through the vestibule. This time it was about a dozen of us. We went up, we were walking fast, there was not even parishioners or anybody else to react to us. We went up to the vestibule, by this time the doors were closed. I went directly for the door and I put my hand on the bar and as I put my hand on the bar this big ol'—later we found out it was an off-duty sheriff that grabbed me and took me away from the door, but by this time the doors were opening, they were automatic. Then the rest of the guys were coming in, then all hell broke loose.

MG: This is when the ushers get involved?

GAR: Exactly, they were LAPD [sic, sheriffs].

MG: What happened? Scuffles?

GAR: Yeah, I guess you call it *chingazos.* By this time the doors were open . . .

MG: So more from the outside were able to come in?

GAR: They do come in, there was actually physical fisticuffs in the vestibule. They do push us out again.

MG: You guys never got to the sanctuary?

GAR: No we never got in the sanctuary because there were too many cops. They had batons. They do get us out again.

MG: This includes by that time not only the undercover, but the regular LAPD come in?

GAR: I think they were there pretty quickly. Then we're chanting outside, "Let the poor people in." There might've been chanting even by the time we got up to the vestibule. Later on as we're out there again, the doors do get broken.

MG: Someone breaks the door?

GAR: They get kicked in, a kick breaks them.

MG: It wasn't a rock being thrown?

GAR: I don't know, there might've been more than one door broken. I know that at least one was broken by a kick, by a good patada [kick].

MG: You guys never got back into the vestibule?

GAR: Gee, I don't know that I ever tried to back in. There were too many cops. As I was going down the street on the sidewalk, one cop threw a baton at me, I ducked, it missed me, but gets a girl right behind me. I found out later that her arm was broken by that blow. There was actually a lot of use of force by LAPD officers.

MG: Then they began to arrest people?

GAR: No, they don't arrest that many, most people were able to leave that scene.

MG: You weren't arrested?

GAR: No, I wasn't arrested. I had a goatee, and I went home that night and shaved the goatee. That morning, my wife, who didn't go with me, woke up screaming because she thought there was a strange man in bed with her.

MG: Why did you shave the goatee off?

GAR: Well, I knew that there would be people who would accuse me of things. I thought it was best to shave and change my appearance. Sure enough, they held me up for three months. They doctored up some photographs with a bandage on my nose to try to infer that I had been involved in the violence, whether I was or I wasn't, they were never able to prove it. They did put a bandage on my nose and they had an informal hearing with McClosky, I just remember his last name. Ben Margolis, a very fine lawyer, represented me *pro bono* and he requested an informal hearing to view the evidence against me and McClosky said, take a look at these photographs, what do you have to say about that? I looked at the photographs and saw my face with a bandage on my nose, and I'd never had a bandage on my nose, this was at a demonstration the day after St. Basil's in protest of those who had been arrested and beaten, and I didn't have a bandage on my nose at that demonstration across the street at an empty lot. I said, Mr. McClosky, take a very close look at this photograph, when have you ever seen a bandage on a person's nose that goes into the nostrils? Whoever doctored that photograph, I'm not sure if it was the criminal conspiracy section guys, Castrita and Cevallos, because they were always tailing us. They also discolored the nostril part of the nose. He looked at it and he certified me to practice a week after that meeting.

MG: You were not part of the 21 arrested later?

GAR: I was not arrested. It might've been because I shaved my goatee.

MG: I get different views on the role of Zeta Acosta that evening, as you know in his The Revolt of Cockroach People, he puts himself with the group that was struggling with the undercover ushers in the vestibule.

GAR: He was one of the persons who went with me . . .

MG: So his account of him being in the vestibule was an accurate one?

GAR: It is except he takes credit for having found the place. He takes credit for having found that door and leading the group up to the vestibule.

MG: When I interviewed Raul Ruiz he said he didn't remember Oscar being in the vestibule.

GAR: He did go with us, but I take credit because for some reason, I just became curious, and I found that side entrance. But Oscar was one of those I told. But I also told, Joe Razo who was very key. He had a lot of respect from all of us, he's not a big guy, but he's a gutsy guy. He always was very sincere, everybody had a great deal of respect for him. I believe it was Joe who I first approached, when the doors were closed. I said hey Joe, I know how we can get in, there's a side entrance. We knew each other very well, we trusted one another very much. Then we sent the word to other key people. There was a group of about ten or twelve who went to the side. I knew how to get in. I read Cockroach People and Zeta takes credit for a lot.

MG: But it is true he was part of the group who went into the vestibule?

GAR: He was one of those who went into the vestibule.

MG: Did you guys anticipate troubles with the police?

GAR: It was always in the back of our minds that at any demonstration the police would be there, and that very easily things could get out of hand. It was always anticipated because we were always followed by the criminal conspiracy section. They knew us by first name, they knew us by sight, and we knew them as well. We knew that there was infiltration and they were always spying on us.

MG: Tell me about the events on the following day. You went back to protest on Christmas day?

GAR: Yes, I believe it was the following day, it might've been two days, we needed a little bit of time to organize, I don't think that we had much time to organize the following morning.

MG: My sense is that it was the following day, because it would've been Christmas Day and the picketing went on while the Masses were being held.

GAR: We had a pretty good telephone tree. We might've gotten word, there's a demonstration, Richard might've called me, somebody else might've called me, whomever, and we were ready to go. I know that it was within a day or two. There was an empty lot and we had a demonstration.

MG: Was the empty lot across from Whittier or on the side street?

GAR: It wasn't right across the street, but . . .

MG: I mean Wilshire, not Whittier.

GAR: It was on Wilshire, very close, not necessarily right across from the church, but maybe a forty-five degree angle. Very close to the church.

MG: There was picketing outside of the church?

GAR: Yes, and of course Gloria Chávez went in with the golf club?

MG: Please tell me about that. Some people remember it, some people don't.

GAR: I remember it, I didn't witness it, but I know Gloria Chávez very well, she was one of the movement regulars. She was a real gutsy woman, one of her favorite sayings, it would crack us up, she would come into meetings and say "*Manos pa arriba, calzones pa abajo*" [Hands up, underwear down]. It would crack us up. She was gutsy. She went in, I didn't witness it, this is what I've heard from others, and of course she was prosecuted for it because she went in with a golf club and royally tore up the place. That was very much Gloria, she was gutsy with a lot of *huevos* [guts].

MG: Did you actually ever see her carrying the golf clubs?

GAR: No, I didn't see that.

MG: From there on, shortly thereafter McIntyre retires . . . did you guys feel that the events around St. Basil's were a success?

GAR: We definitely felt it was a success. There was a lot of pressure brought on the Church. I think it was an international event, it was not just reported here in Los Angeles. There was an all points alert, and it was considered a riot.

MG: So you did see it as a success?

GAR: Certainly. McIntyre was axed, we took credit for that. And of course Bishop, what's his name . . .

MG: Bishop Manning replaces him. And he would actually meet with Católicos. Were you at that meeting?

GAR: Yes.

MG: What do you remember about the meeting?

GAR: I know we presented demands, we always presented demands. It's more money for students for scholarships, more [Chicano] priests, [Chicano] people in high positions in the Church.

MG: But you felt Manning was more amenable?

GAR: Yes, he was more approachable. He did meet with us. McIntyre, the closest we got was I told you, "call the police, call the police." Manning was approachable.

MG: Then there were the 21 who were arrested. Did you attend some of the trials?

GAR: I did attend some of the trials of course. Oscar represented all 21 of them. At that time we didn't have many attorneys in the community. But there were other attorneys who I think would've been able to be part of the team. I think it would've been a more successful effort. I think it was too much for one attorney to represent 21 people. As students we had no perspective of what a legal defense was like and the responsibilities. Had we had a perspective we would've said Zeta, you need help, it's just not enough, c'mon guy, we better see who else could jump in and be part of a legal defense team and it would've been a bigger circus and then probably more people would've been acquitted.

MG: What do you remember of Acosta's defense and how he approached it and his famous antics?

GAR: He was a very forceful advocate. He was not a traditional attorney. His arguments were not traditional. His approach was not traditional. He was very much of a confrontational individual

MG: Do you think Acosta put up a good defense?

GAR: Well no, I mean there was no way [one] attorney could represent twenty-one defendants effectively. That's the perspective that I have now as an attorney having done cases. I represented Carlos Montes, I don't know if you know about him or his case, but it was an eight week trial, and there were two of us, Steve Sonora and myself, and it was just one individual and we had our hands full. For one attorney to represent twenty-one individuals and to be able to keep track—Oscar was not that organized of a guy. During the trial, the prosecutor brought up the fact that he had not paid his bar dues. I think he was suspended for a short period of time until he paid his dues and was again able to practice law and continue the case. Zeta was more of an organizer, a very strong community advocate, physically he was a strong man. He didn't take shit from nobody. I remember one time we were having a Chicano Law Students California convention and he was a speaker at USC and he said something that made a few people laugh, and that ticked him off completely. And he said "The next motherfucker that laughs I'm going to kick your ass." There was complete silence. Nobody wanted to take Zeta on, he was a big guy.

MG: All of the stuff that he writes in the Cockroach People, is that really Zeta or is that a lot of embellishment?

GAR: There's a lot of embellishment , but I'm glad he wrote it, and he's a good writer. We needed that exposure, in terms of we hardly had anybody who was doing any writing. I'm very pleased that Zeta, he fictionalized the events, but it focused attention on the events just the same. I wish he was still with us, he'd definitely be in a position of leadership, he'd be pushing and not just following. That's what he always was. He was a leader, he was the head of the pack, he deserved to be followed. He ran for sheriff when people wouldn't think of doing that. Yet, it was a very progressive position for him to take.

MG: How much of an impact did the arrest of the 21 have on the group itself, the Católicos, did it affect how it would sustain and go on?

GAR: Definitely, Richard was convicted, he spent three months in jail, he had an injury, he cut his finger because he was washing dishes. After that he had to spend a lot of energy to be admitted to practice law, he was delayed—I was only delayed three months—he was delayed for a year plus. He went through a very lengthy hearing. I was fortunate that I was able to point out that the photograph was doctored. But he was convicted, he was arrested and convicted so he had to appeal the conviction.

MG: One of the last events that Católicos had was later in August, '70, the burning of the baptismal certificates. Were you part of that?

GAR: No. I didn't burn my certificate. I was probably there when they did it, but I didn't even have my certificate to burn, I was born in Mexico.

MG: How central was Richard's leadership in hindsight to Católicos?

GAR: He was the key. He was the spark plug. He was the one who kept things moving. Otherwise I don't know if Católicos Por La Raza would've ever happened. He had a burning desire to get the Church to become more responsive, probably his Catholic education, what he went through, gave him that perspective. There was nobody who felt as strongly as Richard did. Católicos was organized in large part . . . because of Richard.

MG: How central was identifying as Católicos as Catholics to the organization? Was this primarily a political move? Did religion or faith have anything to do with Católicos?

GAR: There were a lot of us who were not very religious and didn't attend church, but we believed in the concept and philosophy of Católicos Por La Raza. Which was basically the Mexican-American community is overwhelmingly Catholic, contributes on a daily basis towards the operation of the Church, we contribute money every Sunday, the ones who leave us and leave their properties to the Church, the great number of Catholics in southern California are Mexicans, are Latin, so the Church needs to be more responsive to those that comprise it, which is us. We didn't have to be very religious or oriented toward the Church to see that concept and believe in it.

MG: Was that where Richard was?

GAR: I think he was more in terms, there was something about it that burned that desire that happened while he was growing up and while he was going through Catholic school, I believe. Also, he was a philosophy major so I think it was that that did something to his psyche that made him such a strong leader, that we really appreciated his thinking. He was also very personable fellow; he had quick wit, so for example, he would tell me, "Oh Miguel, you're beyond charming," to this day I still tell people. I say, "you're beyond charming." I like that about Richard, he was very personable, very joking, I appreciated his humor.

MG: Did you guys address him as Richard or Ricardo?

GAR: I called him Richard because that's how I met him. I think he took on Ricardo when he got involved with the movement.

MG: What can you tell me about the role of women in Católicos? Were women centrally involved? Marginally involved? How would you describe it?

GAR: Women were involved in Católicos Por La Raza the same way they were involved in other organizations in the movement and there were plenty of them. During the Christmas Eve demonstrations, one of the people standing next to me was Alicia Escalante. She was a very strong leader, she was one of the strong leaders who happened to be a woman, but welfare rights organization was one of the strong organizations in the Chicano movement and Alicia was the leader of that. She was a leader not only in her own organization but in the movement in general. Irene Villalobos, her sister was also a strong supporter. Gloria Chávez, she was not so much in the leadership position, but she led by example. She was always there and she was always strong.

MG: Some of these women would participate in Católicos, like coming to meetings and participating in demonstrations?

GAR: Definitely.

MG: So they identified as part of the group too?

GAR: Católicos Por La Raza, you know what, all the organizations at that time, there was the leadership, and then you drew from the movement in general when you needed to have a demonstration. It was a core group who would organize and then you would run the word and people in the movement would support it.

MG: In terms of the core group were there any key women involved?

GAR: I think so. Carmelita Ramírez, who is now an attorney, was part of our core group. There was also Nora Martínez.

MG: Miguel, what else can you tell me about Católicos?

GAR: I think you've pretty much sapped my memory.

MG: Thank you for your assistance.

Part 5

Richard Cruz, circa early 1970s.
Courtesy of Special Collections, Davidson Library, Univ. of Calif. Santa Barbara

Richard Cruz: People's Attorney

TO: Rev. Charles C. Casassa, S.J. , President (Rev. Donald D. Merrifield)
4/23/69
Loyola University[1]

Father Vachon, Dean (Mr. O'Brien)
Loyola Law School

Board of Trustees
Loyola University

FROM:	Richard Cruz	Loyola Law School
	Michael García	Loyola Law School
	Al Sierra	Loyola Law School
	Lee Lucero	Loyola Law School
	Robert Fernández	Loyola Law School
	Joseph Aragón	for USC Law School
	Ralph Ochoa	for UCLA Law School
	Frank Hidalgo	Loyola UMAS

Dear Sirs:

As previously noted in our letter of March 6, 1969,

1. There are approximately 650 students enrolled at Loyola Law School.
2. Of those, less than 1% are Mexican-Americans.
3. There is but one Mexican-American in the third year day class; one Mexican-American in the second year day class.
4. In a county where 12% of the population is of Mexican-American background, the under representation of the Chicano community is on its face discriminatory and an open affront to the one million Mexican-Americans who populate Los Angeles County.
5. The existence of this intolerable situation is especially aggravating in the view of the fact that Loyola University is the only Catholic institution for legal training in Los Angeles County; and by the fact that it is a Jesuit institution which, despite its namesake, has for over 48 years not been responsive to the needs of the poor Mexican-American segment of the population.

[1] Ricardo Cruz/Católicos Por La Raza Papers.

6. UCLA law school has committed itself to enroll 25 Mexican-Americans in its next first-year class; USC law school has recently committed itself to enroll 10 Mexican-Americans and provide financial assistance to them on an as-needed basis.

It was our sincere hope that the letter and our many private discussions would result in what is fair and just, namely

1. That Loyola University School of Law as a matter of official public policy guarantee that the Mexican-American community be adequately and fairly represented in the student body of the Law School.
2. That the guarantee of adequate and fair representation be achieved no later than the beginning of the next academic year.
3. That the guarantee include financial assistance in such amounts as may be needed by entering Chicano students.

The response to our letter, dated March 26, 1969, indicates that the Law School will not guarantee adequate and fair representation until the "financial problem is alleviated." This is a totally unsatisfactory response for the following reasons:

1. It has been the Law School policy for 48 years;
2. It assumes that all Chicanos who apply lack adequate funds;
3. It neglects the fact that, if accepted early enough, a student may be able to make his own financial arrangements;
4. It completely ignores the fact that, unlike USC and UCLA, Loyola Law School has an evening division which allows the most needy students to support themselves through full-time employment;
5. It results in a refusal by many Chicano law school applicants to consider Loyola for legal education.

For these and other reasons, on behalf of the Mexican-American community we are left with no choice but to publicly demand the following:

1. That Loyola Law School commit itself, in concrete terms, to adequate and fair representation of Chicanos in next year's student body;
2. That this commitment be made no later than 2:00 P.M., Thursday, May 1, 1969 ("Law Day").

PEOPLE'S DECLARATION OF APRIL 29, 1972[1]

Richard Cruz

We, the people, on this the 29th day of April, 1972, declare with the voice and one spirit that the courts of the United States:

- Have stolen our land; but the land (La Tierra!) remains ours . . .
- Have treated us like trash; but we are not trash . . .
- Have shown no respect for us; but we remain respectable . . .
- Have separated our families; but our families remain united . . .
- Have treated us like criminals; but our only crime is poverty . . .
- Have humiliated us in public; but we retain our pride . . .
- Have herded us like cattle; but we remain human beings . . .
- Have used impressive legal words; but we remain unimpressed . . .
- Have law schools for the rich; but the poor are excluded . . .
- Have hindered us from organizing; but we will do so anyway . . .
- Have violated the Treaty of Guadalupe Hidalgo; but it shall be revived . . .
- Have denied, not only our civil rights, but also our human rights; but they will be reclaimed . . .
- Have jailed our leaders; but have not broken their spirit . . .
- Have made a mockery of justice; but justice will not be mocked . . .

For these, and for so many other reasons, we the people on this 29th day of April, 1972, in front of a law school that teaches but words, do openly and proudly and courageously declare that the courts are illegal and an affront to the people; we further declare that justice resides within the hearts and minds of the people and shall not remain the unwilling captive of a rich few; finally we declare that from this day forward we the people shall openly and actively commence the campaign for justice. Justice has no price! It belongs to the people! It shall be returned!

[1] Ricardo Cruz/Católicos Por La Raza Papers.

Courtesy of Camilo Cruz

Richard Cruz elected Chair of La Raza Law Students, late 1960s.

THE FIGHT FOR MIGUEL GARCÍA AND RICHARD CRUZ[1]

The purpose and intention of this message is to let the public be aware of Miguel and Richard's plight, thoughts and feelings.

What has happened to these unfortunate individuals is a tremendous INJUSTICE; we hope that those of you reading this will read it with an open mind. So here it is . . .

The victims of Injustice are MIGUEL GARCÍA Y RICHARD CRUZ. Both of them graduated together in June of 1971 from the Loyola Law School in downtown Los Angeles.

Before any person can practice law in this state, one has to first: take and pass the state Bar Examination, and secondly: be approved and determined a "qualified person" by the Committee of Bar Examiners. This committee of Bar Examiners is made up of 15 lawyers, hand-picked by governor [sic] Reagan.

Miguel and Richard have both taken and passed the State Bar Examination on August 1971. But, the Committee of Bar Examiners has denied them their "certification", or rather their authority or license to practice law in California courts. Miguel was finally granted certification, but not until this year, normally it would be soon after passing the Bar Examination. Richard, to this date still has not received his certification.

The Committee of Bar Examiners has given no reason whatsoever for not granting Richard Cruz his certification, all they have revealed is that he is presently under "investigation."

[1] Unpublished and undated document probably in 1972 in Ricardo Cruz/Católicos Por La Raza Papers.

WHAT ARE THEIR REASONS????

Both Miguel y Richard were and are not guilty of any crime, except that they are Chicanos that fight against and within the "system." por nuestra RAZA. Are they dealt with unjustly because they have dedicated so much time and efforts to working and fighting for La Raza?

If these two men had not fought for their RAZA and went the way the MAN wanted them to; they would not have gone through the hassles they are presently going through, or the ones they have already gone through! The Committee of Bar Examiners knows that Miguel and Richard helped and worked with many Chicano organizations and Barrios before they had even graduated from law school. The C.B.E. must also be scared that Miguel y Richard will continue to do the same kind of work, except this time with lawyers degrees and certification. What this means is; we will have some heavy people fighting the MAN in court and defeating him LEGALLY: playing it "his way." They are afraid that we will have too strong a voice in the courts!! THE CHICANO OF TODAY SHOULD NOT LET ANYONE DICTATE AND CONTROL THEIR LIVES especially when it comes to the kind of tactics that the C.B.E. is trying to use against Richard Cruz. As it is we have no political voice; now the MAN is trying to prevent US from acquiring TOO MUCH legal voice!!!

Now, it is up to US (the people), to work together, somehow or other, to get the certification for Richard Cruz.

Richard might only be one person, but surely he can speak for many!

If the Committee of Bar Examiners get away with this, what's to prevent them from doing this to other Chicanos that try to make it as legal attorneys?

If we can win this other struggle, we not only will help these individuals but rather, the entire RAZA; the entire RAZA because Miguel and Ricardo have and will continue to fight por La RAZA

CHICANO LAWYER—ACTIVIST SUBJECTED TO CALIFORNIA STATE BAR HEARING

By Manuel Barrera[1]

During the past three months the State Bar of California has been holding hearings into the so-called moral character of Ricardo Cruz, Chicano Movement Lawyer, who passed his state bar exam last January but still has not been allowed to practice law in California by this organization. This hearing, set up by the State Bar of California and, being conducted by the Committee of Bar Examiners subcommittee hearing officers, has brought out the racism and bureaucratic conformity-like practices characteristic of this organization.

Two issues are at stake in this hearing: (1) Who should determine who should practice law—Lawyers only, or the people in the community who will be affected directly by lawyers' practice? (2) Richard's moral character—characterized by his successful community legal organizing activities, which include Católicos Por La Raza, leading to two misdemeanor charges on Ricardos' person. Will the bias of the Bar members towards Ricardo's community organizing activities be fair?

Ricardo's hearing has set a precedent in the history of the State Bar of California; in that, Ricardo: a bold, honest, and dedicated lawyer has waived his right to hold the Committee hearing on his case in confidence (private). Thus Ricardo has opened his hearing to the public—never before done in California. His

[1] As published in La Raza, vol. 1, no. 10 (Fall, 1973), pp. 22-23 in Ricardo Cruz/Católicos Por La Raza Papers.

reason was to permit the public to see first-hand injustice being committed upon his person and that of future Chicano lawyers who only seek justice for our people.

An idealist in word and deed, Ricardo, graduated in philosophy and law; was born in the barrios of Los Angeles 29 years ago. A Chicano who understands well the discrimination suffered by our people in the United States, he decided to become a movement organizer for La Causa.

Always active in high school as a born leader, he decided to attend college facing financial handicaps. Law was to be a major tool in helping alleviate the problem of our people.

For the last five years, Ricardo has been very instrumental in recruiting Chicanos to go into the field of law. This recruitment was done by his skill in organizing successful groups of individuals sympathetic to the needs of Chicano realities. From a few (seven) statewide Chicano law students in 1967, this number of students has grown to a present 500 plus.

Ricardo realized success by exposing the hypocrisy of law schools—Catholic law schools in particular—who did nothing in the way of recruiting Mexican Americans into that field. When one considers the Los Angeles Archdiocese, the wealthiest (one billion plus, second only to New York; a diocese that was founded by Mexicans; has a membership of over 70% Mexican American make up; has no Mexican Americans in its hierarchy; and whose former Archbishop Cardinal James McIntyre (The Bookie) had the "gall" to call the Mexican American lay membership "Rabble" on Christmas eve of 1969—then it is not difficult to understand why Ricardo picked the Roman Catholic church as a prime example of the exploitation and abuse agent that has used the Chicano and Latinos throughout the Americas.

Perhaps the State Bar of California feels threatened by Ricardo's plan to open free legal service in the barrios so that our people might have some representation before the courts instead of being herded like cattle into prisons to rot and be forgotten forever. Recently, the United States Federal Commission on Civil Rights issued its findings on Justice and the Mexican American in the Southwest. The findings concluded with an affirmative "Mexican Americans never have a fair day in court." Findings in the field of education were also negative in nature.

You should know that in California, thousands of lawyers passed the bar exam like Ricardo—but unlike Ricardo, possibly only he has been dealt this gross injustice of a hearing into his moral character. Minorities, especially community activists, seem to be singled out for shaking the shoddy political boat.

Now we arrive at the hearing secessions that have been going on the past months. The attorney representing the state, and, special interests in the city, have paraded their classic assortment of undercover agents from Los Angeles Sheriffs and the Los Angeles Police departments. Their testimony, trying to discredit Ricardo, is found to be full of holes, and obviously rhetorical. The State Bar

Examiners seem to be interested in two misdemeanor charges (inciting to riot and disturbing a religious ceremony) that Ricardo received as a result of a peaceful protest rally and Christmas Mass celebrated Christmas Eve 1969 by the Catholic poor outside the steps of St. Basil's church (a four million dollar edifice otherwise considered the Fort Knox of the West.) The violence reported by news media was the result of undercover sheriffs officers who were placed inside the church foyer Christmas Eve to make sure no Chicano be let in. At midnight, the law personnel attacked young women and children alike who were entering the church to continue the Christmas service.

Ricardo Cruz served several months in jail for the misdemeanor charges. The fact that he was willing to go to jail for "just" principals to benefit our people, gives further credence to his commitment of struggle for the poor and voiceless.

Letters of recommendation for Ricardo to be accepted to practice law in California have been submitted to the hearing committee. All letters supporting Ricardo are from distinguished community people of California such as: Cruz Reynoso CRLA; Edward R. Roybal, Congressman; Catholic Bishop Juan Arzube; Father Merrifield Loyola President; and, the list continues. Over forty letters were submitted and many of these people have appeared in person to further reinforce Ricardo's excellent moral character. When asked by the hearing officers whether after their having known the specific charges against Ricardo this would change their opinion of him all answered that knowing Ricardo, their support still stood; and added, that, for this, he was better prepared to serve the community from a first hand knowledge.

The community also signed over 4,000 signatures demanding Ricardo be received by the Bar. One should keep in mind that the persecution being delt [sic] Ricardo by the Bar only reinforces heavily the racist attitude by public officials to question the integrity of a Chicano—a practice well known in the Southwest.

These past months have been trying months of inconveniences for Ricardo, his family, and friends. With the very able help of dedicated defense lawyers (Mr. Nate Zahm, American Civil Liberties Union; Mr. Art Goldberg, National Lawyers Guild; and Mr. Antonio Rodríguez, Mexican-American Legal Defense Fund) the hearings have brought to light the gross paternalistic attitude of the State Bar of California.

The time has come for the public to have its say in who will defend the people. Lawyers should not totally be judges in deciding who may practice law in California. Organizational dogma capitalizes on selfishness, monopolizes and passes judgment leaving the public subservient to the bars every wish. Housecleaning is in order for the State Bar of California.

The people of California deserve an honest lawyer like Ricardo Cruz—not Heresy Trials that make a mockery of justice.

The State Bar of California would be serving the public better were it to hold necessary public hearings into the questionable conduct of one if its members such as Superior Court Judge Gerald Chargin (San Jose, California) and his disgraceful racist attitude towards California Mexicans, for example.

ADMINISTRATION OF JUSTICE?

By Richard Cruz and Miguel García[1]

To: State Bar of California and the Committee of Bar Examiners

Gentlemen,

We Miguel García and Richard Cruz took and passed the California Bar Examination (which ordinarily entitles one to practice law) in August of 1971. However, as you know, Richard has not been certified to practice law because he is being "investigated" by your Committee of Bar Examiners at the present time. And Miguel, who was also under "investigation", was not certified to practice law until February 18, 1972.

The purpose of this letter is to make out [sic] thoughts & feelings clear to not only you, but to the public at large. It is an "open" letter because we have nothing to hide. Indeed, we are anxious for the entire community to know what is happening regarding our certification status.

Since you have seen fit to investigate us, much of what we tell you is not new. You know, for instance, that we both attended Loyola Law School in downtown Los Angeles, and graduated together in June of 1971. You also know that Miguel was the Chapter Chairman at Loyola of La Raza Law Students Association and that Richard was statewide chairman of the same organization. Presently, we are part of an organization called Abogados de Aztlán (Lawyers of Aztlán), which is a group of Chicano lawyers and law students dedicated to the creation of a People's Law Office for barrio residents. These things you gentlemen know.

[1] As published in La Raza, vol. 1, no. 8 (April, 1972), pp. 12-13 in Ricardo Cruz/Católicos Por La Raza Papers.

What you don't know is that much as you have studies [sic] law students, we—Miguel and Richard—have studied lawyers and the Bar Association itself since we entered law school. And we have many questions to ask of you lawyers which we hope you will also answer openly, as we have answered yours.

Our first question is quite simple. When we began studying law in 1968 we were the only Chicanos in the school. In fact, we were the only poor persons in law school. And there were several hundred (at least 900) law students enrolled. That was at Loyola law school. At the University of Southern California law school that year there was not one single Chicano law student. At the University of California Los Angeles there were maybe five (all of whom, by the way, are presently members of Abogados de Aztlán). So of the approximately 3,000 students enrolled in the three accredited law schools of Los Angeles, about seven were Chicanos when we began studying law. These absurd statistics despite the fact that over a million Chicanos call Los Angeles their home. Our questions, then: If the Committee of Bar Examiners is so zealous in its study of law students and their activities, did it not know that Mexican-Americans were grossly underrepresented in the law schools of California and in the legal profession in general? And if it knew, then why didn't it act? Or at least, perhaps, conduct an investigation as to "possible" racism in the law schools? Is not the Bar Association interested in all peoples participating in the process called the "Administration of Justice?" We will assume you are, of course. So maybe the problem was merely one of lack of communication. Miguel and Richard and the other Chicano law students, you will be glad to know, went ahead anyway. And we are happy to report that after a sustained and oftentimes bitter struggle, there are approximately 400 Chicano law students statewide who call La Raza Law Students Association "theirs". So, let bygones be bygones—we should have notified you of the problem. Nonetheless, would you please answer the questions?

Our next area of inquiry relates specifically to the reasons you have for not presently allowing Richard to practice law, and for not allowing Miguel to practice law for such a long time after he passed the Bar Examination. Essentially, as we understand it, a law student who passes the bar is eligible to practice law unless for some reason, he is considered "unqualified" by the Committee of Bar Examiners. Now Miguel and Richard have not been told that we are "unqualified" or otherwise not fit to practice law. We have merely been told that we are "under investigation." Thus—to use words lawyers like to use—is our status "pending?" That is question one under this subjection of inquiry we shall—to continue our use of lawyerlike words—label "What Reasons Does the State Have For Not Letting Richard Practice Law and For Not Allowing Miguel to Practice Until February of

1972." It's not that we have any particular objections to "pending" around for a while. After all, as most Chicanos—indeed most poor people in this society—we have become quite used to a "pending" status. Whether it be awaiting trial, or the landlord, or the police, or the immigration officials.

Indeed, our people even have a word—"pendejadas"—to describe our present predicament! The "pendejo" is the man who creates the "pending" status. In this particular matter, Miguel and Richard are the "pendejees" (to continue our use of lawyerlike words). But, and we ask this in all sincerity, tell us clearly if we are not "qualified" to practice law in the barrios of East Los Angeles. Don't tell us merely that we are under "investigation". Because we have no longer realized that our commitment to the poor and oppressed and victims of injustice and racism will mean that the rest of our lives will be "under investigation." Nothing new! What are the charges? Will there be an open hearing? When? And where? Can the public attend? Can the press? Please answer these questions. And answer them as honestly and clearly as we are asking them. After all, as the men who administer and regulate lawyers, and the legal profession in general, are not you public servants?

Also, we understand that the Committee of Bar Examiners is especially interested in our activities in the barrios. Well, quite frankly, we are proud of them. And we will list the organizations we are a part of as best we can remember:

Miguel García:

1. SALUD (Chicano social workers who did their best to straighten out the bureaucratic mess engulfing and preventing efficient services to the poor. Miguel was a co-founder.)
2. Latin Gents (a barrio social club sponsored by Judge Leopoldo Sánchez. Be sure and check with him—if you haven' t already.)
3. Congress of Mexican-American Unity (CMAU) (This organization was a means of uniting Raza throughout Los Angeles County).
4. Católicos Por La Raza (This was a barrio organization comprised of students, workers, priests, and nuns who actively demonstrated that the Catholic Church failed to meet the needs of barrio residents).
5. La Raza Law Students Association.
6. Abogados de Aztlán.
7. Mexican-American Legal Defense and Education Fund. (A Ford Foundation—founded legal services program—check with the Ford Foundation for details, or with Mario Obledo, the program Director, whose phone number is (415) 626-6196).

8. Miguel is also a member of a "blue-ribbon" committee in Los Angeles conducting hearings on police-community relations. (Ed Davis, Chief of Police for Los Angeles, is also a committee member; [as] is Peter Pitchess, Los Angeles County Sheriff. We don't have their phone numbers, but perhaps you gentlemen do).

That's about it for Miguel. Except we should add a little bit about his personal history. He was born in Zacohalco de Torres, Jalisco, Mexico. His blood is as Mexican as it can be. He is Chicano by virtue of the historical accident called "la lina"—the "border". He came to the United States in 1954 and has resided here ever since. And, by the way, he is part of the familia García which to this time has borrowed, scrapped and struggled to see him through law school. His present indebtedness, because of law school, is approximately $6,200.00. Did your investigation include this statistic?

As to Richard:

1. La Raza Magazine (A barrio publication in East Los Angeles dedicated to tell the truth to barrio residents. The "regular" news media has always distorted the facts so the barrio cannot rely on it. Phone number—(213) 261-0128).
2. Congress of Mexican-American Unity.
3. Católicos Por La Raza.
4. La Raza Law Students Association.
5. Abogados de Aztlán.
6. Reggie-Poverty Law Fellowship (Richard is presently assigned to and working out of the East Los Angeles Legal Aid Office, 5528 Whittier Boulevard, L.A. Phone 266-6550.)
7. Trinidad Iglesias Defense Committtee (Trini is on trial in Norwalk Superior Court, Dept. "N". The attorney of record is Ben Margolis, phone 380-1900.)
8. Justicia O . . . ! (A bilingual newspaper describing the court process and telling barrio residents of their legal rights. Distributed—free—by Chicano law students throughout the barrio. P.O. Box 20568, L.A. Calif.).

As to Richard's personal history, he was born in Los Angeles. His father, Don Ramón Cruz Magallanes, is from Zacatecas, Zacatecas, Mexico. His mother, Celia Durán Cruz, is from Arizona but her parents at one time resided in Chihuahua, Mexico. So, as you can see, Richard is also part of the family of peoples called Mejicanos! Present indebtedness of the Cruz family for Richard's legal education: $5700.00. Did your investigation include this statistic?

Alright, so that's what Miguel and Richard have been up to while we were in law school. As we say, we're proud of our inclusion in our people's struggle for self-determination. Perhaps we should not have been so active while attending law school. Nonetheless, and we're not sure if you will understand this, but our love for our people left us with no choice. Perhaps, you may think, we are fools for having gotten so involved. It certainly would have been much easier to go through law school like the majority—a cocktail party here, a seminar on "social issues and the law" there. And a lot of study in between. But, does the love men show for their people and for JUSTICE constitute a reason to disqualify them from practicing law? Please let us know.

This leads us to our next line of inquiry. What standards are used in determining who is qualified to practice law? Miguel and Richard for example, have shown an interest in their community, its problems and the resolution of those problems. Ironically, these are the very reasons you have used to investigate us! Our questions, then, are these: Should not lawyers serve not only JUSTICE, but also the people who reside in the community in which the lawyers intend to practice? Have not Miguel and Richard demonstrated a concern for JUSTICE and for the people in the barrios in which they live and in which they intend to practice law? So what's the problem? Does JUSTICE cost? How much? Why has the State Bar or Committee of Bar Examiners never studied or "investigated" the lawyers of all communities who habitually charge hundreds of dollars to plead people guilty (which the client could have done for free!)? And why have the above state organizations never seen fit to investigate the lawyers themselves—their concern for the community in which they practice and their concern for JUSTICE? Please answer these questions. And in doing so, keep in mind that you have seen fit to question Miguel and Richard's "qualifications" to practice law despite their involvement in the community and concern for JUSTICE.

We can go on asking a lot of questions. And in fact, we will. But let's reconsider for a moment the nature of the problem. The State Bar of California is the official state agency for lawyers. It is comprised solely of lawyers yet one of its functions, oddly enough, is to make sure that lawyers serve the people. Now the lawyers have chosen a Board of Bar Governors from among themselves. This Board is compromised of 15 men and is supposed to run the State Bar. The Board has then itself selected another group of lawyers, called the Committee of Bar Examiners, which is supposed to screen applicants and make sure they are "qualified" to practice law. What we want to know is why, if lawyers are supposed to serve the people, the people themselves are not allowed to be members of the Board of Bar

Governors, or of the Committee of Bar Examiners? We also want to know if the Committee of Bar Examiners represent the people in the barrio? We are prepared to present to the Bar or Committee a lot of Chicanos who have been very unhappy with lawyers. In fact, we are anxious to show that we are not joking when we say that we are part of the people and their struggle. Have you men ever been in the barrios of East Los Angeles? But we want you tell our people that you are speaking for them when you don't let Richard practice law, or have decided that Miguel could not practice law, or have decided that Miguel could not practice law for a long time after he passed his examinations.

Enough for now. We anxiously await your reply.

Miguel García
Richard Cruz

RICARDO CRUZ: PEOPLE'S LAWYER[1]

April 25, 1973

Board of Governors
State Bar of California
1230 West Third Street
Los Angeles, California

Open Letter

Gentlemen,

I address you as a Chicano and as a member of the State Bar of California. I wish to remind you gentlemen that injustice in the barrios and other poor areas of Los Angeles are tremendous. As you undoubtedly know, governmental and private documentation and research make this fact beyond dispute. Landlords, police, merchants and yes, lawyers, daily exploit or abuse the poor. Indeed, it is a common complaint of a complete radical and cultural cross-section of peoples in this city and throughout that people in power have become arrogant and distainful [sic] of the common people. The barrios, compromised of millions of Mexican and Chicano people feel these injustices, these exploitations and abuses as much if not more than any segment of the general population.

For these reasons I write to you gentlemen. I realize that your power is limited. On the other hand, as lawyers and as Governors of the State Bar of California you do have tremendous power which can be used for the betterment of Chicanos and other poor peoples. Clearly, it seems to me, the State Bar of California does have a tremendous responsibility to serve all people in their quest for justice. My sincere request, therefore, as a fellow lawyer and a member of the State Bar, is that

[1] In Ricardo Cruz/Católicos Por La Raza Papers.

you turn the full power and influence of the State Bar of California toward the cause of social justice as it relates to Chicano and all poor peoples in Los Angeles and elsewhere in the State of California.

Specifically I urge you to turn your full attention to two pressing problems:

1. Bar Examination: The poor people of this city are in desperate need of conscientious Chicano, Black, Indian, Asian, women and other minority lawyers. A despicable situation presently exists in that literally dozens of such law school graduates are presently not able to practice law because they have not passed the California Bar Examination. In my opinion, the Bar Examination is therefore doing a grave disservice and injustice to the minority peoples of this State because it acts to prevent otherwise qualified and property trained people to assist their communities by the practice of law. To my knowledge the Bar Examination has not been justified of [or] validated or otherwise proven to be of merit as compared to the severe and detrimental effect it is having on the administration of justice in Los Angeles. I request, therefore, that you take immediate action toward either the elimination of the Bar Examination or establishment of acceptable alternatives. I needn't remind you that Mr. Janofsky, past president of the State Bar, has publicly recognized the existence of a problem in this regard. Action is needed and needed now. Please let me know what action will be immediately taken by the State Bar toward solution of this problem.
2. Character Hearings: As you may know I have previously not been allowed to practice law because my moral character has been deemed questionable by the State Bar (the Committee of Bar Examiners). I passed the Bar in August of 1971. I must emphatically make you gentlemen realize that I am not unique and that literally dozens of presently Black, Chicano and other minority law students have been arrested or convicted for either their political beliefs while participating in demonstrations or have found themselves under arrest because of the mere fact that they have grown up, lived and worked within communities where to not be arrested may very well be the exception. My complaint in this regard is that very possibly, to take my case as an example, moral fitness hearings can deprive the minority communities of conscientious and dedicated lawyers. It is my urgent request that you gentlemen do all in your power to see to it that law students from poor communities who have suffered arrests and convictions because they grew up in the barrios and ghettos or because of their political beliefs do not be singled out for "character" scrutiny. I emphatically declare that arrests alone do not in any way indicate a lack of commitment toward social justice or lack of ability to practice

law. Please let me know what policy will be adhered to by the State Bar as it relates to "moral fitness" hearings of Chicanos, Blacks, Asians and Indians who have suffered arrests or convictions.

People need lawyers more than ever. As a Chicano and a member of the State Bar I do request that you gentlemen take immediate action on Bar Hearings and the Examination itself as they relate to depriving people of legal counsel. I take this communication very seriously and request reply as soon as is practicable.

Sinceramente,
Richard V. Cruz
Attorney at Law

Photo by Ray Cruz. Used with Permission.

Richard Cruz, USC Law Day, March 13, 1972.

ABOGADOS DE AZTLÁN[1]

[Attorneys of Aztlán]
by Richard Cruz

A radical discussion of emerging concepts as the Chicano and other poor people's lawyers deal with the administration of "Justice" in Los Angeles and elsewhere.

PART ONE: THE CHICANO LAWYER HIMSELF . . . WHAT SHOULD HE DO?

The Chicano finds himself in need of a lawyer. Maybe he has been placed under arrest, or is being evicted or otherwise is within the grip of court action. Assuming, as is hardly ever the case, that the barrio resident is able to secure competent counsel, he will be eager, indeed anxious, to delineate the nature of the problem to the lawyer. He will have a very clear idea of why he has been arrested, whether he is guilty, why the landlord is evicting him—in short the barrio Chicano will very intelligently be able to understand the legal problem, the facts themselves. "I've been taken, robbed, by the auto dealer," may be his presentation of the case to the lawyer. Or he may tell the lawyer: "The police unlawfully arrested me because I am demonstrating and they don't want me to speak out about injustices . . . "

The barrio resident, then, has not only fully assessed his problem by the time he gets to the lawyer, but more importantly he is ready, willing and able to participate in the solution of the problem. After all, it is the Chicano himself who finds himself confronted with a problem. It is the Chicano as complainnant [sic] or defendant who has the greatest interest in the solution of the problem and, therefore, the greatest desire to participate in the solution.

But he cannot participate. The minute he relates the facts to the lawyer his participation ceases. The dynamics of this are pretty obvious and can be delineated. First of all, it must be understood that the legal complex has been designed

[1] Ricardo Cruz/Católicos Por La Raza Papers.

to exclude the people from its inner workings and machinations. And this grand exclusion is hardly accidental. The people, in a very real sense, are implicitly told that the lawyer's office is as far as they can go insofar as their active participation. Even if a trial or other formal hearings take place, the Chicano or other client is relegated to the status of observer whose presence or non-presence is of little consequence.[2]

Aogados De Aztlán

Probably, for example, the majority of Chicanos who have had the misfortune to experience the legal process have found themselves saying as few as five, maybe 20 words, throughout the entire courtroom proceeding. A series of lawyer-prompted, pre-determined "yes" or "no's" is the extent of most client's [sic] involvement in the determination of their fate. It must be emphasized, furthermore, that while non-participation may be a common experience to all peoples, certainly the Spanish-speaking or bilingual Chicano doubly feels the reality of insignificance in the English-speaking proceedings.

Having stayed a bit, let's get back to the assertion that non-participation is not mere historical accident—but is instead part of a design to ensure that Raza and other poor peoples have no say in the administration of justice. This contention is well documented and stems from both the economic philosophy of the courts and the deeply ingrained racism in the courts.[3] The economics of it is that the courts are the protectors of the status quo, the entrenched interests and the rich class of people. Thus, by seeing to it that poor people cannot follow their case beyond the lawyer's office, the rich individuals and corporations have a guarantee—promoted and defended through the courts, law schools, legislative bodies and numerous Bar associations—that only men of similar economic standing and orientation can control or direct the legal process. A recent case in the East Los Angeles barrios will demonstrate how this works.

The case is called "Los Tres del Barrio" by residents of the barrio. It involved three young men, Alberto Ortíz, Juan Fernández, and Rodrigo "Rudy" Sánchez. The

[2] Its almost like a Kafkian novel wherein the client hears his name spoken, his problem discussed and his very guilt or innocence bandied about - yet the actors in the neat little drama never once concede to his presence, let alone his very existence as a concerned human being.

[3] The reader is especially urged to read two recent paperbacks to get a "from-the-horses-mouth" view from radical lawyers themselves as to the racist and economic principles guiding the courts and lawyerism in general: (1) Law Against the People, ed. Robert Lefcourt, 1971, Vintage Books; and (2) Radical Lawyers, ed. Jonathan Black, 1971, Avon Books.

three had been very active in the Pico Gardens Housing Projects of Los Angeles. Their main thrust was to rid the immediate vicinity of drugs—mostly "colorados" (reds) and "blancas" (whites). They were working voluntarily out of the Casa de Carnalismo (House of Brotherhood) which is a Chicano center for activities and residents of the Housing Projects. The incident and resulting court activity is well described by La Raza Magazine, excerpts of which are as follows:

> "One day in July, 1971, Rodolfo Sánchez got a telephone call from a man called 'Bobby' who told him that he was interested in buying heroin. Rodolfo saw the opportunity to know another person involved with drugs. He invited Juan Fernández and Alberto Ortíz who went armed because of the danger involved when talking to a person whose interest is in heroin and big money. Different the guy pushing 'reds' or pills, he is selling death cheap to make a living. Rodolfo and 'Bobby' decided to go to another place to make the supposed transaction followed from a distance by Alberto and Juan. Rodolfo asked the man if he was using. "Bobby" answered that he did not. Rodolfo realized the man was a drug dealer, one of those who destroy lives.
>
> "It should be known here that Rodolfo Sánchez had been a drug addict who was in prison for a number of years because of his addiction. The fact that a younger brother of Rudy's died of an overdose of drugs had a tremendous impact on this man. When he was in prison Rodolfo analized [sic] his life realizing that his people are living mindless by the pills and drugs setting his goals to try to stop the flow of drugs in the barrio.
>
> "Alberto and Juan approached the other two men and Juan told 'Bobby': 'give me your money and don't come back to our barrio to score heroin, if you come back something bad is going to happen to you.' Bobby said: 'looks like you mean business.' Bobby made a move to get off his motorcycle at the same time putting his hand to his waist making an attempt to go for his gun. Juan surprised by Bobby's move, jumped back took his own gun and fired. Almost instantly another shot was fired and Bobby fell to the ground. Hours later these three Chicanos were arrested and accused of shooting a federal narcotics agent and of robbing monies trusted to a 'public servant' to deal with heroin. This agent Roberto 'Bobby' Canales was sacrificed (used) by his superiors and we'll tell how come and why this agent is paralized [sic] from the waist because of a gun shot. Some of the highlights on the administration of 'justice.'
>
> "The prosecution has used a law, the Jessie James Act, a law made to protect postal carriers in the 1800s which carries a sentence of 25 years for that

charge alone. A day before the trial October 18, 1971, three agents went into the home of some members of Carnalismo to try to terrorize these witnesses. A report in which it is established that even though police personnel and equipment have been increased police have failed to stop the increase in drug traffic. People also refuse to report drug peddlers because of the danger involved when dealing with the police.

"Defence [sic] lawyers were refused to use the term Chicano in the trial. A law graduate working as an investigator for the defense caught the court interpreter translating testimony in a favorable manner to the prosecution. This investigator (a Chicano) was threatened with contempt by the judge for interfering with court proceedings. An affidavit signed by a police informer who since 1968 was forced to be an agent informer for the Treasury Department, Bureau of Narcotics. His duty, to infiltrate Chicano organizations and inform of drug activities among other things. Judge Lydick stated he did not believe agent Frank Martínez was a police informer, refusing Frank Martínez as a witness for the defense.

"This informer reported to his supervisors days and weeks (that the members of the Casa) were involved in an anti-drug campaign, his supervisors told the informer this was a lie and that the government had intentions of closing La Casa de Carnalismo by any means necessary.

"Here we establish without doubt how the superiors of agent Canales discriminated when it comes to sacrificing their agents. Knowing that Carnalismo organizers were stopping drugs and pushers in the barrio, sometimes in a forceful manner, Canales' superiors did not hesitate to use Canales to entrap Los Tres del Barrio. Why didn't they use an anglo agent?

"Composition of the jury, one gringo of Mexican descent, one house negro and ten anglos. A reality that Mexican people have never been represented in the judicial system, the policemen are anglos, the judges are anglo and the jury has always been made up of anglo people, mostly middle class.

"The judge said in the trial that us Chicanos are white and were represented in the jury. More than 25 witnesses who tried to testify for the defense were excluded, among them a college professor. An expert in police-community relations was also refused as a witness.

"Los Tres del Barrio were found guilty of conspiracy, shooting a federal agent and robbing government money.

> "To what point may the police be used to oppress people.
>
> "Must a race defend themselves from oppression, imprisonment and genocide?"[4]

The economic bias of the courts—their class consciousness and allegiance to the status quo—is well demonstrated in the case of Los Tres. Had there been Chicanos of political awareness in the office of District Attorney there might well have been indictments sought against not only the various government agencies that nurture the very possibility of gunplay, but—even more importantly—against the various procedures of drugs who with almost total freedom are able to filter their products into the barrios. Only the most naïve still believe, with any sincerity at least, that the government is truly attacking the "drug problem." All the government is attacking, through its Busches and Hoovers and Youngers, is the street level of drug traffic. They are attacking the petty victims of narcotics who, unknowingly, are political fodder for the aforementioned types of men who, especially at election time, decide it is time for a "crackdown on drugs" and conveniently see to it that the L.A. Times and other local media carry this important "news". Had the trial jury, not to mention the federal Grand Jury, been comprised of even two Chicanos from the barrio, certainly these two would have paid close attention to the overall dynamics of the case. And what about the exclusion of the evidence as to the overall government intent and manipulation of the situation? Would a Chicano from the barrio—assuming the law school and collegiate experience had not thoroughly brainwashed and distorted his human, political and economic awareness—have systematically decided as judge that the excluded evidence and testimony was "irrelevant?" Finally, if the courts would truly protect and encourage those like Los Tres who seek the elimination of drugs, there would be no need for the myriad of "law enforcement" officers, etc., whose very livelihood depends on the existence of a "drug problem." This factor points out the courts' role in seeing to it that the warped and corporate—controlled economy be not brought to the forefront by the literally hundreds of thousands of men who would otherwise be unemployed and stirring if it weren't for the courts and government-nurtured "drug problem."

The case of Los Tres, then, is only one of a multitude of cases involving Chicanos that stands for the proposition that not only are the courts the handmaidens of the rich and established, but are equally, in furtherance of the economic objectives, hell bent on the systematic exclusion of Raza and other poor peoples from the legal process itself.

[4] La Raza Magazine, Vol. 1, no. 7, (Jan, 1972).

This exclusion is also a function of racism. For not only are the judges, DAs, PDs, POs, and other lesser court bureaucrats part of the economic class they intuitively must protect, but they are at least institutional racist as well. "How the hell can these Mexican people—these Chicanos—have any part in our cherished and tradition-wrought system of jurisprudence?" "After all," the middle-class or rich lawyer or judge would continue to ponder, "we civilized these people and taught them the richness of common-law thought and process!" Such thoughts, despite the grand protestations of liberality and intellectualism, constitute the attitude of the overwhelming majority of those who control the administration of justice in Los Angeles and throughout Aztlán.

And so into this milieu of racism, economic bias and resultant exclusion of Raza from the process of law itself steps the recently-graduated Chicano lawyer. What should he do? How is he to help his people?

At the outset the Chicano lawyer or law student should assess and understand the nature of the various employment opportunities available to him upon graduation. Roughly and ridiculously described as "law reform" or "service" group, the opportunities are entitled (in Los Angeles, at least): Legal Aid Societies, Western Center on Law and Poverty, Mexican-American Legal Defense and Education Fund, Model Cities Program ("Center for Law and Justice"), the OEO-financed Reggie Fellowship for "poverty law", and, statewide, the California Rural Legal Assistance. Such lawyer groups have the immediate commonality of being funded by various branches of the United States government or by the Ford Foundation (MALDEF). They also constitute what can be termed the "keep-busy-like-you've-never-been-before" centers with the subtle goal being to ensure that the lawyer or law student never has time nor the incentive nor the encouragement to assess the legal system itself. In other words, the government has—with all its expertise and centuries-wrought experience—designed the various programs to keep the Chicano enthralled with the myth that he is thinking or being creative or making change. When in reality the hooked Chicano is merely the living perpetuation of the court process itself. Under the ruse of "law reform" and "service" to the people, the well-meaning Chicano lawyer becomes part and parcel of the process of systematic exclusion of the people themselves from the administration of justice. And, especially if the particular program is well administered, the young lawyer has never even realized that he has become a puppet in the racist and class-conscious overall court system. The lawyer is led to believe that he is "making change" in the law. But because he has never—from his entering law school to acceptance of employment—been challenged to radically assess his role, i.e., to see the courts and legal process in the light of their pre-determined racist and economic function, he fails to realize that change in the law is an absolute impossibility, from within at least.

One real change in the law, for instance, that the OEO—or Ford-controlled man at most gives lip service to, is the previously- described revolutionary process itself of having the people, the masses, have total participation in the solution of problems. This type of change is real change. And real change is the complete antithesis to government-sponsored and controlled "service" and "reform" programs.

Law school was, of course, no help in preparing the Chicano lawyer-to-be to think and assess from a truly objective and external viewpoint. To think other than from within the legal structure. The dehumanizing process, well-nurtured already by the college experience, is accelerated in law school. The law student is daily told to "think like a lawyer."[5] He is made to feel like an elite human being who only is able to assess social and legal problems and see them through to resolution.[6] The emerging Chicano lawyer, then, finds himself in a spiritual dilemma if and when he first confronts the total dynamics of lawyerism from a radical perspective. To be human being is to renounce himself as lawyer. To be a lawyer is to renounce himself as human being. Yet, primordially at least,[7] he understands that the questions he is beginning to ask can only be answered by the human being as human being. Certainly the concept of justice—one of the noblest and most eternal of mankind—cannot be understood, in a way that makes a difference to the poor and oppressed at least, by only an elite handfull of men who, by virtue of distorted egos and warped education, consider themselves the keepers of the keys. And equally certain is the fact that to begin the systematic attack on the rigidly—enforced economics and racism of the courts—to make real change in other words—demands that one be much more than mere lawyer!

The fact of the matter, then, is that the people don't need more lawyers, even more Chicano lawyers. They need men and women who unfailingly and without hesitation are willing and able to (1) assess and expose the present legal process in its complex and systematic exploitation and exclusion of the masses; and (2) suggest—in both thought (writings, e.g. Justicia O . . . ! and orally) and deed (e.g., People's Law Offices, "issue" cases taken to the people themselves around which they can organize, and life style)—viable and human, i.e., radical and revolutionary, alternatives to the status quo. The rest, of course, is up to the people.

[5] Which is really not to think at all!

[6] Unlike most Chicanos in law school, this ego-building technique is especially effective in Chicanos who - like almost all Raza - have experienced deep psychic emasculation in this racist and oppressive society. "Lawyerism", and its attendant opportunity to achieve notoriety and a sense of pride - especially in the field of criminal law—is attractive because of its ego-inflating propensities. "Give some Chicano lawyers their first big case and press conference," a Chicana law student said, "and he is long gone to not only himself, but to his people." [sic]

[7] En los huevos!

But to the Chicano lawyer himself goes the initial burden of nurturing and creating the conditions and climate within the revolutionary conscious of the people can develop and thrive. The Chicano lawyer, especially as a member of Abogados de Aztlán, will have done his job if he can see to fruition the above-delineated goals. He will have defined THE PLAN, THE GRAND SCHEME which for centuries has been used to systematically steal both the lands and minds of our Raza. In short, the Chicano lawyer will have come back home to his people. He will have begun the process of destroying (forever?) the contemporary myth called the administration of "justice" in the United States. The process, once begun, will perhaps enable the Abogado de Aztlán to someday soon unite in voice and spirit and intellect in declaring:

> "When we swore to justice, we were sincere; and it was our very sincerity which led us to realize that she is indeed blind and can see neither government nor flag; so our oath and allegiance did not blind us to any government—least of all that which our people are presently incarcerated.
>
> "The lawyers of Aztlán have found that justice is more than just a lady. Es una mujer—she is a woman. And as all women, she cannot be captured, nor bound, nor imprisoned—only loved. She finds no love under a flag of red, white and blue. Perhaps there is no justice to be found under any flag!
>
> "So our allegiance is to justice. Not to a judge or court or government. Our people are our only government. They are our only flag. They are our only border. The United States be damned . . . "

Abogados de Aztlán . . .
C/S

With humility yet pride, carnales
Respectfully submitted,

Richard Cruz,
Abogados de Aztlán
January 27, 1972

SOME NOVEL CONCEPTS: LAWYERS & SOCIAL CHANGE[1]

Richard Cruz
Chairman, Abogados de Aztlán

For Members of Abogados de Aztlán

As we continue to progress from lawyers as individuals to a collective of lawyers on the threshold of actual experimentation in the field of social change, it is most beneficial, I feel, that we zero in on specific areas of concern so that we firmly understand the difference between critical analyses which leads to action and romantic generalizations which lead nowhere. We do as little of both right now and the resultant confusion leads us to frustration.

In this paper I want to analyze, as best I can, the requirement that each and every one of our activities as lawyers must in some way reflect a goal. What I am assessing, in other words, is the process itself that must be mastered so that when we choose cases it is not by accident, but by design; when we say "my" case is "relevant" we know what we mean; and when asked or pressured by camaradas or associates to handle "their" case, we can say yes or no with firm assurance that we are making the right decision. Presently we are found with but vague and romantic conceptions and notions as we begin to deal with these problem areas.

In the first place we must understand, as most of us do already, that the goal is social change. This is the foundation, the absolute if you will, upon which our many levels of choices and dilemmas must be resolved. A concrete example will help make my point clear. Presently several of our members—of Abogados de Aztlán

[1] In Ricardo Cruz/Católicos Por La Raza Papers.

that is—are pursuing an appeal for Los Tres del Barrio. Juan, Beto, and Rudy, all from Cuatro Flats in East Los Angeles, comprise Los Tres and have been convicted and presently are doing federal time for their role in the shooting of a "narc" in the barrio. The three men actually had been actively engaged in street-level efforts to keep hard drugs out of the barrio. In any event, this involvement on our part more or less "happened" in that traditional customs and habits, traditional peer pressure and barrio influence, and traditional and human respect for the activities and persons of Los Tres—and of course other—less defined influences—motivated us to get involved in this time-consuming litigation. The essence of our involvement, however, was neither critically defined nor strategically understood from the perspective of social change. In retrospect, as will be seen, there may have been any given number of reasons related to social change why the appeal should indeed have been undertaken. But my point is simply that we do not firmly control our undertaking from the beginning. And this we must do.

Back to Los Tres. And let's proceed to initiate what we'll call a socially comprehensive exercise in assessing the merits of our involvement. The goal being social change, then of necessity our first question must always be: What, if any, social change is involved in the undertaking of this case? Our second question, then, is naturally (assuming social change is involved): Is the degree of social change of such quantity that it should be undertaken? The third question which we might very well ask as members of a collective group, is: Does the matter of social change attendant to this case blend with and advance the level and area of social concern presently defined as priorities by the overall collective?

Let's proceed to answer these questions, however awkwardly, remembering that the purpose of this paper is not to derive answers but to introduce an intellectual process—a framework or mode—which is a prerequisite to the creation of a functional and successful "law office" dedicated to social change.

(1) What, if any, social change is involved in the undertaking by our members in the appeal of Los Tres del Barrio?

The very asking of this question forces us to ponder our definition of social change. What <u>is</u> social change? We must for the first time perhaps, by the very act of posing the question, not only admit that we probably don't know what social change is, but, furthermore begin to come to terms with this awareness. This phenomenon is essentially us working from reverse in that for the first time do we really take stock and begin to criticize and assess our work. We return to our cases for the answers which should have been taken care of before we committed ourselves so thoroughly to these cases. By looking at Los Tres, for example, in an analytical way for the first time, I am able to see that its effect on social change is the freeing of Juan, Beto and Rudy—who as men of action and revolutionary fervor, are catalysts and movers. These men are needed, and needed very badly. Not only does the barrio need them, but we need them. This, in my opinion, is the only justification, of substance that is, that calls for our involvement in the case of Los Tres as lawyers committed to social change. It may seem obvious and it may actually appear "that we knew that all along." But the beneficial aspect of this critical questioning—this exercise—is that we clearly come to grips with the relative importance of our involvement, not in an intuitive and fuzzy way, but in a conscious, controllable and well-defined way. We are then better able to look at our other cases and activities, and also more prepared to look at each others' activities. We can start to honestly come to grips with our effect, if any, on society. "Why do we need this exercise?" you might ask. Because a present tragedy among us is that as long as our members delude themselves into thinking that their legal activities are effecting social change—as some are—or, worse yet, as long as members have not even bothered to ask if their legal activity is purposeful and effective—as other members continue to do—then our hopes and aspirations for dynamic and vital collective of Chicano and Chicana lawyers are doomed to defeat. So not only must we be able to ask this question, but we must also be honest and sincere enough to accept the answers. For, in reality, the majority of our involvements don't really have much substance vis a vis social change. They really don't make a difference.

Let's proceed to the second question, however, namely:

(2) How much change is effected by this case? Should we do it? The asking and answering of this question of necessity assumes standards, i.e., that we have developed a range of values and priorities with which we can compare. For example: the value of welfare cases (and for that matter, the value of most cases lumped under the "legal aid syndrome"), from the viewpoint of their relationship to social change, is very minimal compared to the value of freeing dynamic men from imprisonment. While on the other hand, the value of a school case—fully exploited by our members in terms of exposing schools and having students mobilize—may indeed outweigh both other cases. It's relative. Yet we must begin to evaluate cases toward the goal of collectively making ourselves pick and choose. (In short, we must begin to realize that a selectivity, and the discipline to become selective, must be nurtured. Otherwise we spin our wheels and the so-called collective becomes the same old individualistic and tension-ridden association). We must be able to ask whether we should do a case and then be able to follow through and

say yes or no. "How much social change can come about by the case called Los Tres?" "Enough," we will hopefully say, "to require (or not require, for that matter) my involvement." "The school case," we might continue, "because it potentially can involve hundreds of students and expose the courts as the anti-educational monsters which they are, is therefore much important at this time than either Los Tres or welfare cases."

The third question, as to the relationship of our cases to our priorities, does not at this time require much discussion. This is for the simple reason that it is premature, considering our level of development as a collective, and our level of awareness as politically and socially involved individuals, to ask and answer this question. Let's explore the first two first. The fact of the matter is that we have an awfully long way to go. But as we begin to start asking the right questions we at least get a glimpse and taste for where we want to go!

Part 6

Richard Cruz, late 1960s or early 1970s.
Courtesy of Special Collections, Davidson Library, Univ. of Calif. Santa Barbara

Richard Cruz: Pensamientos and Other Reflections

CHICANOS IN MEXICO: SOME EMERGING THEMES[1]

Richard Cruz

It's remarkable how little we—as Chicanos involved in the life and death struggle called "el movimiento"—discuss the importance of Mexico and Mexicans to the struggle. Perhaps the freshness of our renewed love affair with ourselves as Chicanos—de Los or San Jo, or de Texas; or of La Raza Unida Party, Moratorium Committee or MEChA—has temporarily prevented us from seriously shifting our eyes and hearts to the south. Whatever the reasons, we are foolish if we do not establish actual and ideological revolutionary relationships with the Mexican who, by virtue of blood and history, is tied to us and we to him as brother to brother to brother, or Mother to son.

Various factors or themes are emerging—on both sides of "la frontera"—which must be taken into consideration. First of all, the embryonic notions we as Chicanos display, the notions of "carnalismo," La Raza Unida (unity)", of "Aztlán", for example, demand that we consciously and actively see ourselves as ONE PEOPLE with ONE DESTINY which can only be achieved by the same REVOLUTIONARY STRUGGLE. To shout Que Viva La Raza!, por ejemplo, as we do at our countless demonstrations throughout the Southwest, and not be thinking of and feeling the countless masses of our people to the south who are at a bare subsistence level, is to be provincial to the point of treason. It must be understood, in other words, that the Chicano is a Mexican without a nation; or stated conversely, the Mejicano is a Chicano with a home . . . with land that he can call (for the most part) HIS.

I'm not suggesting that we lose sight of ourselves as Chicanos; that we forget (as if we could) that we are practically surrounded by a foreign people and civilization (Western Civilization). I am merely suggesting that we nurture our

[1] Unpublished and written in 1971 in Ricardo Cruz/Católicos Por La Raza Papers.

consciousness as Mejicanos, as ONE PEOPLE. The Zacatecano, for ejemplo, with all his pride in the culture, traditions and music of the state of Zacatecas, does not view himself as anything but part of the Mexican existence and family. Our beauty and emerging consciousness as Chicanos (the northernmost Mejicanos) does not in fact separate us from the historical fact of our blood and history. Are you any less a Mexican than your tía in Chihuahua or your primo in Nayarit merely because of the historical accident called la liña [the border]? Are you any less a Mexican merely because you don't speak Spanish or, if you do speak it, it is of the Pocho dialect? Of course not! To say so is to completely ignore the fact that literally thousands of Mexican Indios y mestizos don't speak any Spanish at all. To say so is also, more tragically, to make a mockery and hypocrisy of the precious words—"la familia, la raza unida, carnalismo, etc. . . ." Moreover, as will be discussed subsequently, to ignore in our hearts and minds our identity as Mejicanos and to think of our problems as "ours" and those of the Mexicans as "theirs" is to give conscious legitimacy and recognition to the border as a legal and valid phenomenon. We become handmaidens to the separation of our peoples (LA FAMILIA) as perpetrated by the original and continued rape, by the U.S., of the Treaty of Guadalupe Hidalgo.

This brings us to another consideration, namely: what do our caranles to the south think of us, of "el movimiento?" Our noted philosopher, Octavio Paz, has written that . . .

> "The pachuco tries to enter North American
> society in secret and daring ways, but he
> impedes his own efforts. Having been cut
> off from his traditional culture, he asserts
> himself for a moment as a solitary and challenging
> figure. He denies both the society
> from which he originated and that of North America." [2]

This assessment, of course, is of the pachuco. As Chicanos y Chicanas struggling to free our spirit, to purify "el movimiento", it needs to be emphasized that we retain little ideological similarities to our former selves as pachucos. We no longer—in thought or deed—deny both the society from which we originated and that of North America. Only the latter society, its indices of western civiliza-

[2] Octavio Paz, The Labyrinth of Solitude, 1950, p. 17.

tion (basically European) grossness and barbarianism, are being subjected to active and increasing rejection by the Chicano. Indeed, as Chicanos in 1971, we are nurturing our spiritual essence as men and women and families of the Mexican experience and blood. It is not insignificant, Chicanos, that as this discussion proceeds "La Marcha de la Reconquista" winds its painful way from Calexico to Sacramento. We are quite literally reconquering our primordial essence as LA FAMILIA MEJICANA.

So, do the words of Paz ring true in 1971? Does his assessment of the pachuco, insofar as they may reflect the feelings and thoughts of Mexico in general, retain validity as regards the Chicano?

Several recent occurrences suggest that, insofar as the government of Mexico (PRI), its elite and its pseudo-intellectuals, its creoles (Mexican-born Spaniards) and property-owning bourgeoisie are concerned, the Chicano is considered legally a "citizen" of the United States and spiritually a rejected (doformed?) child. We are something, in other words, that one in the above circles "best not speak of." At least not officially. The brutal murder of Guillermo and Guillardo Sánchez (primos), on July 16, 1970, in Los Angeles, at the hands of government agents ("la placa") is one such occurrence that comes to mind.

Both Guillermo and Guillardo were "nacionales". Their deaths prompted numerous anit-police demonstrations. At one such demonstration a contingent of approximately 100 Chicanos diverted to the Mexican Consulate in Los Angeles. They demanded not only Mexican official recognition and assistance in denouncing the local government's handling of the matter—but also that Mexico as a nation recognize the plight of the Chicano. The Consul's response was of the glib, hands-off variety that we have been accustomed to from the mouths of gabacho officials. When the office of [President] Echevarria finally did respond (months later), it constituted complete faith in the local court system as the proper dispensers of "justice." (Needless to say, there never has been justice for la familia Sánchez). On July 16, 1970, therefore, the powers-that-be in Mexico cheapened Mexican (Chicano) blood to a tragic level. As Chicanos, we realized our solitude.

The entire handling of green-carders and "illegals"—both in the campos and urban jungles—is a constant reminder of the willingness of both governments to use the starvation and plight of the Mexican and Chicano masses as pawns in the international game called "make the rich richer." When the United States needs cheap labor—cheaper than even the Chicano can supply—la frontera mysteriously opens and the surging masses of our landless carnales struggle forward to become the beasts of burden for agribusiness and the industrial complex. The very need of the poor in Mexico to seek out the border is brute testimony to the failure of the above circles to carry out the revolution. If these elite think so little of the

Mexican "citizen", no wonder they feel such little compulsion to consider us, the Chicano, as members of LA FAMILIA MEJICANA.

The masses, on the other hand, insofar as they suffer from the lack of land, and insofar as Chicanos firmly demonstrate that our struggle is not a civil rights movement, need no reminder that the goal is nothing less than the reunification of LA FAMILIA with LA TIERRA. The poor know the unity of poverty. They know the absurdity of a border. But what the poor in Mexico may not know is the ultimate destiny Mexican "leaders" may have in store for them. This suggests another consideration in our analysis of the Chicano and Mexico. The consideration of Chicanos as mirrors of the future. Not only to our brothers to the South; but mirrors to all those indigenous peoples of the American continents.

As the northernmost member of LA FAMILIA MEJICANA we are acutely and painfully aware of the tragic consequences of a conquered people. Of a people enslaved. And, moreover, as loving members of LA FAMILIA MEJICANA, it becomes our spiritual duty to expose our pains and scars so that our collective peoples may remain constantly on guard and vigilant lest the same fate befall them. Thus, for example, it is we who can best illustrate the pain of a people without land we can call OURS.

Schools, por ejemplo—we have none. Our children merely "do time" in the brick and concrete institutions which serve merely to brainwash our youth to the point where many of our young actually believe that Columbus "discovered" America.

Jails and penal institutions of all variety—they have become our home away from home. A way of life . . .

The campos—mere factories under the sun. Where our origins as a people of the land are frustrated; where our essential understanding of LA TIERRA as our Mother who loves and feeds us is distorted by the gabacho who sees land (its trees and its animals) as profit and money-engendering DEVICES.

Government—slaves never have government. Nor do they have laws, justice or other indices of social growth and interaction. The Nixons and Agnews, the Youngers and Reagans, are but the official slave-mongers of Western Civilization.

The consequences? Need we look beyond the sadness in the eyes of our Mother? The tragedy of our youth on "coloradas" y "blancas"? the [sic] plaintive and desperate poetry of our pintos? The emasculation of our men as they take—not to the gun—but to proposal writing! These are but some of the consequences of the advantage of the gringo upon our TIERRA and our RAZA. And it is precisely this message of results and consequences; precisely this foreboding of evil that the Chicano must communicate to NUESTRA FAMILIA MEJICANA.

Is the warning premature? You may think so, but I do not. The Los Angeles Times of June 7, 1971, for example, displays the headline: EASING OF BAJA CAL-

IFORNIA LAND LAW BRINGS BOOM—Coastal, Border Areas Opened to Foreign Capital. The article states:

> "A presidential decree permits direct foreign participation in tourist and industrial development of previously restricted lands in the border and coastal areas of Mexico has started a land rush in Baja California.
>
> "Since President Luis Echeverría Alvarez released details of the law May 1, land values have soared more than 200% in some areas of Baja.
>
> "Limited to tourist and industrial development, the law sidesteps a provision of the constitution of 1917 which prohibits foreigners from owning land within 100 kilometers of an international border or 50 kilometers of the seacoast, and limits leases within those areas to 10 years."

The last "Boom" was called Manifest Destiny. The Chicano still suffers the resulting alienation from that rape of land and culture. And it is not as if we need look only at this most recent development for guides to the future. For decades, por ejemplo, the Mejicano y Chicano have been denied access to the beautiful playas between Tijuana and Ensenada; in Acapulco tambien. The "tourists" are here to stay. If we let them. Puerto Vallarta increasingly becomes the home of the gabacho "jet set". One need but look, furthermore, at the social pages of any cosmopolitan daily newspaper to see what the "beautiful people", as the gross gabacho socialites call themselves, are buying, selling, building, ect., [sic] in the lands of NUESTRA FAMILIA MEJICANA.

So, while the Mexican elite would ignore our plight, we, the Chicano know with the sagacity of those who have already experienced something that our love and our warnings are primarily for the ears and hearts of the landless and suffering Mexican masses.

The Chicano experiences definitely looms more and more the potential future of LA FAMILIA MEJICANA. The barbarianism called Western "civilization"—with its disdain for land and humanity, its life-destroying compulsion as reflected in Vietnam and pollution of land, air and water—will not stop with the Southwest. Its greed and rapaciousness is a lust. And it looks to the South . . .

Thus, with increasing numbers of Chicanos journeying to Mexico, it is good and timely to provoke serious thought and action with regard to the southern FAMILIA. A review of ourselves as the conquered Mejicanos will hopefully assist us in formulating practical plans of action. Especially action by the MECHISTA who, by far, is the most mobile of "movimiento" Chicanos. And who, by virtue of the historical significance of students to development of revolutionary understanding and activity, must develop into something more than "educated Chicanos", or "fund raisers" or "Chicano militants."

Thus, Chicano students in Mexico become absurd symbols of contradiction and confusion if they view themselves as "tourists." One simply cannot be a tourist in his own home. Nor does the visiting MECHISTA do a service to LA FAMILIA MEJICANA by identifying solely with the students of Mexico. Certainly it would have profound effects if Chicano and Mexican students would unite in principal; for instance unity of students on the principal of non-recognition of la lina, or recognition of AZTLÁN; or unity of students as petitioners to the Mexican Government for simple recognition of the plight of Chicanos . . . But, be that as it may, it is to the struggling masses that our message of impending disaster and carnalismo must be carried. As visiting Chicanos—by word, deed and life style-the twofold message of mutuality of need and struggle must be projected.

Mutuality of need in that La Raza in the southwest cannot possibly sustain itself, its struggle, as a third entity—not quite Mexican yet certainly not gabacho. Mutuality of need in that the Mejicano must understand the Chicano as his carnal closest to the enemy. It is we, the Chicano, who can strike and are striking the first blows, not for "Chicano power", but for the very continuation of LA FAMILIA MEJICANA! As previously noted, moreover, it is the Chicano who need but display his wounds and scars as human beings to the Mexican in order for the Mejicano to realistically assess his probable predicament if current trends continue.

Mutuality of struggle also must be communicated. This means several things. It means the recognition of La Frontera as nothing more than an inhuman mechanism with which both governments are able to play the suffering Chicano campesino and barrio dweller against the Mexican "illegal" for profit. It means the recognition of the essential unity of October 2nd with August 29th. Tlatelolco with Salazar Park. Blood with blood. LA FAMILIA MEJICANA united against the bedfellows called PRI and "American democracy." But most importantly it means that the burden is on the Chicano to show our FAMILIA that we really are involved in a revolutionary struggle for LA TIERRA. Then our carnales in Mexico will takes us seriously. And they will look and listen and see that our enemy is theirs. And they will embrace the Chicano con gritos de QUE VIVA LA RAZA Y LA FAMILIA MEJICANA . . .

We will have come home . . . and our philosophers will not be afraid to speak the truth.

Untitled

—RICHARD CRUZ[1]

It's time we come to grips with ourselves both intellectually and as intellectuals. Our youth having been rediscovered we reverse the process and grope toward maturity. And "the spectrum begins." The return to youth is the revolution.

Standards do come hard as of necessity, frustration—whatever—the socially defined self disintegrated and weakened as our other bursting identity demanded blow after blow on the social (real) institutions—church, culture, school, factory, etc.—which had given us birth. Literally the attack upon ourselves had begun. Always, then, the only question for us at least can only be: where, having begun a war, a spiritual rebirth and a revolution, is it going?

"The spectrum" can only begin with myself. Only from the self (spectrum) can the epistemological (western civilization) question—knowledge & power—be entered. Entry it is.

"Power to the people"—as rhetorical as it sounds—is and always has been the only goal. As individuals we can only begin to understand the mandate of power if we have power—personal power. And this can only be made possible by travel along the spectrum.

The individual spectrum is the entire existence.

Thus do and did we enter the rebirth, revolution and reality. Full of wonder and fear. We fear ourselves. Rightly so. "Fear of the unknown." The revolution, then, is knowledge of ourselves for the sake of conquering fear.

What else might the revolution be? Evolution or revolution? Does it really matter? Evolution to the termites as they continue to live. Revolution to the dinosaurs as we view his remains. What does it mean to us? Who are "we" and "us" by the way—are we the "intellectuals?"

What difference do we make? That, as good as any, is the question. "So what!?!"

The whatness, the whyness, the whoness. The principles of life. The only philosophical understanding of a revolution is as a socially meaningful principle of

[1] Unpublished, untitled, and undated (circa 1970s) in Ricardo Cruz/Católicos Por La Raza Papers.

life. The revolutionary is a warrior for the survival of the race. The ultimate principal of life for the revolutionary is survival. From this understanding do we have to understand ourselves as intellectuals. The spectrum is 360 degrees—it's not duality nor trilogy. Neither Hegel nor Jesus. Good nor evil, nor right and wrong. It is the "I" in rediscovery. The spectrum, quite simply, includes intellectual power.

Fulfillment is the spectrum is power. On with the show.

Artist: Life is a painting.

Musician: A picture of music.

Poet: Words in action.

Lawyer: A reflection of justice.

Priest: God's reflection.

Philosopher: Life is a question.

Gentle person: Life is gentle.

Warrior: Survival to the fittest.

Mystery prevails to the mystic as Wisdom engulfs the understanding.

The spectrum continues. The fog and the eternal pattern of the drums hold hands. Harmony prevails—despite. Passion flows, humor laughs, the heart pumps blood and our wisdom nods at all. We are so many yet we are one.

Keep but one face. The spectrum is one. Not many. Power and knowledge, in that order. . . . To confuse is to be confused. Most confuse. Too many faces.

Reason, as the emotions and the bowels, can be mastered. Of course. Mastery or reason moves us along. The "I" disappears. The I becomes immaterial—indeed nonexistent. Hegel would have us understand that the I becomes the "We" upon mastery of reason. In reality, however, the "we" itself becomes the cabbage or smog, the freeway pavement and the spoken word—the sense and the nonsense—in all forms and manifestations as reason wilts in the sunlight.

To humans the spectrum is the totality of human experience. To mice, strawberries and snails its [sic] the same. All for one and one for all as they say on campus.

Student: "What school do you go to?"

Mestizo: "La Universidad de la Tierra."

Brujo [Witch]: "Dame mammon, cabron"

Student: "Don't either of you work?"

Mestizo: "When I have to."

Brujo: "All the time."

Student: "What's your position, ideologically speaking, on social change and revolution?"

Mestizo: "I belong to the land."

Brujo: "It depends on my nose."

Student: "Your nose?"
Brujo: "Most definitely."
Mestizo: "¿como?" [what?]

Untitled

RICARDO CRUZ[1]

How ugly the pain of the conquered. We can barely see ourselves!

Mirrors one and all. Our laughter but sounds, our tears are water, our laughter w/o happiness.

Our music isn't ours. No wonder we can't sing.

When we're alone, then we feel. Que loco!

So we march & shout & feel what we want. No more. More would frighten us!

But when alone we cry for each other. And we wish things were different. We dream our private revolutions—words of happiness & true love of human beings who feel—and we're so stupid we don't even know that at that time of lagrimas—not tears—we are with the masses! And they w/us!

But only when we're alone. Que triste raza! We think we're chingones! Yet no tenemos huevos para gritar con lagrimas—our souls have only reached our mouths. Como gabachos! That when we're alone we are together. Maybe my lies to myself are through a mirror?

Our blood is mixed, raza. Can we survive that?

Can you understand how I feel carnales? Do you feel like me? Que gaucho, si no! Que gaucho si no puedes!

Just make sure you pass the bar, mother fuckers. Give us your hand. The land & blood know about books! And MECHA . . . when's our next dance on campus? "Que viva La Raza guys . . . MECHA, MECHA, RAZA, RAZA, CLF?!? Chicano Liberation Front in English! Kill the man, carnales, but organize our language. We've been to his schools, he's never been to ours. He won't understand. Enough said. You do, and maybe the B.Bs will take off the berets out of respect.

A la brava, carnales! The cameras are gone. We're by ourselves. We used to joke about how the revolution won't be televised & now we find that the mans T.V.'s don't care about la sangre de la tierra! That's like la tierra after the rain. Con los pajaros—our souls loose in the dark—where no one can see us.

Los tres! The 13! Católicos 21! Los Siete!

[1] Ricardo Cruz/Católicos Por La Raza Col.

Tijerina, César, Corky, Talamantez, Los seis de la Capital, Zapata, Villa, Montez, primos Sánchez, you may be alone.

Our people can't cry anymore!

So get your degrees, assholes. And cruse Whittier. Sell your defense fund tickets, write your proposals and wear your berets (beanies). Win your case—Zeta—and get your praise. Sal's in Hollywood representing los pobres. The circus goes on.

We dance & sing. That's like the movies.

Our souls on a trip we've never seen with dope. Our spirit drunk with confusion. Borrachos somos, but we boycott Coors!

Our best poetry says we are a little of everything—pachucos, campesino, Mex-Am, B.B., LUCHA, mestizo, indio, y Joaquin—but fuck our masks! We're either the same people or we're not. Are we?

I don't know Raza. If I lied you would know. And you do know. So give the answer to me! Si tienes huevos!

And that's why we use the word "Raza." It signifies the unknown—the devil—and the known—the gods.

We use it to say what we're not. Maybe we know what we are—somos cabrones?

Los romplejos! Los romplejos!

The cockroach y los sapos! They'll see all of us to the grave. What looks like love is revolution. Shakespeare was Chicano: "full of sound & fury, signifying nothing." It's all a joke. No wonder we laugh through our tears!

Los gatos y los perros—our superiors by far. Our chingones brag about their welfare & EOP & HEALTH TASK FORCE & other easy (ripoffs), and our "pets" laugh.

Las pulgas have seen our blood more than the enemy! A tale to a flea—nuestra sangre!

We just can't see ourselves. Our mixed blood has turned to a course! It has weakened us.

—RICHARD CRUZ[1]

Que triste [How sad]. To be conquered & cry alone. To listen to our music that isn't ours. To fear myself! And you! And you me!

Then we love at night. Where there are no mirrors to see our bodies . . .

The joke's on our liars whose love for the people went with the lights No more make-up man, no more revolutionary! A deal's a deal, like the Jews say, [with] their hands up your ass. And you shit your money. But no cameras then. You suffer alone. You've earned your solitude. You—the Mexican American.

[1] Unpublished, untitled, and undated (circa 1970s) in Ricardo Cruz/Católicos Por La Raza Papers.

RICARDO CRUZ[1]

Somos indios, somos mestizos! [We are Indians, we are mestizos!] O god our land is gone—no wonder we're dead. It's all we know—we can just feel it.

When we're alone! No mirrors! Listen, though. Listen to our familia de la tierra en lost campos [family of the land in the countryside]—they can still cry & sing & laugh—and we fucked up pendejos [idiots] in the city actually call our own people in the campos [countryside] "impoverished."* [*and out go the Chicano law students to give "civil rights" to our families! Pendejos!]

Cruz, Raza! Cry together. As we do when we think we're alone.

Our bodies have become jails. They have locked us in. It's like our bodies fear us as the unknown is feared. Or is it the other way around? We fear our bodies because they are the land!

No wonder we barely know that we're still Mexican-Americans. Even you, los batos locos [street dudes]. We can barely see ourselves.

But we do when we're alone. Don't we?

And our so-called vanguards! (Our so-called "vanguards"—pendejos que son—even call themselves "vanguards.") Desgraciados! [Disgraced ones] Our vanguards of the mouth. Comé caca! [eat shit!]

Sometimes we feel cold & inhuman, and maybe we are.

[1] Untitled, unpublished, and undated (circa 1970s) in Ricardo Cruz/Católicos Por La Raza Papers.

RICHARD CRUZ[1]

Not too long ago a bunch of us Chicanos and Chicanas began getting out of law schools. Que loco! [how crazy!]

We were actually "movement babies" because the "blow-outs" and other open turbulence swelled within the hearts and thoughts of our people as we began our law studies. This was in 1967 and 1968. What a strange feeling it was in those years to be studying law in classrooms and simultaneously see law as it was applied: Sal Castro and the others indicted for the crime of demanding education for our children; the CPLR [Católicos Por La Raza] "21" arrested, tried, convicted for demanding that the Catholic Church practice what it preaches; the "Biltmore" heroes for confronting "our" governor faced felony indictments and two to three years of appeals before they were cut loose.

Photo by Ray Cruz. Used with Permission.

Richard Cruz, 1972.

[1] Untitled, unpublished, and undated (circa 1970s) in Ricardo Cruz/Católicos Por La Raza Papers.

CHICANO INTERVIEW: CHICANOS, CATHOLICISM, AND POLITICAL IDEOLOGY (1976)[1]

Richard Cruz

1. Sex: Male Female
    - Male
2. Age of respondent?
    - Thirty-three
3. What is your occupation?
    - Lawyer
4. What is your religious affiliation?
    - None
5. If none, did you ever have a religious affiliation?
    - Catholic
6. If yes, why did you cease to be a Catholic?
    - Personally, it has no relevance to my life, and secondly, as a member of a growing number of Chicano activists, I see it as a detrimental value—or a detrimental effect on the political and historical aspirations of the Chicano people.

        (In what way?)

[1] Ricardo Cruz/Católicos Por La Raza Papers. It appears that this interview was done by Lawrence J. Mosqueda for his dissertation and later book Chicanos, Catholicism and Political Ideology (Lanham, Md: University Press of America,1986).

Well, there's so many ways. Eventually I would want to share then [sic] thoughts in our discussions on religion in general. I don't see the word even, or the discussion of it, or the need for religion, you know—not what I consider to be types of problems facing all peoples, let alone the Chicano people, you know. I see that there is mysticism as a reality that I accept. There is spirit. There is power. There is reality. These are words I like and respect very much and consider them relevant for all people, and certainly the Chicano people; but I don't see the word, or the life called religion as necessary. In its rituals, in its teachings, and in various forms . . . well, its manifestations in other words—the effect it has. Both the word itself and the meanings and then the rituals and the trimmings of what it means to be religious. And I don't think the Chicano people ultimately deep down come from a base of life, or values, or cultures that really relate to religion as it's been interpreted and put into their lives. In other words, post-Columbian and pre-Columbian. And I think the minute the Spanish stepped on the new land they used the sword and religion to conquer the people and I think the people are still conquered because of religion.

7. Did you attend Public, Catholic, or other schools?
   - Catholic schools.
8. If Catholic, how many years did you attend a Catholic school?
   - Well, let's see. High school, one year of college at St. Mary's College, and then LACC [Los Angeles City College] and Cal State, Los Angeles so those weren't Catholic. And then Loyola Law School, a Jesuit law school

     (So most of your education was Catholic?)

     Yes.
9. Would you like your children to attend a Catholic school? Why or why not?
   - I would like them to meet philosophers. I think there is a tremendious [sic] amount of good philosophers within some of the best traditions of the Catholic teaching orders, such as the Jesuits. Actually I'm a Christian Brothers product and I'm very proud of some of these men who I consider spiritual; and I think as a result philosophical—as great teachers they went way beyond religion themselves even. They went to Mass and all these things but they sure as hell knew reality when they saw it. They related to reality more than they were to any trimmings and trappings and pushings, and what I call the dark ages and dark mentality of religion.

     I wouldn't mind my kids relating to those kinds of teachers and the kind of morality that is discussed in Catholic schools. One thing good about Catholic education, or religion—an unfortunate thing—is that it's about the only thing that talks about morality—good and evil—and all these things—and I consider that important. But essentially—my kids—I hope they would just relate to a lot of different levels of schools and things, including Mexico and whatever I could do, I would think.

10. Please tell me which statement comes closets to expressing what you believe about God?
    1. I don't believe in God
    2. I don't know whether there is a God.
    3. I don't believe in a personal God, but I do believe in a higher power of some kind.
    4. I find myself believing in God some of the time, but not at other times.
    5. I know God really exists and I have no doubts about it.
    6. Don't know.
    - Again, I think that reality, and power and spirit are the best three words that come to the top of my head that could describe what I mean if I'm going to use the word god. I prefer not to use the word "god". I prefer to say to intimates, friends, strangers, or anybody—I don't believe in God. I believe in reality, power, spirit—these things. I find myself going through life a lot happier, a lot more down to earth, a lot more able to relate to the problems of life and the solutions to the problems of life by being a realist, and a powerful person, and a spiritual person, not ever relating to God or this or that religion.
11. All in all, how important would you say that religion is to you?
    - Not at all.
12. About how often do you attend religious services?
    - Never.

    Here is a list of things that some Catholics do. During the last two years have you managed to:
    1. Go on a retreat.
    2. Make an Easter duty (confession and communion).
    3. Make a day of recollection.
    4. Read a spiritual book.
    5. Make a mission.
    - Well, I do a lot of those things. But I don't do anything in the purview of religion or the name of religion.
13. How do you prefer to call yourself, and why?

1. Spanish speaking	4. Mexican
2. Latin American	5. Chicano
3. Mexican American	6. Spanish American
	7. Other ( )

- Chicano.
  (Any particular reason?)
  Well, it's a good enough label. I tell my friends I'm an Arab. It's just a good enough label, but it is the label that allows myself and our people to relate to all kinds of things—our culture, to this, to that—to food, to sex, to a lot of things. Chicano—I like the word.

14. Could you tell me why you became involved with Católicos Por La Raza, and were you a founding member? It's not still active, is it?
    - Right. It's not really active as an organization or as a social—political—religious thrust anymore. I became involved: 1) I was organizing in Salinas, California and I was a law intern, student. I was a law student with the California Rural Legal Assistance, and that allowed me to meet César Chávez. And at that time the grape boycott was really just getting going. It was quite a life and death struggle then for the farm workers. Meeting Chávez in Santa Barbara, California at a secret meeting of many of his lawyers and other people. I was just a student and really was just there, and people thought that I should meet him. And I realized from watching this meeting, and what was going on, that the Church had not, and they were very much concerned that the Church had not officially backed up the boycott. So I pretty much made a promise to him. I said, "César, I'll do my best, whatever, I know you can relate to that. I mean I don't know you and you don't know me and I couldn't care less anyway who you are or anything like that. But I think the Church should back it up." So that was one reason I came back to Los Angeles. That would be about 1968 or so. And the second reason is, of course, personal in terms of my own feelings and religion. I was a super, super religious person almost all those years. I was very mystical, very religious, and I still consider myself related to the mysteries of life. But I am definitely not a religious person. So it was my personal religion that made it clear to me that there was just no way on earth that the Church wouldn't of course get behind Chávez once they understood what was happening with a little pressure. Those were militant times, those were fighting times, and the Church was being ignored, you know. So the religion of it as I understood religion, and I understood it excellently because I had all the teachers, led me to really in a sense come to this position. What I'm really saying then is: practice what you preach. So 1) a promise to the farm workers, with respect to one specific, to get the Church to back the boycott. 2) Let's call it the "practice what you preach" syndrome—all these people in a sense have pure ass hypocrisy. Talking all this love and yet they wouldn't back up a boycott. I

couldn't believe it. 3) Reasons that we touched on a little. Historically I guess to me the Church—the Catholic Church—of course more than anything allows or forces our people to be submissive. No matter what, with or without farmworkers or practice what you preach attitudes, the Church had to be looked at, exposed, to me personally and to my opinion, to anyone who wanted to really get down to the serious question. What the hell is religion? What is its relevance? Is it needed? What is it? In other words, an attitude of freshness, a radical attitude in the philosophical sense of the word "radical". To allow myself at least personally to ask the big question: Is it relevant and who are these people, and are they Christian even, let alone good souls? 4) At that time I was at a Catholic law school. I knew as much as all the other peoples who were related to education that the Church had almost zero input in terms of the real good education of the Chicano people. Certainly it had some high schools; grammar schools and high schools. But after that you've got to have your money or that's it—off to Santa Clara or Loyola or the very rich schools and you've got to have a lot of money. Education is a very big thought in my mind. Especially then with the high school blow outs going on and all kinds of things happening. The Church in other words to be pressured to back up and put its money where its mouth is and start paying for scholarships and all these things.

So these are early thoughts that led to my input into an organizing efforts as a law student using the Chicano law students' association which I also helped to create as a base.

When I came back to Los Angeles, then, very coincidentally some MEChA students at LACC were independent—I didn't even know them—were pretty much thinking along the same lines. ALL on their own, not necessarily related to Chávez or farmworkers or anything—just a matter of it being time we looked at the Church. The schools were being looked at then, and health, and some of the other things. So a little coalition started developing of law students and college students and it ultimately led to laborers, welfare mothers, and brown berets. And the coalition grew and grew and ultimately organizers such as La Raza magazine and other people like that. Really just people themselves. Immaculate Heart nuns. The organization just spread like wildfire. It turned out that everyone was willing to look at the Church—especially, specifically, Cardinal McIntyre's domination of the Los Angeles Church.

(Was it primarily local or did it have some national ties? Did it have branches, say, in Texas or up in northern California?)

Well, it was primarily Los Angeles. But it had activists and members and supporters and affiliate types of groups all over—wherever there's Chicanos. I know in San Diego actually before anybody ever heard of St. Basil's in terms of the Chicano movement and the riot that occurred there—the ambush I call it—a bunch of Chicanos took over a retreat in San Diego, for instance. And that inspired an awful lot of us. And they just sat in that place until the welfare nuns, or whatever they were, decided to meet their demands. A year later or before, or sometime around those years, probably 1970 I would think, MAYO had a big meeting in Texas—I forget which group it was, I think it was MAYO—they painted the Virgin brown and did many symbolic and actual things. And I think they took over a church also and that type of stuff. So there's all kinds of stuff related to religion and the struggle against or for, or with respect to, the Catholic Church. Católicos was definitely Los Angeles-based, and made up of Brown Berets, the law students, welfare mothers, high school students, regular people and organizers. And just all kinds of people—nuns, ex-nuns, priests, ex-priests, and all kinds like that.

(How large did it get? How big was its membership—people that were actually involved in going to meetings and demonstrations?)

Right. Well, altogether we're talking about a year and one- half, almost two years.

(When was the time period when it actually existed?)

Within that time, starting with essentially a press conference when it was announced that demands would be made on the Church. I forget the specifics–that's why I want a copy so I can look at all that stuff. I've got all kinds of photos if you want, everything.

(Yes. If you've got something I can look at.)

So if we get a copy of that we can refine it—dates, even copies of whatever you want, the first press conference. I don't know, whatever you want. But I remember that Ruben Salazar was the only reporter that showed up for that press conference and I think he was with the L.A. Times. That would have been probably three, four or six months before the Christmas Eve of 69. So we can think of the middle of 1969 to the end of 1970, about a year and a half, from a press conference, a demonstration, to petitions, to of course a big riot, of Católicos Por La Raza activity. And in that year and a half there was a minimum of between 3 to 5,000 people related, whether they demonstrated or picketed, or wrote letters, or fasted or so many things that happened. There was a baptism of fire when 15 to 20 people including myself and my brother and some of the others burned our baptism certificates. There was a midnight march from downtown—from the chancery itself, the headquarters of the church—to where the cardinal was living at that time; and there was over a thousand people in that particular march. It was a fantastic march, we couldn't believe it. It was midnight, we had a midnight march. I don't know who called for it and all of a sudden there was a thousand people there from all over West L.A. The cops couldn't believe it. I know we couldn't. Like I say, there was an absolute minimum of 3,000 people involved. High school students really were with it, just so many people in a year and a half.

(It's been seven years now since Christmas Eve 1969. What do you think has changed in the Church? Has anything changed? I saw the list of demands in La Raza magazine. Have any of these demands been implemented? Has anything happened in the Church?)

Well, the tremendous, tremendous success. 1) The Pope fired McIntyre. McIntyre was both the symbol and reality of the completely turn-of-the-century mentality—paternalism with respect to the Chicano people. No matter what any historian ever says, no matter what the Church may say, we know that the Pope sent the delegate to can McIntyre's ass. So Chicanos fired his ass—the Pope fired this ass. 2) The Church—for the first time ever the Chicano people had a Bishop Flores and a Bishop Juan Arzube. In other words, Latinos. Bishop Arzube is not a Chicano; he's a South American. So immediately the first time ever, we made it clear to the Church: "Look, you Polish Church people took care of each other, your Irish sure as hell did, your Italians did. You all have your people, now where's our Chicanos, in other words?"

So they responded. We see then groups like Padres and others, and the Chicanos within the Church itself. Nuns and priests came to us and let us know very clearly that we really helped them, and finally they recognized that they were embarrassed of their own racism among themselves, and that they could stand up and organize and put pressure on the Church and start at least being active. Like I say, the Polish religious people were, the Italians and others. Everyone takes care of their own. So we see then two things: The appointment of two bishops; the first time ever in the history of the Southwest—and most importantly, and this I'm proud of and apparently Chávez has publicly recognized that with Católicos the Church did get to back the boycott. That was huge and very important thing in the farmworkers' struggle.

As compared to us, in other words. Those "mean radical" Chicanos. In those years you know Los Angeles Chicanos were fighters. So the

Church compared us to the nice farmworkers and definitely backed up publicly and became part of the boycott. And we feel that that very much helped. We understand that several millions of dollars, as much as a half a million, was pumped into the farmworkers' struggle.

(From the Los Angeles Diocese , nationally or California?)

We would really have to look and spend hours to find exactly what. Essentially the Campaign for Human Development was begun, CHD. That stems exactly from Católicos Por La Raza. Which adds up to finally the Church getting into the funding business. We made it clear the Episcopalians sure are with the Chicanos. And the Jews and everybody was with the Chicanos but the god-damn Catholic Church. So literally millions of dollars went into that in terms of once a year collections of all parishes apparently all over the United States. And all that money goes toward CHD. Which to this day I have no idea how many community groups or programs have benefitted from it. But we know that literally dozens and dozens have. In other words, Church money is going right to social growth of the Chicano people, social-political programs. Católicos Por La Raza also inspired many many priests and nuns to quit and grow up, or to stay within and grow up because they saw what the Church was all about. But I guess personally to myself and quite a few others, what it did was allow many of us to really once and for all get down to pre-Columbian and post-Columbian realities of who are we. Do we need religion? You know my answer. I've given it already. And I'm not asking anybody, nor did Católicos Por La Raza ask anybody, to relate to those ultimate questions.

So we can think of some real big things and some small things. Whatever personal, social-political, that were the result of Católicos Por La Raza. It educated a hell of a lot of people. All of us were educated like crazy.

(Also as a result of your activities was that when you passed your bar exam you weren't going to be allowed to be a lawyer. Now you're obviously a lawyer. What happened to make the bar change its mind.)

It took a year and a half of bar hearings, about 23 hearings, and that was another issue not really related to the Church.

(Did the Church back you up any?)

Bishop Arzube testified as to my moral character. And Father Marafield and the Jesuits were and always have been loyal to myself personally and to the issues that the Chicanos had presented to them. Even against their own Church. Fr. Marafield, who's now the President of Loyola also testified on my behalf.

But the bar hearings were really not a Church thrust. This was no longer organizationally and politically related to the Church so much. Other than the instances when the Church had to come out anyway, even though we had quote "attacked it" which was not the truth, they supported by their testimony. That was the law instead of religion, that was law. Lawyers and law students.

15. Who would you say are the three Anglo people who have the most power in this city (county if rural), and what do they do?
    - Oh, I really can't comment on that. I mean there's so many. It's an Anglo world. It's an Anglo city, and I don't know. It's always behind the scenes anyway, so I don't know. I'd have to find out.
16. Have any of these people helped or hurt Chicanos? How and why?
    - There's a tremendous amount of true sincere help by all peoples with respect to the problems that relate to the Chicano people. I work very very closely with American Civil Liberties Union, with city attorneys even. I've had a great base myself. I've understood people, like Father Marafield has always been a tremendous man in my opinion. Just all kinds of people, people in law, in religion, in schools who aren't Chicanos have been very helpful to the causes that Chicanos have to relate to.
17. Have you ever heard of the term "El Movimiento"?

    yes no

    If yes, what does it mean to you?
    - It's a struggle for identity and political, economic power. That's how I see the word, that's what it means to me. So "El Movimiento" is very relevant and thinking about it, I really just see it as identity. For instance, why I've had to, myself, relate to religion. Everybody also, in terms of Católicos Por La Raza, started realizing that the true understanding of themselves as a human being, a human animal, had better understand who their gods are, if any. If they're from Europe, Israel, or whatever the hell their gods are from. And I consider that part of the movement very much so. El Movimiento called, with respect to the Catholic Church, that it was part of the movement. It's identity, I think as much as any of the Chicano activities—whether it's the moratorium, or the partidos [political parties] or La Raza Unida. Probably their thrust with respect to the Catholic Church may be the best example of identity being sought. El Movimiento is very much so in terms of political-economic power. I see it in those three words.

18. Can you name any projects presently going on in this state aimed specifically at improving the condition of the Chicano (Mexican American, Spanish, etc.)? (e.g. housing, health, education, etc.)

    yes no

    - Well, there's multitudes of them, thousands of them, I guess. But including the farmworkers, for instance.

      (Are you a participant in any of these projects?)

      Well, right now I am relating to a trust, a hopeful beginnings of legal power. There's a whole base of Chicano lawyers, all from the sixties. All from the Chicano Law Students Association. Each of whom, statewide, are relating to the political—legal power—with respect to their practice of law, whether agencies or public defenders or even city attorneys or District Attorneys, or like myself. There's apparently about seven of us who we consider to be the real key to the future, our own businesses, we call it, meaning no government, no foundations, no Church, nobody's money—just me and my people. There's about seven private law officers, as I'm defining it, related to the very important hope of justice for the Chicano. Plus the base to back it up. So I'm related to law. That's the great thing happening. A bunch of young Chicano lawyers, maybe as many as fifty statewide, are all kicking away in terms of political-legal power.

19. What do you feel are the major public problems facing the American people in general and Chicanos in particular?

    - I see it very very deeply. I see the American people, period. We're all American people, all of us, having to realize that the system is crumbling, is decadent, is designed to lose, is designed to keep only the few people in power. I see the challenge well toward the eighties of this. Whether the American people can understand that this is a new world, and it has to have a new world of thought. And essentially that's going to have to come from the people who grew up here, I think. That is the Mexicans, Chicanos, South Americans. The indigenous peoples have to be respected. The indigenous people will have to find their identity and hopefully translate that in terms of a new world. I mean all fronts of a new world. For instance, law alone. I don't care that there's very few lawyers on this planet. There's been very few lawyers from the get-go as far as the human animal. That's all western civilization. In Cuba they have people's justice. In other places they have people's justice. "Who needs lawyers?" for instance. People have to ask that. Schools: my secretary's just getting started in college, looking at all those catalogs. Wondering what the hell education is all about. Fresh approaches that have to be classified as a new world because anything else is old. I see the third world as a blank and South American peoples having to supply it, the seeds and spirit to develop a new world. If the American people can't see the eighties and the need for a brand new world, in terms of politics of every institution and its procedures then it'll just go on crumbling away to the whatever you call it, the millennium, to the year 2000 or so. Living with the Democratic and Republican parties and the Catholic Church and the Wall Street brokers, and the Howard Hughes' and the CIA's and the same old trash. Ultimately leading to, of course, what everybody is scared of anyway, and that's why they need religion so bad, is the big catastrophic nuclear wars and diseases, and famines and all that.

20. Do you feel that Chicanos are discriminated against in this country? If so, how and why are they discriminated against?
    - Well, that goes back to what I was saying earlier. It's the Chicanos' fault very much, too. Unless he or she realizes the brilliance of the identity, the identity, of two worlds. We live two worlds. We're schizophrenic people. We got the two worlds really. The pre-Columbian, whatever that means, and the civilization that produced whatever we feel in a very deep way. Perhaps best exemplified by Corky's [Gonzáles] poetry, Yo Soy Joaquin. Unless that kind of understanding of one's own identity and the confidence that can hopefully develop, then Chicanos will always be like little slaves or idiots or afraid to be really educated or stand up or understand that they have a say as to justice or to politics and as to what gods they want, if any. Chicanos are at a point where they should create their own gods, create their own heavens. If they insist on it, make their own. Make the Church real to them.

      But also the society at large does discriminate because it also has absolutely no awareness. I don't blame them in a way. If Chicanos have the complejo [hangup] and can't understand their own power and their own identity and own beauty, their own dual civilization—it's twice as good. Then of course the society as it does, the whites and everybody, the Anglos, the majority will just want to relate to Chicanos as inferior people. As people who don't have any identity. So there is discrimination, but it's got to go both ways. The Chicano has to start with God, starting with religion, has to understand who he or she is.

21. Have you ever been personally discriminated against?

    yes no

    If yes, how? What happened?

- It's not so bad now, but I could give many examples. But as a lawyer of course, especially the first year when there was very few Chicano lawyers. Now there's quite a few more. Almost automatically the clerk or the bailiff would want to know, even if you have a tie on, "Who are you, are you the interpreter, are you the bailiff, what are you, you a probation officer?" "I'm a Lawyer." It's very hard for the system to see Chicanos lawyers. That's just one quick example but there's a lot of that you know.

22. What did you learn from these activities that you have participated in? (e.g. about the system, about yourself, etc.)
    - There's so many things you learn but one is that people can unite, can organize. Literally 50,000 and that's an absolute minimum of Chicanos in Los Angeles organized and demonstrated and picketed and kicked ass. Whether it was the Church or politics or schools and I say that as an extremely conservative, historically accurate figure , 50,000. There was at least 20,000 in one of the moratoriums alone, at least 3,000 to 5,000 in Católicos. The blow outs were at least another 5,000 high school kids. And if we're looking at a five year run, there we're talking of at least 50,000 and probably more likely 100,000 people, you know, resulting in some tremendous changes and tremendous growth of the people and tremendous radicalization of the youth especially. And the tremendous political and economic results for the Chicano people. But all really rolling toward the eighties to see what difference it makes now that there are Chicanos growing up—getting their identity, getting degrees, getting in law, getting in medicine, getting Ph. D. programs, getting in all these things. What differences will it make in terms of the eighties and the new world or not, in other words. Or will the Chicano lawyer, the Chicano doctor, the Chicano Ph. D. be the same old three monkeys: see no evil, speak no evil, hear no evil.

      So what I learned was that a new world can be created. It's going to take a fantastic battle first within the souls and hearts of Chicanos themselves first. And then whether they can roll up their sleeves and open that store, open that market, and buy their own politicians like everybody else and create another world. I think another world has to happen. I think it is possible. And the seventies, to use that as a period of demonstrations and obvious political activity, trained me to believe that people can unite, hopefully as doctors, economists, accountants, lawyers, cab drivers—it doesn't matter—but every facet to create a world.

23. Do you think there are any important differences between what the two major parties (Republican/Democrat) stand for, or do you think they are about the same? If differences, what are the differences? If same, why are they the same?

- Well, I say—well back then I used to say, the only difference between the Bank of America and the Catholic Church: there wasn't a nickel's worth of difference between the Catholic Church and the Bank of America. And I don't think there's a nickel's worth of difference ultimately between the Democrats and Republicans. Except that historically the Democrats allow more of course, social issues to be considered and a lot more monies to float to minorities, and are less repressive less fascistic, than, of course, the Republicans. Less racist. So really the most important thing about the Democrats is that we can assume, as we're seeing, that . . . Mayor Bradley is a Black man. We can see that minorities will get little by little trickling toward that White House some day, and Washington in general in terms of national politics. So the Democrats ease up on the CIA and ease up on the facists running the nation. They ease up a little on racism. And they push some minorities out into the communities which people do need. And they push a little more jobs and most importantly they allow—especially these days after the minorities kicked the Democrats all over town—they allow for minorities to get involved, to get more and more upstairs within the party and therefore politics.

  Other than that, the ultimate solutions. I don't see a nickel's worth of difference between the Democrats, the Republicans, the Catholic Church and the B of A [Bank of America]. They're all in bed together.

24. One of the relationships that exist among Chicanos is that of being a Godparent. Are you a parent or a Godparent? How do you view that relationship both to the child and the parents—as social, religious, taking care of the child if something happens to the parents?

- I'm not a Godparent that I know of—No I'm not, I would know.

  (Are your children baptized—so you have compadres? How do you view that relationship, as social, religious, taking care of the children if someone dies—what is it?)

  Well, I'm not a Godparent but to me it's one of the formalities of religion that is imbued now within the culture of what is essentially the Mestizo people, the Indian people that we are, that the Chicano people are. It has taken on a cultural meaning and significance. I don't know one Godparent, my own included, who really has any semblance of knowledge or understanding of religion really. The baptism itself, but after that they go partying. That's what it's all about really. It's internal family politics. That's what it adds up to. Aunt Janie had the baby lately and let's do this, and Uncle Tio meets somebody and "they don't like me, honey, so I don't want him to be the Godfather." This is the real reason people pick these things. The Godfather and Godmother themselves are about as a-religious as anybody who walks.

25. Most people say they belong either to the middle class or to the working class. Do you ever think of yourself as being in one of these classes?
    If yes, which one?
    middle class working class
    - I mean I'm a lawyer so I guess I'd have to be defined as a professional. As the professional class—whatever. Economically I said if I'm lucky $500 a month and one time $1000. But one time here a bunch of partners we had at one time, we divided $400 four ways including the secretaries and everybody and that was the pay for that month. So it's . . . I'm a lower economic professional I guess.
26. Do you feel that you have a lot in common with other Chicanos in this social class? Why or why not?
    - Well, I've always related to the people. I'm proud to be like many of the people in my family, many of the men, a man of the people, in other words. I really don't like my categories. I respect everything I am, in terms of like lawyers, or college graduate, but all I hope that means is justice and education in other words. I don't really relate personally to categories and again why, too, because I feel and have deeply studied my own identity and forced it out, sometimes at great sacrifice including three months in jail on the Church activity. Such that essentially I'm a human being, I'm a human animal, that's all I am.
27. Do you feel that you have a lot in common with other minorities in the United States and people in the developing nations? (Third World Consciousness)
    - Yes, I relate very much to the Black people. I have many intimates and old friends with them, and am fully aware of the problems of charity begins at home. In other words me first, mi raza primera [my people first]. That is my philosophy. Yet I'm not a racist and I do relate to as my clients are. I've got clients of every rung of the racial economic ladder. Obviously I've opened in East L.A., an office here so I relate to most of my clients who are Chicanos.

28. In general, do you approve of the clergy being actively involved in political and social issues? Why or why not?
    - I've got to say yes. In other words, I would love to see clergy relate to the myriad of social issues—sure.
29. Do you feel that the Catholic Church is a benefit to the Chicano community? Why?
    - I think that without the schools we would be hard pressed to find some very important education going on—good education. Because there are some dedicated teachers within the school structure of the Catholic schools. Other than that though, for reasons we've really talked about, I think, I would have to say that the Catholic Church is a detriment to the identity and growth and future of the Chicano people, just as it was when the Spanish first used the gun and religion to conquer the people. I think the people are still conquered slaves by religion. So I can't really think other than that. I know there's some stuff coming—a buck here, and a dollar there, and a donation here and the Church backed the boycott, and the Church has helped farmworkers. So the Church can put a lot of tremendous power, its tremendous power and money and its pulpits to the people. Again to me it's a nightmare because again the real issue is whether the Chicanos can grow up and have their own god if they insist—stay out of Europe and whatever the old world was.
30. Do you think that the Church has a right to teach what position Catholics should take on political issues and make them a moral obligation of the membership? Why or why not?
    - If religion would practice what it preaches, especially Christians. All you've got to do is live—we told them in Católicos—live your so-called leader, the one who says—you say said "Be like me." If they live like Jesus they would just practice what they preach—just do it. Set examples. They don't have to tell nobody what to do. I really don't think the Church should do anything except live the life the Christ said that he was all about. And they say that they started and that's why they call themselves Christians. So live with the poor, feed them, get going in other words. They don't have to tell nobody nothing.
31. Are you familiar with the "Theology or Liberation"? If yes, what does it mean to you? What is your opinion of it?
    - No, but it sounds interesting. . . .

32. Are you familiar with any of the social encyclicals:
"Rerum Novarum" by Pope Leo XIII
"Quadragesimo Anno" by Pope Pius XI
"Mater et Magistra" by Pope John XXIII
"Pacem in Terris" by Pope John XXIII
"Populorum Progressio" by Pope Paul VI
yes no
- I've heard of them with the Catholic education in college and all, but I'm not familiar with any of them.

  (Then you haven't really read any of them.)

  Well I probably have. I probably read one or two anyway, or excerpts, but I can't really tell you which one is which or what says what.

33. The concept of "charity" means different things to different people. What does it mean to you? Do people have a right to expect charity? Is it inevitable that there will always be people who need charity?
- Charity as best I remember it, the Church defining it, is love and I think that's a good word. But if it's not practiced, in other words, then it means nothing. So, charity is not in my opinion what the Church in its active day to day world translates in terms of a buck here, a welfare program there, or an adoption service. I don't think that's charity at all. Charity, if it's love, has to go to the solution of problems, in other words the deep seated reason for problems and the solutions of them. So I don't see any charity in donations and all these kinds of things the Church does. I think charity is love, and if it's not practiced then it's just jive.

34. Some people say that no good can ever come from violent confrontations like those that happened in Los Angeles in the past. Other people say that such confrontations do some good because they make Anglos pay attention to the problems of Chicanos. Which comes closer to what you feel?
- No good can ever come from violent confrontations.
- Such confrontations do some good.

  Why do you feel this way?
- Well, we know that historically and as given Católicos Por La Raza, the ambush of the Chicanos by the Catholic Church, by Cardinal McIntyre and the LAPD and the Sheriff's department—these were his ushers that evening. We know that good has come from violence. I'm not saying that violence is good in itself, of course. Who wants violence? I've seen enough of it myself in terms of barrio politics and that evening, the mace and the clubs and violence is ugly, you know. But historically in the United States alone, the labor unions wouldn't exist without violence.

The political leaders use violence all the time. The Church resorts to violence so let's face it, violence is as much a part of reality as anything else. And like all reality, it has its good and its bad.

35. If the United States got into a war today, would you personally feel that this country is worth fighting for? Why or why not?
    - Well, people, good people are always worth fighting for. That's one thing I would say there. If that's what's happening. I wouldn't be in any damn war anywhere, except for my people. And if the United States goes to war for Chicanos then I'll be the first to suit up, but I don't think that's going to be happening.
36. What does the phrase, "the meek shall inherit the earth" mean to you?
    - It's a trite bunch of words along with "blessed are the poor" that has been used from the day, again, the Spaniards stepped off the boats, whether with their swords and their rosaries, or whatever, to conquer the Mexican-Chicano people and to keep them conquered.
37. How do you view the Virgin of Guadalupe? What does she mean to you? (very real, myth, source of national pride, etc.)
    - Let me give you an honest answer here. I don't have any any personal or religious feelings whatsoever with respect to the Virgin except as a woman who apparently existed and apparently was a hell of a good woman.

      (How about specifics about the story of the Virgin of Guadalupe?)

      It was just a trick, just a trick, used by the Church to fool the Indians who were already being conquered anyway. So they had nowhere to squeeze but into whatever was being offered. And the Spaniards were smart enough and sharp enough and the Pope was brilliant, apparently, to set up the alternative in terms of existing religions. And with swords and death I don't think it meant anything to anybody but as a way to flow into your state of slavery. It really means nothing to me other than just another example of how the pre-Columbian Indian people, our people, ourselves as original people, were duped.

      I'M GOING TO READ SOME STATEMENTS. PLEASE TELL ME WHETHER YOU AGREE OR DISAGREE WITH THEM. I'LL READ ONE AT A TIME AND YOU TELL ME IF YOU AGREE STRONGLY, IF YOU AGREE A LITTLE, IF YOU DISAGREE A LITTLE, OR IF YOU DISAGREE STRONGLY.

- Agrees strongly
- Agrees a little
- Disagrees a little
- Disagrees strongly
- Doesn't know, no comment

38. It is more important to work to get to heaven than to try to improve your life here on earth.
    - Disagree strongly.
39. One has an obligation to forgive and forget when one is wronged, an obligation to turn the other cheek.
    - Well I don't agree in carrying grudges. I agree with that, I guess. I don't believe in grudges. But I certainly don't think in terms of—if we are talking about the Chicano peoples as an entity—we're not to hold grudges but we sure as hell have to fight to stay alive. And fight for social-political power. So I guess I disagree with that in the social-political context of the Chicano people. Personally nobody should carry grudges because you just carry yourself to the grave. That's all you're doing.
40. Suffering is part of one's punishment for one's sins.
    - Jive, that's jive.
41. If our economic system were just, there would be much less crime.
    - I believe that.
42. Poverty is chiefly a result of injustice in the distribution of wealth.
    - I believe that.
43. The law protects property rights at the expense of human rights.
    - Very much so.
44. Most great fortunes are made honestly.
    - No way.
45. A hungry man has a right to steal.
    - Sure.
46. The government should tax Church property.
    - Yes.
47. Workers should have control over their work places.
    - Yes.
48. In general, Church members are better citizens.
    - Better hypocrites, not better citizens.
49. Religion should play a predominant role in one's life.
    - No.
50. One can be a good Catholic and supporter of Capitalism.
    - Well that's almost synonymous. That's pretty much what is happening. That's what the training is of the Church, yes.
51. One can be a good Catholic and a supporter of Socialism.
    - Sure, we would have to again relate to Christ, I guess. And apparently he lived a communistic life, a socialistic-communistic life. In terms of his personal life and whatever social-political activities he got involved in, yes.

52. One can be a good Catholic and a supporter of Communism.
    - Oh sure, one can be religious and a supporter of anything, really.
53. Chicanos have been discriminated against by many groups but not by the Catholic Church.
    - False.
54. It is more important to be active in the Church than to be active in politics.
    - I don't agree with that.
55. Priests and bishops can be trusted to give sound advice on political issues of the day.
    - It's just too general but I get some great advice sometimes by religious people when we're talking politics.
56. The Pope is infallible. He does not make mistakes on matters of faith and morals.
    - Of course, I don't believe in that.
57. Going to Mass helps to solve my problems.
    - False.
58. Powerful people are powerful because God has made them so.
    - False.
59. If the Pope were to issue a political opinion, it should be followed.
    - No.
60. Generally speaking, my parents were more religious than I am.
    - Sure—I'm sorry—I was more religious than my parents. My brothers and I turned my mother on to religion actually. So in my case, no. The answer is no.
61. The way people vote is the main thing that decides how things are run in this country.
    - That's not true.
62. The Catholic Church is a wealthy institution.
    - Yes.
63. There is life after death.
    - Don't know.
64. If you suffer in this world, it is often the result of the wages of sins. God is punishing you.
    - No.
65. Government officials are the legitimate authority leaders of the nation and should be obeyed.
    - The answer's always basic to that..whether Hitler and his henchmen. . . . And a person has to live by what's right. With or without the dictates of the government or the Church.

66. The Catholic Church (religion) is a source of personal strength to me.
    - No.
67. The Catholic Church (religion) is a benefit to the Chicano community.
    - I think it's a detriment.
68. Chicanos should spend more time praying and less time demonstrating
    - False.
69. Violence will never help Chicanos get equal rights.
    - Again the history of this nation and apparently all over the world is violence—as a reality just as much as food and football and anything else that's real has produced results whether anyone wants to relate to it, and that includes me personally in terms of our discussion. I hate violence. I've seen enough of it. But unfortunately that has resulted in results.
70. As a Catholic (if Catholic) I should use political processes to make Christian values standard for the whole nation.
    - [Then] I don't know where the Jews fit in. This is supposed to be a nation of all people. Nor do I know where the Buddhists. No way. No way. I don't think so.
71. The only function of the Church is to communicate salvation by preaching, teaching and administrating [sic] the sacraments.
    - We apparently are stuck with formal religions, huge religions. Catholic, Protestant, Jewish churches. I would hope their function is to practice what they preach, and to live the life of love and the betterment of the society. I think those would be more ? functions. If we have to have religion, it's hopefully made up of society, of real people and needs.
72. A good Catholic supports his country no matter what.
    - A lot of people like that. But that doesn't make sense to me.
73. The demands of the Gospel require that Catholics be involved in political, social and economic affairs.
    - I think there's an awful lot of good cases made up that way. A lot of studies and research. I can't quote them right now I don't remember. I think a tremendous amount of analysis has concluded that the gospel does add up to those types of thinking. But obviously again you can make anything you want when you're dealing with the heavens and gods. You can do anything you want with it. Gison (?), the French theologian, I like what he said "when gods fight gods, men die." So just as equally those who say that's exactly what religion is, should be, in terms of heaven or this or that and non-ethereal, or whatever. But again it can go either way. That's the nightmare of religion. People use it all the time.

74. How do you feel you have changed religiously during your lifetime?
    - Well, once I got rid of religion, then my spiritual self, my identity, my fears, my strengths, my confidence, everything, everything, became much more realistic. No longer was I relating to heavens and hells, good and evils and spooky stories and mortal sins and venial sins. I became what I am—an animal, a human animal. My choices became my own two feet in other words. I had to stand up like a man instead of like I did for many years—praying for somebody to do this or do that, usually with respect to me. Now I make them do it or not, if it's good. It's been a great benefit for me to get rid of religion.
75. How do you feel you have changed politically during your lifetime?
    - Well I'm politically active in a sense, by that I mean, we're all trying to wheeze (?) a lot of good Chicanos. And all kinds of people here in LA are all trying to see political power for our people, and for all people who have good hearts, let's hope. So once I became political I haven't changed in other words. I've been at social-political activities for almost nine years now, maybe ten, I don't know. But I haven't changed since then. But before that I wasn't political at all. (Apolitical?) Just apolitical. Whatever I was—a Democrat, a college student, a playboy, or whatever I was.
76. Do you feel that there is any connection between your religious and political beliefs and/or the changes you have undergone? How about other Chicanos—from your experience—would you say that there is a connection between Chicano religious and political beliefs. If yes what is that connection.
    - Yes, I think we've really already covered all the answers to that without me just saying a lot of the things over again.

      (The same for Chicanos in general—do you feel there is a connection between the religious and political beliefs of Chicanos?)

      Using myself, if I'm any example at all, the less religious I got, finally when I got rid of it, the more political I became. And by politics all I mean is power. I have seen many examples of my power and my ability to use power for the betterment of my people and myself. Charity does begin at home. For my kids even. A direct relationship, or whatever, the less religion, the more political. Religion allows me to live in the heavens, allows us to relate to a god, to Jesus, to Mary to realities that aren't real at all. The more we relate to them for the solutions of problems we are able to be duped. Back to the words "blessed are the poor"; and "the meek shall inherit the earth." The meek don't inherit nothing, nothing at all. Maybe they sleep good and maybe they do add up to a very safe person. But essentially the meek are meek and the poor are poor. If anyone wants to be meek and poor, it's their business, but I sure as hell don't think that that's what it takes for the Chicanos to grow up and have a world that they can feel happy about. So the less religion the better, if we see that there's a translation of power—political power for people. But I don't think that can come about with everybody being super religious.

An Ode to Chicanos & Chicanas

Richard Cruz
August 29, 1975[1]

Selfish, insecure, frightened mother fuckers . . .
Mamonas and Papas, boys and girls . . .
Hate the City but afraid to own it . . .
"All is possible" to one another but to the enemy a different, completely different story . . .
Closet punks the "students" who are afraid to study . . .
Closet punks the "lawyers" who practice injustice . . .
Closet punks the frigid, horny "women" who shout womans "liberation" . . .
Closet punks the "vatos" who ain't scored a piece since their right hand . . .
Selfish, insecure, frightened mother fuckers . . .
Sons and daughters of the indigenous ones, of the land . . .
Afraid of your own shadows.
Brilliant minds. Yet not the discipline to pass the bar or practice a profession.
Brilliant poets and artist and feelers and cries of tears.

[1] In Ricardo Cruz/Católicos Por La Raza Papers.

Untitled Poem

By Richard Cruz[1]

Take it in, take it in.
It pisses you doesn't it?
Or are you too old, weak or
Religious to be pissed off?

Anger frightens the good people.
They eat meat and kill the
Environment and who knows
What else. Not to mention Vietnam.

But they must never get angry.
Jesus—for whom they profess great
Love, grabbed a whip and
kicked ass at the phonies-
indeed in front of St. Basil's-
But never, never be angry or
get pissed off—but [get] motivated
and act!

[1] Ricardo Cruz/Católicos Por La Raza Papers.

Richard Cruz[1]

We're afraid to dream
Because we don't know
If they will come through.

We've been taken so many
times that we can't
help but hate the next
time.

So we're frightened and
Chicanos & Puerto Riqueños
daydream—hour after
hour.

Somos don Quixotes!
But we've lost our
sense of humor! Fear
is stronger than humor!

We say it's a language
barrier . . . afraid even
of words! As if our message
had anything to do with language!

What's funny is that our
message to evolution is
so strong—Like Luis
Valdez said one time
"Chicanos are the master
race! Y sabes que—raza laughed!

[1] Ricardo Cruz/Católicos Por La Raza Papers.

Damn fools that we
are. We know so
much, yet we know
so little! Do you
ever get that feeling?

We talk about so many
things with each other.
But we never talk
about courage or will
or fear or hate . . . so
we never really talk
at all.

Just a lot of words.
We say NO 300 times
a day. And then when
enough are listening
we say "RIGHT ON!!! "

You're waiting for me
to talk to you, well,
shit—pendejo!—I'm
waiting for you!

We know we're a
civilization but we
don't know what
it means. Yet we
live it when no ones watching!

Afraid of yes. They
look so evil. I guess
that's why we can't
see. Why? Why?

It's like the sickness
is the cure. Trip out
loco—I know how
you feel. And that's
why we lose hope!

We feel so alone. Yet
. . . fuck it, we get too
emotional!!!

I can't write poetry when
I'm emotional any
more than I can make
revolution. So let's be one
or the other and quit
chasing windmills!

Like I'm as tired of
going in circles as you.
Don Genaro, from
Don Juan, would laugh
at us as much as he
laughed at Carlos.

CPLR, LRLSA, MECHA,
and let me add, UMAS,
CMAU, LUCHA, y,
¿por que no?, ENCHO!

What they did to the
Indians, they'll do to
us, motherfuckers! Lying,
chickenshit bullshitters!

Mestzos, my dear?
We might as [well] wear
hula hoops, as far
as these savages care.

Civil Rights! Mierda
pendejos! Mierda pero
no puedes ver! And
you read your books
as if they're mirrors!

But you see only words
not yourself, so back
to the fear. And
there's nothing worse
than feeling alone!

Don Juan! Join us
you pinche brujo!
We need your gods!

Pero, tambien. La tuja
y come caca! Such
is our pride! Hijo de
la chingada! Coñio!
como dicen los Puerto
Riqueños! (Luis, y Rosa
y Tomas—y quien sabe
quien mas?)

I lost you for a minute
but you know what
I mean. Our gods
are within us, but
We won't let them
out.

We even invent other
worlds. That's how
removed we are from,
I don't really know
what?

A hundred tribes got
together. And they
didn't even like each
other. Yet you accuse
the carnal of not
"understanding!"

Those tribes were
our forefathers, if you
didn't understand.
The only "civilization"
we are is the one
we make!

5000 years later
the Jews got their
land. How dare
you be anxious?

Show as much courage
as you do anxiety! Or
the man will always
know better. Like
he has since he arrived.

The poet, the artist &
the musician. They all
speak to each other.
Why can't we . . .
the revolutionaries?

RICHARD CRUZ LETTER TO HIS PARENTS[1]

Dear Mom and Dad,

Having recently divorced my wife of seven years, it is especially difficult to realize that I must now also divorce my parents, you, my dear, Celia and Ramón.

It is and will be a difficult task. I have weighted [sic] all thoughts and emotions. I have consulted family and friends. And, perhaps most importantly, I have given two months of conscious deliberation to this task, the task, that is, of deciding whether to be myself and stand on my own two feet, or of being forever the child that yearns for parental guidance . . . help and money before any human and important endeavors are undertaken.

Well I have made my decision. And I am proud of my choice.

Out of respect I am choosing to communicate the reasons as best as I humanly can. Fortunately for myself at least, the single most important reason that exists as the motivation for my one-year removal from each of you is religion or, may I say, so-called religion. I must and will make my thoughts with respect to religion as clear as I can: mom has sold me out for another man called Jesus; dad has sold himself out in the name of religion for the sake of keeping mom around.

By the way, it's not that I am jealous of Jesus. More than any of you have I at one time loved, sacrificed, understood and, a rare thing indeed, also studied the person, life and times of J.C. I was more of a Christian than all of you put together (and that includes Rose). When I sung the <u>tantum ergo</u> the tears of my eyes for the

[1] Undated (circa late 1970s or early 1980s) in Ricardo Cruz/Católicos Por La Raza Papers.

suffering of humanity were the harmony. When I was an alter boy I showed up on time (as usual) and when I beat my chest with the "mea culpa" it was my guilt and sincere belief that it was my fault that people were unhappy and hungry and violent to one another—thus did I, whether at Easter or 6:00 Mass, beat my chest despite the ridicule of fellow altar boys and sincerely hit myself exclaiming (as a child, almost Camilo's age) "it's all my fault, it's all my fault."

I'll never, never forget.

Part 7

Camilo Cruz, Richard Cruz, Paloma Cruz, 1990.
Courtesy of Special Collections, Davidson Library, Univ. of Calif. Santa Barbara

Eulogy of Richard Cruz by Camilo Cruz

EULOGY OF RICHARD CRUZ

BY CAMILO CRUZ[1]

HELLO, MY NAME IS CAMILO CRUZ. ON BEHALF OF RICHARD CRUZ, HIS FAMILY, AND ESPECIALLY HIS THREE CHILDREN I WANT TO THANK MALDEF FOR THIS PRESTIGIOUS AWARD AND HONOR.

THE WORST THING ABOUT DEATH IS NOT THE DEATH ITSELF. BECAUSE WE ALL ARE GONG TO DIE. THE WORST THING ABOUT DEATH IS HOW YOU NEVER REALLY GOT TO SAY THE THINGS YOU WANTED AND NEEDED TO SAY TO THE PERSON WHO DIED WHILE HE OR SHE WAS STILL ALIVE. YOU BECOME FILLED WITH A CERTAIN GUILT AND SADNESS AND FEEL A SENSE OF UNFULFILLMENT IN YOUR LIFE. SO, TO MAKE ME FEEL A LITTLE BETTER WHAT I WANT TO DO IS READ TO YOU, HIS FRIENDS AND COLLEAGUES, WHAT I SHOULD HAVE READ TO HIM WHILE HE WAS STILL ALIVE. IT'S A SHORT LETTER I WROTE DATED JULY 23, 1993.

Dear Dad,

Although I can't embrace you physically, I can embrace what you've done for me and our people. I want to especially thank you, my mother, and all the other brave warriors who challenged and fought the many hateful and oppressive institutions of this country. Because of the rebellion of the 1960's young Chicanos of today and the future have a few more chances at making it in this society. We don't have to worry as much as you did about having a voice, an existence, and about calling ourselves "Chicanos". In thinking of you Dad, I think of the tremendous 1960's and the people you were involved with in creating the beautiful Chicano Revolution. Many things are still wrong of course, but are better now because of what you and others have left for us.

Camilo Cruz Eulogy, July 23, 1993 in Ricardo Cruz/Católicos Por La Raza Papers.

Right now when I think of you, dead at General Hospital, I remember what you told me about death. It was the last time me and you went out to eat at a restaurant by ourselves. I'll never forget it. You told me that your soul as Richard Cruz, your consciousness, would die along with your body. You said that there was no heaven and no hell, only the ground in which you came from. Your energy, you thought, as did our Indian ancestors, would flow back into the earth and would transform into something else of the universe. As I sit here alone in my room, missing you like crazy, I'd like to think of what the energy you possessed for 50 passionate years has transformed into. I could come up with only one thing. Your energy now has joined in with the other forces, to the aspects of the universe which are devoted to freedom. Whether it is revolution of an oppressed people in one country to the notes of the harp sounding over Veracruz you are now there. Whether it's the wings of an eagle or the fins of a whale you are now there. It makes me happy to think of these things, that you are now musical notes and eagle wings. Your deep and profound appreciation and constant struggle for freedom within all realms of the world are what certainly made you a man to be admired and commemorated. You truly knew what freedom was and how to attain it as compared to the many on this planet who go on day to day their whole lives never questioning their oppressive routines and institutions. I have to admit though, being your son I sometimes regret that you knew too much about freedom and wished that it would have been someone else. Someone else to take on the intense responsibility of freedom seeker. But, as the moments pass while I'm writing to you now I know that these feelings are only temporary. I guess these feelings are just a reaction to seeing you suffer and missing you so much. Deep in my heart I don't think that you would have been the Richard Cruz I so idolize if you didn't have such ideas of freedom and justice. You deserve nothing but the freedom you fought so hard for and I know that is where you are right now. Dad, I never told you this, but most of what I love is what you've taught me.

SO, LET'S GIVE MY FATHER, ROSA MARTÍNEZ, AND EVERYONE ELSE WHO FOUGHT DURING THE 1960'S ONE MORE ROUND OF APPLAUSE. THEIR EFFORTS AND ACHIEVEMENTS WILL ALWAYS BE REMEMBERED AND UTILIZED.